Unprotected Labor

Unprotected Labor

Household Workers, Politics, and Middle-Class
Reform in New York, 1870–1940

VANESSA H. MAY

The University of North Carolina Press Chapel Hill

THIS BOOK WAS PUBLISHED
with the assistance of the
ANNIVERSARY ENDOWMENT FUND OF
the University of North Carolina Press.

Library of Congress Cataloging-in-Publication Data
May, Vanessa H.
Unprotected labor : household workers, politics, and middle-
class reform in New York, 1870–1940 / Vanessa H. May.
p. cm.
Includes bibliographical references and index.
ISBN 978-0-8078-3477-0 (cloth : alk. paper)—ISBN 978-0-8078-7193-5
(pbk. : alk. paper)
1. Women household employees—New York (State)—History. 2. Women household
employees—Labor unions—New York (State)—History. 3. Women—New York (State)—
Social conditions—History. 4. Labor movement—New York (State)—History. I. Title.
HD6072.2.U52.N676 2011
331.4′81640974709031—dc22
2010047551

cloth   15 14 13 12 11   5 4 3 2 1
paper   15 14 13 12 11   5 4 3 2 1

For

MOM, DAD, AND PATRICK

Contents

Illustrations

Acknowledgments

I have always loved reading other authors' acknowledgments—tracing academic genealogies and taking note of ways of thanking people that I particularly liked. I looked forward to writing my own. Now I have discovered there are no words to thank adequately the people who have so generously and selflessly offered me their time, effort, and wisdom. I will try to do them justice.

Historians need capable, friendly, and knowledgeable archivists, and I have had the good fortune to meet many. The staffs at Columbia's Rare Book and Manuscript Library, the Newark Public Library, the Manuscripts and Archives Division of the New York Public Library, the Schomburg Center for Research in Black Culture, the New York Municipal Archives, the Tamiment Library and Robert F. Wagner Labor Archives, Ellis Island, and the Schlesinger Library were uniformly helpful and full of suggestions for further research. The Wertheim Study at the New York Public Library gave me a quiet space to write the book. Jonathan Frye at the Lindquist Group opened his company's records to me and showed real enthusiasm about the project. Special thanks to Ellen Belcher at John Jay College, Maida Goodwin at the Sophia Smith Collection at Smith College, Steven Siegel at the 92nd Street Y, and Curtis Lyons and Patrizia Sione at the Kheel Center at Cornell University. Their friendliness and generosity made research a pleasure.

This book began at the University of Virginia, where I was lucky to be part of a vibrant scholarly community. The Corcoran Department of History and the College of Arts and Sciences funded the project with travel grants, teaching assignments, and a fellowship. Grace Hale and Brian Balogh read my work and advised me with good cheer, and I am glad to have had the benefit of their insights. I am especially lucky to have worked with Cindy Aron. Her readings of my work were both numerous and meticulous. She could always, as if by magic, put her finger on exactly what would make my argument stronger and my prose better. She continues to be an unfailing source of support, practical advice, and warm encouragement. She is the model of a teacher, scholar, advocate, friend, and mentor that I will look to for the rest of my career.

I also benefited from the companionship of brilliant graduate students. Particular thanks to the Junto, Andrew Torget and Erik Alexander, who read and critiqued my very first and feeble efforts at writing in graduate school and have remained (I hope) lifelong friends. Their wives, Alexandra Torget and Carrie Alexander, are long-suffering listeners to discussions of historiography and research.

I am particularly grateful to Kristin Celello and Melissa Estes Blair, both of whom have read and reread much of this manuscript. They have also happily delivered a wide array of pep talks when the going got rough. Kristin and Carl Bon Tempo are always ready with good advice, no matter how frantic or long-winded my questions. Both are brilliant scholars and truly amazing cooks. I am a lucky beneficiary of both talents.

Scholars outside of the University of Virginia have also been extremely generous. Eileen Boris is a fierce advocate of my work and has read the full manuscript at least three times. Her revision suggestions were always excellent, and I am in awe of her grasp of the literature on this (and, really, every) subject. Despite the fact that she has no official responsibility for my career, she has always readily offered advice and support. I am grateful to count her as a friend and mentor.

Rebecca Edwards read the entire manuscript and bears responsibility for sending me to graduate school in the first place. Miriam Cohen also read a chapter and has been very encouraging. Leigh Ann Wheeler and Dorothea Browder also offered excellent suggestions for revision of part of the manuscript. This book is better for their ideas. Sian Hunter, Beth Lassiter, Kate Torrey, Paula Wald, and countless others at the University of North Carolina Press have been incredibly patient with me, and I am grateful for their help and support in moving this manuscript to publication. Rebecca Sharpless read the manuscript carefully and helped to improve its argument and prose. Madeleine Glennon came through in the clutch and tracked down a last-minute citation. Members of the Brooklyn writing group have offered careful readings, excellent company, and delicious wine and cheese. They are Charlotte Brooks, Richard Greenwald, Anne Kornhouser, Jonathan Soffer, Jeffrey Trask, Lara Vapnek, and Tim White. I am also happy to thank my colleagues at Seton Hall University who have welcomed me into their department, namely Tracey Billado, William Connell, Larry Greene, Williamjames Hoffer, Nathaniel Knight, Dan Leab, Maxine Lurie, Maxim Matusevich, James McCartin, Murat Menguc, Mark Molesky, Dermot Quinn, Thomas Rzeznik, and Kirsten Schultz.

My family members are constant champions, and this book is for them. My dad, Derek May, has been unfailingly enthusiastic about my education, even asking for a framed copy of my doctoral diploma to hang on his wall. My mom, Catherine Harkins, has read almost all of this manuscript, and her advice, much as I may have been reluctant to admit it, was almost always right. My brother, Jonathan May, always helps keep things in perspective. Elizabeth Nogrady has known me for so long she might as well be family. She has been an excellent companion for our adventure in academia. My husband, Patrick McDonough, deserves special mention. Being married to an academic is a little like being married to someone in the army, an institution with its own rules and traditions and with immense control over your life. Patrick has soldiered on. He traveled to visit me all three years that I lived in Charlottesville and then for another year when I lectured at UVA. He gave good advice about how to handle this or that situation. He made me laugh. He vacuumed and did the dishes. Most of all, he loved me even when I am pretty sure I was not all that lovable. He should know that being last is the place of honor.

Unprotected Labor

Introduction

At the end of the nineteenth century, Vassar College historian Lucy Maynard Salmon suspected that something was rotten in the kitchens of America's middle class. Whenever she was in the company of women, talk always turned to the problem of paid household labor. At parties and in quiet social gatherings, Salmon observed, "with whatever topic conversation begins," discussion among middle-class women "sooner or later gravitates towards the one fixed point of domestic service."[1] This conversation did not take place just in middle-class parlors. In the late nineteenth century, the popular press printed these private whisperings and invited experts on domesticity, labor, and morality to parse the labor relations of the private home for the benefit of a voracious readership.[2] Then, in the late 1880s, Salmon embarked on an ambitious project. She distributed over 5,000 questionnaires to both employers and domestics, inviting recipients to discuss domestic service in general and conditions in their households in particular. As a historian with a reverence for firsthand accounts, Salmon hoped to go right to the source of the "servant problem."

Salmon's inquiries elicited a torrent of response from both workers and housewives. Household workers objected to the low wages and long hours that prevailed in private homes. Had they chosen factory work, domestic servants complained, they would have had some time to themselves at the end of the workday. In private homes, however, "you are," one worker objected, "mistress of no time of your own."[3] Middle-class employers were equally unhappy. A housewife in Brooklyn decried the "numbers of untrained, discontented girls who seem to have little appreciation of a good home, but leave on the slightest provocation, disliking any supervision but wanting their own way, even if wasteful and careless."[4] Domestics, employers complained, were unfit to work in middle-class homes. Middle-class housewives, domestics retorted, were unfit to run them.

Faced with these results, Salmon concluded that it was high time that domestic service cease to be a labor relationship worked out privately between household employers and domestics. Instead, Salmon argued, "reform in domestic service must be accomplished along the same general economic lines as are reforms in other great departments of labor."[5] Salmon urged women's organizations to include domestic service in their labor reform agendas, which were beginning to coalesce at the turn of the twentieth century. Some of the responses to Salmon's survey, however, held clues that reform would not be easy. Among the thousand or so surveys and letters that flooded Salmon's mailbox, a few expressed household employers' indignation at even being asked about what went on inside their homes. One Yonkers housewife replied to Salmon's inquiry with a terse note that "the questions are so decidedly personal that I decline to answer them under any considerations."[6] Another employer, although she welcomed Salmon's efforts to address household labor problems, declined "to give any detailed information as to my private affairs to those who have no business to be advised of them and where the good to be accomplished is exceedingly dubious."[7]

Projects like Salmon's were part of the fabric of an important public conversation about paid labor in private homes that began at the end of the nineteenth century and extended to the public policy debates of the New Deal. Although historians have tended to dismiss this discussion as middle-class griping, the controversy over the "servant problem" made up a political debate that would shape the largest sector of women's employment into the 1940s. This book explores the public debate over domestic service, labor regulation and reform, and labor activism between the late nineteenth century and 1940 in New York City and its environs. I argue that the public discussion of domestic service in middle-class homes, where circumstances were usually closely guarded as private, turned the middle-class home inside out. Private problems became public, and widespread anxieties about urban iniquity, labor conflict, and government regulation threatened to invade the middle-class private sanctum. At the heart of this debate was the middle-class home. Domestics, in a variety of public forums, argued that middle-class homes were workplaces. Meanwhile, employers insisted that their homes were private spaces, over which they should have complete control. This discussion among domestics, legislators, journalists, employers, and organized women's reform groups shaped government labor policy and put the private middle-class home at the center of urban political debate. It also had a profound impact on both domestic employees and their working conditions. Not least among these consequences was that household workers were entirely left out of the protective labor legislation that women working in industry achieved relatively easily.

Domestic service was the largest employer of women until after 1940, and its story is therefore vital to the history of both working women and the middle-class women who employed them. This book weaves together three narratives to form a political history of domestic service in the urban North. First, it traces the history of workers who toiled in middle-class homes. Second, this book recounts the story of middle-class women, both ordinary housewives who employed domestics in their homes and organized women who created, lobbied for, and debated protective labor legislation for women workers. Third, this book examines how the categories of public and private shaped activists' approach to domestic service reform and workers' resistance to the occupation's worst conditions.

New York is a particularly good place to study the public and private dimensions of paid household labor. First, examining the politics of domestic service in just one place illuminates how national policy debates played out in smaller contexts. An examination of state-level battles for protective labor legislation, for instance, reveals divisions among women's groups over regulating domestics' wages and hours that have been lost in discussions of national policy.[8] Second, focusing on New York changes the national story in important ways. For example, scholars often argue that domestics were excluded from labor laws by racist southern congressmen who wanted to maintain a cheap source of African American labor in the South. These legislators, historians argue, blocked domestics' inclusion in the federal Fair Labor Standards Act of 1938.[9] The roots of domestic workers' exclusion from labor laws, however, stretch back to the nineteenth century, when labor reformers began to create separate reform agendas for domestics and other working women. Then, in the 1930s, household workers lost a two-year battle for state-level labor legislation in New York, a progressive northern state with not a single Jim Crow legislator. We are, therefore, forced to rethink how the largest category of working women was excluded from basic labor protections. This book expands on narratives of domestic service that focus on individual relationships between domestics and employers to include interactions among domestics, employers, labor reformers, and the state.[10] In a study like this one, domestics suddenly appear less passive and middle-class reformers seem less united and, importantly, less selfless.

There are other reasons to choose New York. New York City was the nation's social and economic capital and a center of urban growth, immigration, and African American migration. The number of domestics among the population of women in New York City and Brooklyn remained high throughout this period. In 1880, there were over 700,000 women working in domestic service or taking in laundry in these two cities, representing over 40 percent of wage-earning women.[11] As the occupational options for women increased in factories and shops, the number of domestics as a percentage of the overall population of working women declined. Domestic service, however, still represented the most likely occupation for working women through 1940, and middle-class families continued to employ, and complain about, domestic workers.[12] New York City also mirrored changes going on in other northern cities during this period. Like Chicago and Boston, New York experienced a great influx of western European immigrants who worked in domestic service between 1870 and 1915. Like Washington, D.C., and Philadelphia, New York City housed a small community of African Americans, which grew exponentially after 1915. New York also served as the nerve center for women activists interested in reforming women's industrial labor, immigration, southern migration, and domestic service. For example, sociologist and reformer Frances Kellor hoped to use the employment office licensing law that she successfully passed in New York in 1904 as a model for similar laws in other cities. Believing New York to be the epicenter for the "servant problem," Kellor located the headquarters of her domestic service research organization there, creating a model on which she would base similar reform efforts in Philadelphia, Boston, and Chicago.

Although New York City serves as an example of the changes in domestic service going on nationally, it also differed from the national context in instructive ways. New York was in the forefront of political changes affecting domestic service and labor regulation generally. Women activists in New York were experts on labor regulation for women workers and pioneers in the national movement to provide working women with a minimum wage and maximum hours.[13] In fact, New York was on the vanguard of the labor reform movement, offering its industrial workers the strongest hours law in the country by 1935. In the 1930s, New York also had the largest active domestic workers union of any American city, easily outpacing similar unions in Washington, D.C., Chicago, and San Diego. By the time the fight for inclusion of domestic workers in state labor laws heated up in the 1930s, New York had become a center of New Deal political power, domestic worker activism, and middle-class women's reform. Furthermore, unlike those advocating for inclusion of domestics in federal labor laws, New York's middle-class and working-class activists did not face opposition from Jim Crow politicians. In other words, if labor reform for domestics could not be made there, it could not be made anywhere. Protective legislation's failure in New York therefore tells us something important about women reformers' consistent ties to the ideology of the middle-class home and the limits of cross-class coalitions.

ECONOMIC AND DEMOGRAPHIC SHIFTS had transformed domestic service in the North by the mid-nineteenth century, making the occupation a target for labor reformers and state regulation. Before that, most household workers lived in rural areas performing domestic tasks for family friends as part of larger networks of mutual aid between families. Rather than employees, white domestic workers in early nineteenth-century northern homes seemed more like sisters or daughters, eating at the family table with their employers and working alongside the farmwife to accomplish daily chores. Although these relationships were not without conflict, "hired girls" often seemed more like extended family than hired help. Hired girls were most likely the daughters of neighbors and friends who led full lives as equal members of the community, going to school and meeting friends and suitors. Hired girls also performed a variety of tasks that contributed to the household's financial survival, including collecting eggs or making other products for market, in addition to the housework that provided for the family's comfort and bodily needs.[14] Paid housework, before the advent of mass urbanization and immigration, thus existed somewhere between wage labor and rural patterns of mutual aid and support.

Urban growth and the expansion of industry led to changes in both the productive and the familial aspects of paid domestic labor. In northern cities, domestic workers were no longer members of neighboring families. Instead, they were strangers who performed housework in return for a wage. As "productive" labor increasingly took place outside the home, domestics also stopped performing tasks that contributed tangibly to the family economy. Instead, they focused all of their energies on housework. By the middle of the nineteenth century, domestic workers were no longer the social equals of their employers but rather wageworkers, separated from their employers by a gulf of socioeconomic class. Very wealthy families built houses with back stairs and separate living quarters to limit social contact between household workers and employers. But even when workers used separate stairways, their responsibility to clean and care for their employers necessitated personal and bodily intimacy. For middle-class families living in small apartments with only one maid, even this minimal separation was impossible.[15] Families' discomfort notwithstanding, standards of cleanliness and refinement continued to rise in middle-class and elite households. Not employing at least one domestic seemed inconceivable, even if conflict between employers and workers also seemed inevitable.

By the late nineteenth century, when this book picks up its narrative, domestic workers in the urban North were likely to be immigrants. Native-born women refused to take domestic work, leaving employers with no choice but to hire foreign-born workers.[16] Although Scandinavian and German women also found jobs in private homes, Irish women particularly gravitated toward domestic service. In fact, in 1900, 41.2 percent of white servants nationwide had been born in Ireland.[17] Irish women began leaving their homeland in the wake of the potato famine in the late 1840s, but Irish immigrants, and particularly Irish women, continued to pour into America long after the famine had ended.[18] By the 1880s and 1890s, newcomers from eastern, central, and southern Europe vastly outnumbered Irish immigrants, but that does not mean the Irish stayed home. Although Irish immigration fell as a percentage of total immigration in those years, the actual number of Irish immigrants went up. For example, Ireland sent 436,871 immigrants between 1871 and 1880, representing 15.5 percent of total immigration. Between 1881 and 1890, Irish immigrants represented only 12.5 percent of total immigration, even though 655,482 Irish immigrants had arrived in American ports.[19] More than half of these newly arrived Irish immigrants were women, and the majority were single. Since Italians and eastern and central Europeans often refused to perform paid housework, the Irish and a few other western European immigrant groups continued to occupy most domestic service positions.

Frederick Opper, "Our Self-made 'Cooks' — From Paupers to Potentates," *Puck Magazine*, January 30, 1881. (Courtesy of Michigan State University Museum)

The conflict between middle-class housewives and their domestic work-ers was therefore as much about ethnicity and race as it was about class. Although Irish women did not face the same legal segregation and dis-crimination that African American domestics faced in the South, the Irish did not quite qualify as racially white to most native-born New Yorkers. Nineteenth-century Americans generally viewed race as a series of biologi-cal traits tied to a person's ethnic or national background. The Irish, by this logic, were a race unto themselves and were inherently and biologically different from the Anglo-Saxon, or British race, from which most native-born Americans imagined they descended. Not only were the Irish differ-ent in many native-born Americans' estimation, but they were also inferior. Writers and other cultural critics in the late nineteenth century depicted the Irish as brutish and prone to alcoholism and violence. Others alleged that the Irish intrinsically lacked the civic virtue to become good citizens.[20] These ideas were compounded by a deep-seated anti-Catholicism that ran through the middle-class American Protestant psyche. Such racialized ideas about the Irish surely spilled over into the relationships between household employers and their workers. At least newspaper editors thought so. Cartoonists frequently portrayed the Irish domestic as apelike and aggressive, towering over the demure, Protestant lady who employed her.

What looked to middle-class employers like Irish working-class aggression seemed to many domestics like nothing more than self-defense. Household workers sought to control their working conditions in myriad ways. Sometimes they dragged their feet or talked back or burned dinner. Sometimes they quit. Sometimes they argued for higher wages in tense negotiations that took place in the waiting rooms of domestic employment agencies. These efforts all played out in a gendered, ethnic, and working-class context that made immigrant domestic protest different from industrial unionism. Nevertheless, domestics identified themselves as working women, no different from women working in shops and factories, and they did their best to assert their own needs in the face of employer demands. They did so by maintaining networks of support among one another and the wider working-class community. We sometimes imagine domestics as cloistered workers, trapped in middle-class homes and communities far away from the vibrant labor activism of shops and industry. I argue, in contrast, that a sense of working-class community was not limited to the factory floor but could be, and was, maintained within middle-class neighborhoods. This working-class activism, however, was hampered by its exclusion from the legal support that labor laws offered women who worked in industry.

African American domestics took the place of immigrant women in New York and other northern urban centers after World War I. In the late 1910s and early 1920s, the U.S. Congress passed a series of immigration restrictions that all but dried up the supply of immigrants to work in middle-class homes. At the very same time, thousands of African Americans began to leave their homes in the South to travel to northern cities in search of better jobs and more political freedom. Between 1910 and 1940, 1.5 million African Americans made this journey. Once they arrived in cities like New York, most African American female migrants found jobs as domestic workers.

As the women doing the work in middle-class homes changed, domestic service as an occupation also changed. Immigrant women had usually been single and had lived with their employers, but African American women were often married and had their own families to care for. Many black women refused live-in domestic service positions, choosing instead to live with their own families and perform their own domestic chores at the end of the workday.[21] In the first decades of the twentieth century, then, urban domestics in the North changed from immigrants living and working in middle-class neighborhoods to African Americans who maintained their own homes in communities separate from their places of work.

Live-out African American domestics also resisted employer demands differently than did immigrant workers. Immigrant domestics did not live in working-class or ethnic neighborhoods. African American workers, on the other hand, often made their homes in urban black communities. In the 1920s and 1930s, black communities like Harlem were epicenters of a new racial pride and militancy. It was, after all, in Harlem that the scholar Alain Locke found evidence of a flowering and self-consciously African American cultural renaissance, and it was in Harlem that Marcus Garvey began advancing new ideas about black nationalism. It is perhaps no surprise, then, that communities like Harlem also gave birth to domestics who directly confronted employers' control over the occupation. These workers formed unions, lobbied state legislatures for protective labor legislation, and turned out in force to protest health regulations that targeted black domestics as a potential source of disease. This book therefore works not just to uncover the activism of domestic workers but also to document their effect on politics and public policy. In doing so, it tells the story of working-class women alongside that of middle-class activists. Here, working-class women are active participants in domestic labor politics, not just passive targets of middle-class reform.[22]

While work shaped the lives of domestics, nineteenth-century middle-class white women's gender roles tied them to the private sphere, where they were expected to remain submissive to their husbands and fathers, perform the emotional and physical work of motherhood and housekeeping, and exhibit piety and sexual chastity.[23] White middle-class men, meanwhile, went out into the public world of work and politics, where they wielded economic and political power. For some middle-class women, these gender roles were quite limiting, but nineteenth-century gender ideology also produced a rich tradition of women's political reform.[24] Women reformers used their alleged command of the values of the private sphere to make the case that they were uniquely suited to address class inequality and the suffering of the poor, especially if those poor were also women. Beginning in the nineteenth century and continuing through the New Deal, women's groups rallied around issues like school reform, temperance, protection of women workers, and poor relief. Women activists promoted themselves as uncorrupted by the dirty business of politics and commerce and able to bring a feminine and moral perspective to reform.[25] These gendered politics allowed the formation of cross-class coalitions between working-class women and middle-class reformers, giving way to protective labor legislation, welfare, and other Progressive and New Deal reforms.[26] In public and in private, women's association with the private sphere could be an advantage to ambitious middle-class and wealthy women, even as they were ultimately blocked from achieving equal political power.

These reformers, like the ideal of gendered privacy and moral authority they invoked, were, for the most part, white and middle class.[27] The term "middle class" as I use it in reference to women labor reformers, however, includes important class differences among reformers and many varying financial arrangements.[28] Many wealthy, politically progressive women led, funded, or joined women's reform organizations. Mary Dreier, who was active for decades in the Women's Trade Union League (WTUL), enjoyed a trust fund left behind by her father. The membership lists of organizations like the Women's City Club included many New York elites. On the other hand, many of the women who devoted their lives to labor reform, particularly those working in the years between 1900 and the 1930s, supported themselves. Many of these women had advanced degrees and earned their livings as professionals. Often they worked as social workers, lawyers, or sociologists, and they brought those skills to their reform work. Frances Kellor, for instance, earned a degree in sociology from the University of Chicago and spent her life working in government and reform. Some of the women most interested in labor reform had once held low-waged jobs. Many of the women in leadership positions at the WTUL, including Elisabeth Christman and Rose Schneiderman, spent years working in factories before launching their careers as labor organizers and reformers. Finally, many of the rank and file of organizations like the Young Women's Christian Association, the League of Women Voters, and late nineteenth-century benevolent societies derived their middle-class status from their husbands, who worked at jobs that did not require manual labor and paid enough to keep their wives and children out of the workforce.

The middle-class reformers in this book are also mostly white. Organizations like the National Association of Colored Women and the National Council of Negro Women at various times expressed deep concern about domestics' working conditions, but labor legislation was not prominent on their political agenda.[29] More important, middle-class black reformers did not have the same access to government power as white reformers. Even African American women who were part of interracial organizations, like the Young Women's Christian Association, had trouble pushing white leaders to address domestic service from the employee's, rather than the employer's, perspective.[30] African American middle-class reformers depended on the goodwill, lobbying power, and government clout of white women's organizations to get labor legislation for black workers passed. Domestic service reforms, especially after 1920, reflected not just the gendered vision of white women labor reformers but their racial vision as well.

Nowhere were white middle-class women reformers' gendered politics more evident than in labor reform. Women reformers were leading labor activists and key architects of the welfare state that ministered to women and children. Not all women reformers and politicians supported protective labor legislation, of course, but the ones who play central roles in this book all did. These women's organizations wrote and helped to pass much of the legislation that provided women workers in industry and shops with a minimum wage, maximum hours, and regulated working conditions in the early twentieth century. This legislation, buoyed by the passionate support of women's organizations, was extended to all workers involved in interstate commerce with New Deal labor laws. By the end of the New Deal, increasing numbers of industrial and retail workers enjoyed federal and state labor protections. Domestics, however, were specifically excluded from all of these laws. They remained uncovered by Social Security Insurance until 1950. They were not included in minimum wage or maximum hours laws until 1974. Despite their heavy representation among the ranks of working women, they never gained the right to unionize under the National Labor Relations Act, nor did they win workplace health and safety protections. By the 1960s, in fact, domestic service remained the only large occupational group completely excluded from federal labor laws.[31]

Middle-class women's gendered politics lent itself to passionate labor activism on behalf of women industrial workers. But as this study demonstrates, middle-class women's stake in protecting the morality and privacy of the middle-class home impeded the inclusion of domestic workers in protective labor legislation. As a group, nineteenth- and early twentieth-century progressive women's organizations emphasized the importance of the home to national preservation and identified it as the seat of their moral authority to enact social change. Even after the ideology of separate spheres ceased to be the chief organizing principle in women's lives, women reformers continued to identify with a gendered politics that posed women as particularly virtuous and as particularly interested in the welfare of working women and families. Allowing the state to regulate the private middle-class home would mean acknowledging that the home held no special qualities to differentiate it from the public world of work and industry. It would also mean acknowledging that many middle-class women could be just as avaricious as industrialists and possessed no particular moral authority when it came to social justice for the disadvantaged. Protecting their homes from state intervention seemed vital to middle-class women in order to protect their right to participate in public politics. Thus, even as the welfare state opened increasing numbers of poor and working-class homes to state regulation, women's lobbying groups and many women activists did everything in their power to guard the privacy of the middle-class home, including rejecting government regulation of the wages and hours of domestic workers.[32]

Finally, this book explores the concepts of public and private and how they affected both the ideology of middle-class women reformers and the possibilities for resistance among domestic workers. One important facet of the scholarly debate over public and private is some scholars' argument, particularly that of literary theorists, that the use of public and private to explain all manner of historical forces and events has become too broad.[33] They cite numerous examples of the ways in which public and private were intertwined and argue that such strict categorization has lost its analytical usefulness. This literature sets itself in opposition to the work of classical thinkers like Jürgen Habermas, in which the public world of politics and collective citizenry is sharply delineated from the private world of the middle-class home.[34] I, like most other scholars and historians, acknowledge the permeability of the boundaries between public and private in nineteenth- and twentieth-century New York. I also argue, however, that middle-class women did not always see it that way. They invested the middle-class home with enough meaning that they were willing to expend great energy and political capital to protect it. That women reformers and employers thought their homes worth protecting as a private space makes private and public worthy categories for study.

I argue that ideas about what was private and what was public were in constant tension with each other as middle-class housewives, women reformers, domestic experts, legislators, and household workers debated domestic service during this period. Both employers and progressive organized women generally viewed the middle-class home as a private space rather than as a workplace. In this contention they were supported by the view of the middle-class home in law and culture as a gendered private place characterized by intimate relationships rather than by commerce and industry.[35] Domestic labor, both that performed by servants and that performed by unpaid housewives, was widely viewed as part of women's traditional care work rather than as heavy manual labor for which women should be well paid.[36] Thus, even though many progressive women's organizations supported the regulation of personal services like laundry and beauty parlors in the public sector, women labor reformers and employers alike insisted that the middle-class home, as a private space dedicated to the nurturance of middle-class families, should not be regulated.[37]

Middle-class white women's fierce defense of the home as private space was tied up with their ideas about women's role both in the home and in public politics. Women reformers justified their place in public politics by pointing to the moral authority of the middle-class domestic sphere, which they viewed as a space of innate nurturance and morality. For this reason, middle-class reformers viewed the home and its privacy as territory worth defending. But their agenda was fraught with contradiction. Even as they tirelessly advocated for protective labor legislation for women working in industry, middle-class women's groups insisted that government labor protections for domestics represented an invasion of their privacy. Even as they argued that the home should remain untouched by state regulation, they used state power to address the working-class vice, disease, and behaviors that they suspected domestics brought into their homes. The debates over domestic worker legislation reveal more than mere hypocrisy among middle-class reformers. Instead, they illuminate the complexity of women reformers' continued ties to the gendered ideology of the middle-class home, even as they began to take public positions of power.

Of course, early reformers often ignored the role of labor laws and their own reform agendas in creating, or at least allowing, exploitation of domestic workers. To them, the problem was that the occupation was inherently antimodern. Early twentieth-century reformers often portrayed domestic service as an occupation that was fundamentally different from other, more public, forms of labor. These arguments focused on the occupation's supposedly feudal nature. Jane Addams, for instance, called domestic service a "belated industry" in 1896, but she was neither the first nor the last to cast the occupation in these terms.[38] In 1884, the *Nation* argued that domestic service had not yet passed from "status" to "contract." Lucy Maynard Salmon called the occupation an "ancient, patriarchal institution" that needed to be harmonized with modern life.[39] Even modern historians have indulged the feudal metaphor. Scholars frequently refer to domestic service as "somewhat feudal," "pre-industrial," "precapitalist," "anachronistic," or "outside the major paths of modernization and industrialization."[40]

The idea that domestic service is somehow antimodern is problematic.[41]

First of all, casting domestic service as an anachronistic form of labor naturalizes its exclusion from labor reform agendas and state and federal labor laws. Second, it almost certainly reflects the views of turn-of-the-century reformers more than reality. Domestic service was not a static occupation but instead changed in response to the same demographic forces that shaped industry, from mass immigration and migration to the shifting agendas of Progressive and New Deal reform organizations.[42] Finally, the feudal metaphor also rings false because it suggests that domestic service was an entirely private matter, unchanged by the "modern" world developing outside the walls of the middle-class and elite home. To the middle-class women who hired them, domestics certainly linked private homes to the public world and all of its attendant vices by bringing uncouth working-class women into middle-class homes.

Domestic service was, furthermore, demonstrably affected by public politics. Although we often think of domestic service as hidden from public view in middle-class homes, and hence forgotten by legislators, it was in fact a major topic of public debate and reform throughout the first half of the twentieth century. Domestics may have been excluded from labor legislation, but women's groups were not opposed to using government to regulate domestic service for other purposes. Women activists pursued and passed numerous laws designed to provide middle-class homes with better-trained, medically vetted, and morally sound domestic help. Throughout this period, women reformers argued that government should protect their homes from vice and disease but should not regulate its working conditions. The practical effect of such logic was the policing of the bodies and behavior of domestic workers rather than state regulation of their wages and hours.

Middle-class women did not, of course, control state and federal legislatures. Instead, they had to rely on frequently hostile male legislators to make their reforms into law. The battle for women's labor laws was almost always uphill. Progressive women's organizations constantly shifted their strategies and tactics in order to counter near-constant political opposition. That said, legislators and the public both considered women reformers to be experts on social policy concerning working women and children. Beginning in the nineteenth century, middle-class women's organizations created programs designed specifically to address the needs of working women and children. By the 1930s, female policy makers both staffed and ran the federal Department of Labor's Children's Bureau and the Women's Bureau, even though they were excluded from other policy debates. Progressive middle-class women's organizations, especially before the last years of the New

Deal, set the agenda for reform of women's working conditions and proved vital allies for women industrial and retail workers in the fight for better hours and wages. State and federal lawmakers had the ultimate power to structure labor laws, but when it came to laws affecting women workers, middle-class women's organizations chose which battles to fight.[43] Without a demand from middle-class women's groups for domestics' inclusion in labor laws, the continued exclusion of the largest percentage of working women from basic labor standards remained virtually assured.

This book takes both a thematic and a chronological approach to the history of domestic service in New York City and its surroundings. Chapter 1 examines the public discussion about domestic service in the late nineteenth and early twentieth centuries. The middle-class employers, home economists, journalists, and reformers who participated in this discussion posed domestics as ethnic intruders in the middle-class home, who exposed its residents to moral and physical danger. Such depictions lay the foundation for public labor policy debates that focused on reforming domestics rather than addressing their working conditions. Chapter 2 explores the mutual benefit organizations, ethnic dances, and kitchens of middle-class employers, where domestics created a sense of working-class community and identity. There, immigrant domestics vocally and collectively resisted the harsher conditions of service and, in the process, shaped the range of possibilities for the occupation's reform. Chapter 3 investigates middle-class women's domestic service reform efforts at the turn of the twentieth century, which aimed at stemming the tide of urban vice that many middle-class housewives perceived as seeping underneath their kitchen doors. While they lobbied for protective labor legislation for women industrial and retail workers, reformers of domestic service promoted training programs, immigrant homes, and employment societies for the women who worked in private homes. Chapter 4 considers middle-class women reformers' efforts on behalf of domestics as the conditions of household work continued to decline during the Depression. Although organized women opposed state regulation of their household labor relations, they seemed all too eager to use government power to protect their own homes from inept, and allegedly diseased, household workers. In chapter 5, I investigate African Americans' domestic union organizing and labor activism, which included ad hoc groups of domestics who came together to combat the passage of health regulations as well as to form the most active household employees union in the country, the American Federation of Labor–affiliated Domestic Workers Union.

This book tells the story of how domestics were left out of the protective labor legislation that was relatively easily achieved by other women workers in the late nineteenth and early twentieth centuries. Despite its many moments of promise, the story is ultimately one of failure: the failure of imagination on the part of middle-class women who could not see beyond their own needs to address the needs of working women; the failure of domestic workers to make their voices heard in labor policy debates; and the failure of both reformers and domestics to fully integrate the private workplace into public industry and policy. Indeed, the history of domestic service is an anti-tale of social reform, revealing the complicated motives of women labor reformers and the roots of domestic workers' exclusion from labor protections.

One
The Tyrant of the Household

THE DEBATE OVER THE "SERVANT QUESTION"
AND THE PRIVACY OF THE MIDDLE-CLASS
HOME, 1870–1915

Just before Christmas, in 1907, a group of middle-class housewives gathered on the Upper West Side of Manhattan to hear a lecture on domestic service given by I. M. Rubinow. Rubinow was a medical doctor and Ph.D. in economics who would later contribute to the intellectual framework of New Deal social insurance programs. He gave his lecture as one in a series in a course, "Domestic Administration," at Columbia University's Teacher's College. During his talk, Rubinow accused middle-class women of mistreating their domestic employees by, among other things, working them too many hours for not enough pay. Rubinow's take on the issue was not the one anticipated by the New York housewives in his audience. Maybe they assumed he would argue the part of the dissatisfied middle-class domestic employer, many of whom complained that household workers were variously lazy, dishonest, drunk, or sexually promiscuous. Maybe they expected him to echo the gentle admonishments of the writers of prescriptive literature, who advised ladies to be kind in their supervision of the work and morals of domestics but under no circumstances to tolerate bad behavior or incompetence.

What they had not foreseen was Rubinow's statement that no "argument could be offered against the restricting of the servant girl's hours of employment by law other than the inconvenience of the employer."[1] As a *New York Times* reporter wryly observed, one Harlem housewife who had brought her household worker with her so that "'the girl might appreciate the good home she had found with friends' left quite early in the proceedings."[2]

Rubinow's lecture, and his audience's reaction to it, illustrates the warring factions in the public debate over "the servant question" that developed after the Civil War and raged into the 1910s and 1920s. Native-born working women were increasingly reluctant to enter domestic service, leaving middle-class women to complain bitterly of paying inflated wages to immigrant workers for substandard service. A host of experts, ranging from home economists to religious figures, weighed in on what was wrong with servants, and then, perhaps inevitably, on what was wrong with their employers. This contest took place not just on the women's pages of local newspapers but in a host of magazines, newspapers, professional journals, and published muckraking investigations. It was national and public, and it brought to the fore issues more meaningful than the difficulty housewives had in finding good help. This discussion also set the terms for a larger political debate about how domestic service compared to other women's occupations and how the middle-class home compared to other work sites.

This argument had two sides. On the one hand, complaints about domestics' dishonesty, thievery, and sexual promiscuity led experts and pundits to blame domestics for ushering the problems associated with working-class tenements into the middle-class home. According to the experts, middle-class domesticity was in shambles. Employing at least one domestic was vital to any claim to middle-class status. But domestic service, by carrying urban ills and class conflict into middle-class kitchens, threatened the privacy that undergirded the nineteenth-century domestic ideal. On the other hand, some critics focused not on the moral conditions in working-class tenements but rather on the working conditions in middle-class homes. By the turn of the century, some journalists, reformers, and professional experts had come to the conclusion that the "servant problem" was not a problem with servants at all. Instead, they argued that the real problem was that domestic service lacked the standards and organization that would make it as attractive to working-class women as the store or factory. Commentators offered a laundry list of criticisms of women's management of household staff. Women, they argued, failed to pay domestics' wages completely, on time, and in cash rather than in kind. Female employers filled long days with constant and unpredictable requests, demanded humiliating subservience, isolated their employees from friends and family, and provided inadequate food and inferior living conditions. These analyses redefined the "servant problem" as a mistress problem.

Neither of these points of view served the interests of middle-class women, especially the members of the burgeoning women's labor reform movement. In the last two decades of the nineteenth century, these reformers had begun to make the case that they shared a natural gendered interest with working-class women and that they had both a special ability and a special responsibility to advocate on their behalf. They argued that their class and gender role, which held up middle-class wives and mothers as refined nurturers, made them ideal candidates to help create a community driven as much by a gentle, feminine vision of social justice as it was by the profit motive of male industrialists.[3] White middle-class women's politics and their domestic roles were inextricable. Women reformers would find no comfort in either assessment of the problems with domestic service. In one version, the middle-class home was run by vice-ridden, working-class servants who terrorized their mistresses rather than accepting their gentle reforming influence. In the other, middle-class women were not pious ladies who smoothed working-class women's rough edges and Americanized immigrant workers but rather slave drivers who treated their employees little better than machines. Middle-class women, especially those who looked forward to political careers, could not have been pleased with either of these two gloomy domestic visions.

Middle-class women reformers weighed in on this discussion, but like other observers, they did not fall neatly into two easily articulated camps. Instead, middle-class housewives, domestic experts, journalists, and reformers at various times all referred to both domestics' poor working conditions and the tenement vice and corruption that they believed workers brought into middle-class homes. For example, sociologist and Progressive reformer Frances Kellor, whose ideas are discussed in detail in chapter 3, often made both arguments simultaneously in her written work. There was no clear divide between those who championed the rights of domestics and those who worried over the effect of paid domestic labor on the middle-class home.

As the tone of this public discussion heightened, these warring ideas began to give shape to an urban political agenda. The contest over domestic service was thus tied up with other political debates about women's paid labor, government labor legislation, women's reform, and middle-class privacy. Rather than middle-class grumbling, turn-of-the-century discussion of the "servant problem" was part of a much larger public policy debate about paid domestic labor in private homes and its effect on both workers and middle-class families. Equally significant, the debate over the "servant question" created the political lens through which reform organizations would filter their labor reform agendas.

Domestics and Domesticity

The most pressing part of the "servant problem," according to late nineteenth- and early twentieth-century New Yorkers, was that there were not enough native-born, well-behaved women willing to enter domestic service to fill middle-class families' growing demand. Working-class American women generally considered domestic service to be an occupation of last resort. In factory work, even poorly paid women enjoyed defined hours and tasks. Domestic service, in contrast, required isolation, endless chores, and constant employer surveillance. The occupation was, to say the least, unappealing to those with other options.[4] As social reformer Jane Seymour Klink put it, "The native-born American objects to being placed in any position where there is not at least the semblance of freedom."[5] Another woman who had done paid housework before entering factory labor said she left domestic work because of "the long hard hours, shut off from everything and everybody." If reformers and employers wanted to know why native-born workers refused positions in private homes, she offered, "send them to me and I will give them a hundred and one reasons why."[6] The result was a dearth of native-born women willing to take work in private homes. One journalist reported that the difficulty of finding suitable workers united employers "from one end of Manhattan to the other . . . in a chorus of grief which is echoed from Brooklyn [and] Staten Island" to "the Bronx."[7]

By the last two decades of the nineteenth century, domestic service and the comfort, security, and privacy of the middle-class home had become inextricable. Middle-class and wealthy women depended on domestics to make their households run smoothly and to reinforce their class status as a family who could afford to hire help. These families needed workers to answer the door, announce callers, and serve at the table, while also performing life-sustaining tasks like cooking, cleaning, and child care. New Yorkers who were far from wealthy understood that employing at least one, and often two, domestic workers was vital to their material comfort and to the maintenance of their class status.[8]

Middle-class housewives further depended on domestics to free them from housekeeping tasks so that they could concentrate their energies elsewhere. Middle-class women in the urban North increasingly participated in political reform and charitable activities outside the home in the late nineteenth century. But even if they never left the house, middle-class women were responsible for nurturing children. Child rearing was a full-time job, which required women to exercise consistent guidance in shaping children's characters. Hiring domestics allowed women time to perform the emotional labor of wife and mother.[9] Domestics, thus, made turn-of-the-century notions of middle-class domesticity possible.

A shortage of suitable domestic workers posed a real problem, then, for middle-class and elite families. It is hard to be sure if there was an actual shortage of workers willing to enter domestic service or merely a shortage of workers whom employers considered ideal. Certainly, the numbers of newcomers from immigrant groups most likely to take jobs in private homes were rising during this period.[10] Whether the problem was real or imagined, employers and the popular press in the late nineteenth century feared a crisis in American middle- and upper-class homes. A correspondent for *Outlook* noted with horror in 1894 that the "home life of hundreds of families in this country is destroyed because working women, willing and skillful, cannot be found to enter domestic service."[11] The middle-class home and family depended, both ideologically and materially, on paid household labor. A New York housewife warned that it was "an open secret . . . that domestic help was never so utterly demoralized as it is at present" and that the "home as an American institution is fast disappearing from our country."[12] By 1910, the situation had deteriorated to the point that one housewife was allegedly so "in despair of getting the house 'kept'" that she "burned it down."[13] Domestics' labor was vital to the middle-class home, and the difficulty of attracting women to the occupation might, many Americans believed, spell its destruction.

Doing without household workers seemed impossible. Alternatives to domestic service, including giving up private residences entirely, were widely decried as unworkable or, worse, morally suspect. Observers were especially concerned with the oft-cited incidence of New Yorkers, unable to find competent domestic help, "giving up housekeeping" and moving into apartment hotels and boardinghouses.[14] At the turn of the century, the apartment house, offering separate living, sleeping, and dining quarters, provided a respectable solution for middle-class families facing urban housing shortages. Hotels and boardinghouses, in contrast, forced women and children to mix intimately and indiscriminately with single men in shared living and dining rooms.[15] The boardinghouse, like the tenement house, lacked the privacy necessary for the refined middle-class New York family.[16] Other solutions to the "servant problem" also failed because they required forgoing familial privacy. For instance, Charlotte Perkins Gilman's suggestion that middle-class women share housekeeping and child care duties in corporate kitchens and nurseries never came to fruition because families placed too high a value on their autonomy and privacy.[17] Similarly, middle-class housewives worried that commercial laundries, no matter how convenient, might sicken the whole family, when garments from untold numbers and kinds of homes mixed together in common, and possibly unclean, washrooms. In 1881, for example, "KCA," a New York housewife, wrote to the *New York Tribune*, claiming that her family had contracted scarlet fever from "infectious clothes" in disease-ridden laundries.[18] In 1906, Mary Mortimer Maxwell argued that washerwomen infected "cleanly persons" by taking their laundry to tenement homes in "the midst of filth unmentionable, children almost numberless, as well as beetles and the like."[19] Even the patrons of public laundries did not see them as good alternatives to an independent household. Anyone who could afford to hired private washerwomen to do their laundry in their own homes each week. In other words, the privacy and protection of a self-sufficient home was central to the maintenance of virtuous middle-class domesticity, and domestics seemed central to the maintenance of the private, middle-class home. An alarmed journalist explained with ominous logic that the "home cannot exist without separate households, and separate households are impossible without domestic servants, and domestic servants are now all being metamorphosed into shopgirls and mill hands."[20]

Middle-class New Yorkers agreed that hired help was a crucial part of both the cultural definition and the physical upkeep of their homes. The number and kind of paid domestic workers in homes varied depending on the size of the home and the wealth of employers. Families with only a little disposable income hired just a laundress. Her job was so time-consuming and hot and required so much heavy lifting that the term "Blue Monday" referred not just to the bluing used to keep clothes bright but also to the depressingly arduous manual labor demanded by laundry day.[21] In fact, laundry took all day, leaving the next day for ironing, another time-consuming, hot, and heavy task. Solidly middle-class families, who could not afford large staffs but were not willing to go it alone, often hired just one worker, a general houseworker. The general houseworker performed the duties for which wealthier households hired a chambermaid, laundress, cook, and waitress (and sometimes a scullery maid and a kitchen maid too). General houseworkers performed all of the household chores, from cleaning the house, to making the meals, to serving at table, to doing the dishes, to answering the door, to sweeping the porch, to walking the dog, to doing the laundry.

Occasionally an employer might help with the dishes or with making the beds, at least on laundry or ironing days. There were, however, no guarantees. As domestic adviser Mrs. L. Seely acknowledged, "No two households are alike. Rules differ very much."[22] The work was so labor-intensive that general houseworkers often got only one afternoon off per week plus every other Sunday. Families who could afford to do so hired two workers. One acted as the cook and laundress and the other as chambermaid and waitress. The waitress served at table and kept the pantry stocked and the dining room running smoothly. The chambermaid cleaned the family's rooms, made their beds, laid out their clothes, aired out their rooms, and, if she had time, polished the silver. The cook started at six in the morning and was responsible for all three meals and doing the dishes, as well as for buying the groceries and keeping the kitchen clean and orderly.[23] Employers with young children often hired a nursemaid, who took care of the children during the day and often slept in the same room with them at night. New middle-class and wealthy parents hired a wet nurse, who breast-fed her employers' children, often to the detriment of her own.

General houseworkers, nursemaids, waitresses, and cooks allowed middle-class and wealthy families to live in private homes or apartments, but middle-class privacy was not just about keeping families separated from one another. In New York City, the middle-class home also gave its residents respite from the vice that seemed endemic to the city. At the turn of the century, the wealthiest New Yorkers lived along Fifth Avenue above Fourteenth Street. Dwellings then decreased in prosperity as streets extended toward each river, the East River on the one side and the Hudson on the other, forming what one historian refers to as a "class sandwich."[24] Working-class New Yorkers, meanwhile, lived in tenement districts, which grew up around factories on the riverfront and by the ports in Lower Manhattan. In Jacob Riis's famous phrasing, tenements appeared "wherever business leaves a foot of ground unclaimed; strung along both rivers, like a ball and chain tied to the foot of every street," or, as one tenement resident more bluntly put it, the "nearer the river the nearer to hell."[25] Conditions in tenement districts were notorious. In the late nineteenth century, the Tenement House Committee of the Working Women's Society reported children playing in trash piles amid a "sickening . . . stench" in Lower East Side tenements, which also played host to prostitutes, drunks, and criminals.[26] Dr. S. Josephine Baker, who would later help capture "Typhoid" Mary Mallon, described her work in the Irish district of Hell's Kitchen on Midtown's West Side as a parade of "drunk after drunk, filthy mother after filthy mother and dying baby after dying baby."[27] The horror with which reformers described life in the tenements highlights the social and geographical distance that well-to-do New Yorkers put between themselves and the benighted working classes. Indeed, the middle classes defined themselves not just by their privacy from neighboring apartments but also by their ability to afford residences spatially separated from the blight of working-class neighborhoods.[28]

The "Servant Problem" and the Middle-Class Home

Middle-class women may have lived in neighborhoods far away from tenement districts, but they were often forced to cross these urban class lines in search of domestic employees. According to social reformer Frances Kellor, more than three-fifths of employers found their domestics from one of the 313 employment agencies, or "intelligence offices," in turn-of-the-century New York.[29] While some of these offices were located in the middle- and upper-class neighborhoods which they hoped to serve, many specialized in domestics of specific nationalities and established offices in tenement apartments on the Lower East Side and near the Battery in Lower Manhattan.[30] Hiring a domestic from one of these offices, observed one journalist, required that prospective employers "climb grimy stairs to grimier front rooms" of tenement houses or to "rear tenements, top floors," sometimes finding "merely a frowsy boozing-den for the most impudent and worthless dregs of servant-girldom."[31] In fact, one late nineteenth-century intelligence office advertised its difference from the usual tenement fare by talking up its "prominent location" and "separate and well-appointed rooms," allowing prospective employers to "avoid the annoyance of coming in contact with a crowd of servants."[32] It was, wrote a reporter for the *New York Tribune*, "a repulsive," if also necessary, "task for a woman of refinement to wander about the slums, climbing dark and dirty stairways and exploring unsavory alleys."[33]

Unlike their charitable forays into working-class neighborhoods, middle-class women did not have the upper hand in their interactions with the working-class patrons of intelligence offices. As a *New York Tribune* reporter

A middle-class couple exits one of this New York City tenement district's domestic employment agencies. (Courtesy of Brown Brothers)

noted, women's encounters with tenement conditions in the course "of charitable or mission work . . . might have been tolerable, but as a matter of business it was most unsatisfactory."[34] Public accounts abound of the distinct disadvantage employers faced in procuring a competent domestic at a fair wage. A "humorist" for *American Magazine* described the scene at a Swedish intelligence office on Fourth Avenue, where housewives were "menaced by the powers of Europe" and where he witnessed "a rangy brute of a Norwegian laundress . . . giving a timid little lady from the Bronx a bad five minutes."[35] Middle-class women also believed that employment offices deliberately sent morally suspect women into their homes and neighborhoods. One employer who claimed to have had nineteen different domestics in as many months complained that the intelligence office sent "the most extraordinary riffraff. . . . Many of the girls were drunk when they came to the house; one was a morphine eater and locked herself in the room, [and] made a frightful scene."[36] Although this situation was probably extreme, evidence shows that such claims were at least possible. One employment agent allegedly sent the same woman to twenty-eight different employers, where she remained long enough for the agent to collect his fee and then returned to the employment office to be placed again.[37] Intelligence office managers, Frances Kellor argued, had only quick placements (and quick fees) in mind, not the best interests of the middle-class home. Kellor accused intelligence offices of purposeful neglect when proprietors sent domestics "so intoxicated that [they] must have known it; when chambermaids and waitresses are sent when cooks are ordered; when negroes appear, though whites are distinctly specified; when Catholics arrive in place of Protestants; and incompetents for competent—no end."[38] Not only did elite women bear the risk of leaving their neighborhoods and homes in order to procure domestic help, but once there, they did not have the authority to change the working-class environment, as did benevolent reformers. Although their class status gave them a sense of moral authority on missions of reform, middle-class women who wandered tenement districts in search of domestics were at the mercy of working-class employment office managers. They needed domestics, and only the intelligence office, which they suspected did not have their best interests at heart, could provide them.

That conditions in tenement employment agencies were not up to middle-class standards was perhaps to be expected. Commentators weighing in on the "servant problem," however, worried over the consequences of bringing domestics from these conditions into middle-class neighborhoods and homes. After all, one reporter argued, domestics inevitably came out of tenement offices "with a store of bad habits" and no shortage of "opportunities for work."[39] Middle-class fears about their domestics' personal histories were not unfounded. Domestics were frequently admitted to jails and other institutions for problems that included alcoholism, mental illness, and criminality.[40] Frances Kellor, for example, cited statistics that, of the 1,451 prisoners held at Blackwell's Island, a New York City prison, 1,298 had been domestics before they were arrested.[41] She worried about the effect of these workers "upon the employer and her home," asking, "Can employers afford to accept household workers who come from such dirty, disease-laden, vermin infested, and immoral places . . . ready to contaminate all with whom they come into contact?"[42] As Helen Campbell, a journalist, social investigator, and advocate of tenement reform, reminded New York housewives in the late 1880s, tenements produced "hundreds of our domestic servants, whose influence is upon our children at their most impressible age, and who bring inherited and acquired foulness into our homes and lives."[43] Campbell believed that unsavory domestics who had been reared in the tenements and presumably found employment in its offices to be "powerful and most formidable agents in that blunting of moral perception which is a more and more apparent fact in the life of the day."[44] An employer who wrote to the editor of the *New York Tribune* agreed that many working-class domestics had been so "contaminated by contact with all that is vilest in this world as to be a dangerous element in a pure household — unclean, unfit."[45] As employers traveled to tenement districts in search of domestics, many observers feared that the conditions of the tenements might be carried back to infect middle-class homes.

Ideally, Americans everywhere believed, the refining influence of the middle-class home would ameliorate these early bad influences. Middle-class and elite employers, not to mention the many industrial labor reformers who tried to persuade women working in factories and shops to enter domestic service, saw the middle-class home as fundamentally different from other workplaces. Unlike industrial jobs, paid household labor, reformers and other experts hoped, would promote a utopian vision in which domestics experienced moral uplift under female middle-class guardianship.[46] After all, domestic adviser Christina Goodwin reminded housewives, "it is as offering a good home that domestic service makes its special claim."[47] Goodwin's idea of a "good home" was characterized by a class hierarchy in which middle-class women provided working-class domestics not just with "food and shelter" but also with a "glow of kindly interest and the felt influence of a right view of life and its duties."[48] This kind of moral guidance, housewives and labor reformers argued, could not be found in any factory, no matter how high the wages. Magazines, newspapers, middle-class employers, and writers of prescriptive literature lauded the middle-class home as a school to Americanize immigrants and inculcate working-class women with the ideals of middle-class domesticity. Even Frances Kellor promoted the idea that the middle-class home might counteract domestics' early pernicious influences. It was the middle-class employer's duty and privilege, she wrote, to endow her domestic employee with "knowledge, efficiency, culture and a democratic spirit."[49] A journalist for the *New York Times* agreed that the American home could elevate its servants both "socially and morally."[50] The home was, in these formulations, totally unlike more public workplaces, and middle-class women were totally unlike commercial employers. In an ideal world, the middle-class home might serve as a microcosm of progressive women's wider reform agenda: working-class women transformed under the gentle tutelage of middle-class wives and mothers.

It was not, however, an ideal world, a fact that public commentators frequently pointed out. Refining domestic workers was nearly impossible, middle-class and elite women complained, when domestics wielded more power in the kitchen than did their employers. Businessman, lecturer, and prolific essayist Edwin P. Whipple went so far as to declare the independent, voting man a myth, since, "as soon as he proudly leaves the polls and enters his own house, he is no longer an independent citizen . . . but an abject serve [sic], utterly dependent on the caprices of his domestics."[51] In a letter to the *Tribune*, a New York housewife chimed in, claiming that "as a rule it is the employers who are domineered over by the servant girls." She went on to point out that domestics had the power to alter their employers' household routine, forcing middle-class families "to change their habits, to eat dinner at unconventional and depressing hours."[52] Still another housewife pronounced every employer "at the mercy of her cook or maid," also known as "the tyrant of the household," and a "Downtrodden Mistress" declared herself "in hopeless subjection" to her household workers.[53] Even domestic expert Harriet Spofford had to admit that "if our domestic regulations are not made for us by Bridget and Nora, they cannot at any rate be carried out without their consent."[54] In reality, middle-class and elite women were hardly servants to their servants. Employers could and did fire domestics without reason or notice and without a reference with which to procure future employment.[55] Still, middle-class housewives who wrote in to New York newspapers clearly did not feel that their reality matched the ideal image of middle-class women exerting a gentle influence on women workers.

It seemed clear to many that domestics disrupted the tranquil ideal of middle-class domesticity by bringing working-class behaviors into middle-class kitchens and living rooms. If middle-class families had encountered what they viewed as less than civilized behavior on city streets, they might have chalked it up to the lack of refinement among New York's lower classes and moved on without concern. But the middle-class home was an intimate space where working-class domestics were a constant presence. Indeed, inviting domestics into the most intimate moments of family life was part and parcel of conducting a middle-class household. Domestics laundered the family's dirty linens, cleaned bedrooms, cared for children, and tended sick family members. Moreover, their duties brought them into contact with the family's most private business. They were present for family arguments, marital spats, and moments of crisis. They were not, however, part of the middle-class family. Neither were they bound by the same class-based behavioral standards or sense of family loyalty as middle-class members of the household. Middle-class employers often complained that domestics did not respect their privacy. After all, one *Harper's Weekly* writer noted, "if you get up very early, or stay out very late, you may see a group of these old women chatting in front of almost any Catholic church near a fashionable neighborhood. . . . Those are Mary and her friends discussing us. . . . Did you ever wonder how news flew so quickly from house to house?"[56] As middle-class observers constantly pointed out, employers, despite their social and economic power, did not entirely control domestics' interaction with their families. This working-class intrusion in middle-class homes, however necessary to their material comfort, was profoundly threatening.

The list of allegedly working-class behaviors that observers believed domestic workers ushered into middle-class homes was long. Even the Protestantism of middle-class and elite homes seemed under threat. Fears of Irish Catholic nursemaids secretly baptizing Protestant children in their care were reportedly widespread among employers.[57] One journalist warned middle-class women of the alleged Catholic belief that, with careful and consistent religious guidance, Catholics could convert any Protestant child who was under seven years of age.[58] Worse, Mary Cusack, an Irish nun, reminded young Irish women entering domestic service in America "how happy it would be" for them to convert "some Protestant to the one true Faith!"[59] Although Cusack intended conversion of employers by example, middle-class Protestant readers would have been appalled by any plans for Catholic conversion. Even if Catholic domestics kept their religion to themselves, their devotion disrupted the Protestant families for whom they worked. Irish domestics were often unmoved by pleas to skip mass to attend to unexpected guests or some other pressing domestic chore. As Harriet Spofford remarked, "Bridget" made "the whole family feel the bitterness of having kept her" home from church until, finally, "you let her go and be done with it. Be done with it? She is never done with it. For unexpected saints' days and days of obligation play a perpetual havoc with your affairs."[60] New Yorkers associated Catholicism with the lives and rituals of the immigrant working classes. Catholicism, which Protestant New Yorkers imagined demanded a slavish devotion to the pope, was also a marker of immigrants' ethnic and racial inferiority.[61] By hiring household labor, employers resigned themselves to inviting Catholic influence into Protestant middle-class homes.

But the delinquent behavior that observers of the "servant problem" were most concerned would infect middle-class homes was what they viewed as domestics' pronounced proclivity for sexual vice. In an effort to maintain their stake in what one historian calls the "*desexualized*" middle-class and elite home, female employers spent much of their time policing domestics' sexual liaisons with working-class men, or "followers."[62] Domestic expert Christina Goodwin counseled employers to prohibit the "visits of bad men and women," although, as she gently reminded her readers, it would be unreasonable to insist that "temperate, hard-working Michael shall not come to see Bridget."[63] Distinguishing "bad men and women" from the temperate and the hardworking, however, was easier said than done, and middle-class women and their advisers suspected that most of the men domestics brought home were up to no good. As one domestic complained in a letter to the *Tribune*, "If your clergyman calls to see you . . . you are afraid of being caught with a man in the house, breaking the laws of the house, which forbid 'followers.'"[64]

To middle-class eyes, however, relaxing restrictions on "followers" opened their homes to a literal invasion of the sexually charged working classes. In a fictional tale, University of Chicago–trained sociologist Annie Marion MacLean wrote of a youthful heroine who brought two men to her employer's home, where she shared liquor from the men's flasks. She then expressed surprise at her employer's reaction, exclaiming, "My! it was awful the way she looked."[65] Stories like this one were not always fictional. Annie Ware Winsor Allen, who taught at the prestigious Brearly School in New York City and was a member of New York's Social Reform Club, the Woman's Municipal League, and later the League of Women Voters, expressed dismay when her domestics invited two men into her kitchen. Allen lamented that the two workers, Bridie Kennedy and Helen Tangney, chose men "of whom they knew nothing except that one lodged with a woman shopkeeper." Of this encounter, an eavesdropping Allen could hear only "long silences . . . broken by sudden smothered shrieks or giggles from the girls, or cries of 'oh dear'—in laughing tones." She sent the two women back to the employment office from whence they came, proclaiming herself "not willing to assume the burden of trying to reform these girls."[66] Allen was not the only employer to lose a worker in a dispute over sexual propriety. Johanna Erickson abruptly quit her position as a cook in Henrietta MacLauren Richards's kitchen after the two got into a "fuss" over the man Richards had discovered in Erickson's bedroom.[67] Keeping the middle-class home from falling into moral disrepair demanded constant vigilance.

Media stories and middle-class concerns about domestics' sexual promiscuity were not without support. Experts widely suspected domestic workers of being especially inclined toward prostitution. In his investigation of prostitution in New York City, George Kneeland confirmed earlier studies finding that domestic service was the most likely occupation for former prostitutes housed in rescue homes, refuges, and asylums.[68] The alarmingly inevitable conclusion, commentators warned, was that these institutionalized fallen women very well "may have been girls who worked in your kitchen or that of the woman next door."[69] Students of "the servant problem" focused on the idea that domestics brought sexual vice from the tenements into middle-class homes. In fact, Frances Kellor's most effective evidence against tenement employment agencies was that they funneled domestic workers into brothels and allowed prostitutes to mingle among the workers in intelligence office waiting rooms. Until they addressed these problems, employers "could never be sure" that their new employee, as Kellor put it, "has not been the rounds."[70]

Domestic service experts saw household workers' potentially promiscuous pasts as more than just an intellectual problem. Domestic and social experts viewed sexual immorality as something akin to a virus, sure to spread from one member of the household to the rest. Especially since domestics cared for children, it was particularly important to reformers like Kellor that they be virtuous "from both hygienic and moral standpoints."[71] An additional undercurrent of concern in this literature was that sexually aggressive, attractive young women might prove too much for the self-control of employers' sons and husbands. After all, as one employer told a *New York*

Times reporter, "a handsome face and figure are no recommendation to a servant girl—quite the reverse."[72] This theme appeared frequently in magazines and newspapers at the turn of the twentieth century. In one fictional magazine melodrama, a man impulsively attends the wake of a former domestic named Nora and is surprised to meet his son. His first thought is, "'What is Harold doing here?' . . . There was only one answer." He remembers that Harold was sixteen when Nora began working for the family and thinks, "That is the impressionable age, when life stirs in the veins and struggles for expression. . . . And Nora was pretty, she was very pretty."[73] Kellor also related the tale of two sisters who left their positions because the lady of the house "was very jealous." Kellor was further disturbed to hear that the intelligence agent "joked with them in a frivolous manner about the 'chances you stand of cutting the wife out.'"[74] Neither employers nor reformers often acknowledged what domestics themselves knew only too well—that domestics were probably more often victims of sexually predatory behavior than perpetrators.[75] Instead, reformers like Kellor worried that the sexual experience that domestics allegedly acquired in working-class tenements and employment agencies might have the worst kind of influence on their employers' homes.

It was not just domestics' interactions with men that reformers and public commentators urged female employers to monitor. Although domestic advisers frequently counseled women to allow their employees to invite one or two friends or family members to visit while they were not on duty, they also warned that employers' homes might become working-class meeting places.[76] As one householder told Lucy Salmon, "Who wants a dozen strange girls running in and out of one's back door?"[77] A correspondent for the *New York Times* similarly explained that she had "always disliked" the idea that "in my kitchen all sorts and kinds of people from no one knows where were being entertained."[78] Another journalist complained that turn-of-the-century New Yorkers suffered a "crowd in their kitchens," accompanied by "noise, the dirt, the smoke from visitors' pipes, the waste of fuel, the danger from fires and lamps."[79] Indeed, one domestic expert for *Good Housekeeping* instructed her readers that "the use of the employer's food supply by servants when entertaining their guest[s] should be forbidden or properly regulated."[80] After all, it was not unknown for domestic workers to invite quite unsavory characters into their employers' kitchens. In 1880, the *New York Times* published a piece about a household worker who waited for her mistress's absence to invite a peddler into the house. Her guest promptly "made himself at home," and they both drank freely from the family wine.[81]

A middle-class housewife worried that, left to her own devices, her employee would invite "drunken loafers in my kitchen or night thieves in my silver."[82] As early as 1894, the *New York Tribune* declared that the practice among middle-class families of allowing domestics to have company was in decline because it had been "so much abused." The worst of this abuse included "all sorts of orgies, beer-drinking and card-playing."[83] Without strict control over their domestics' visitors, observers warned, middle-class kitchens would become open to a flow of traffic from the tenements, quite literally turning the middle-class kitchen into an urban public space.

It was not enough to supervise domestics' socializing in middle-class kitchens. If employers were not careful, commentators cautioned, domestics' activities outside the home could have disastrous effects on the middle-class home and family. Household workers' effect on the children in their care was quite worrying to the advisers of middle-class women. Readers of the *Ladies' Home Journal* would have been sickened by a story about a "beautiful baby girl" who "broke out with terrible sores all over her face and head." The rash turned out to be ringworm, caused by daily visits to her nurse's family, "where her little sister who had this disease had played with and kissed the baby."[84] Charlotte Perkins Gilman similarly argued that "it is a perfectly natural temptation" for domestics to take employers' children on such visits, even though "there are all those awful risks of diseases and things. Now, if their families were nicer people and lived in nicer places,— but then they wouldn't want to be nurse-maids!"[85] Late nineteenth-century domestics' willingness to live with their employers' families allowed employers to maintain near-constant surveillance over their household workers. But employers and other observers worried that even that was not enough to protect middle-class families from vice or disease.

Reformers and public observers argued that physical disease was not the only blight that should worry mothers with hired nurses. Moral disease was, in their eyes, just as infectious. As servants assumed more child care tasks, experts worried that they would supplant mothers as middle-class children's primary role models. Was it even possible, these experts wondered, for working-class domestics to communicate the proper middle-class family values to the children they cared for? As an advocate for trained governesses put it, "Is a servant the proper person to train a child?"[86] Another observer reminded women that "one or two sentences spoken in the hearing of your child may destroy his character in years to come."[87] Author and lecturer Heloise Durant Rose similarly compared the nursemaid to "a snake in the grass," giving children "their first impressions of morality or immorality, decency or indecency, honesty or deceit."[88] An outraged correspondent for the *Ladies' Home Journal* agreed that the Irish nurse who told her small sobbing charge to "dry up" so that she could spend more time flirting with baggage handlers on a train station platform was not providing the right environment for middle-class child rearing.[89] Gilman also provided examples of the "irresponsible nursemaid." She reported multiple sightings of children's nurses enjoying "gossip, and quite often a flirtation with some passing friend or stranger" in public parks while walking small children. A horrified Gilman also recounted watching "a particularly impatient nurse" stoop down to "bite the soft cheek of the baby in the carriage!"[90] The home that was supposed to shelter the middle class's most vulnerable could only too easily, in the view of these critics, become the site of children's corruption.

Domestic workers' participation in working-class amusements was therefore also disturbing to domestic service's public experts. Middle-class reformers believed that dance halls, saloons, and cheap theaters encouraged sexual promiscuity through unsupervised socializing between young working-class men and women. Vice reformers were shocked by the frank sexuality of modern dances and worried about the close sexual contact that might occur in darkened movie theaters or in dim saloons under the influence of alcohol. They also worried about the spread of this youth culture to young middle-class women, who were beginning to imitate working-class recreational patterns. Reformers worked desperately to put the dancing genie back into the bottle, enacting legislation to regulate commercial amusements and sending vice investigators to patrol the places where working-class youth congregated. They opened all sorts of working-girls societies and social clubs, hoping to lure young working women away from the dance hall and into a more brightly lit space where they could be supervised by middle-class matrons.[91]

Employers and observers of domestic service, meanwhile, worried that vice returned with household workers to middle-class homes after their day out. One reporter lamented the fact that so many domestics insisted on more time off in order "to visit friends, go to the theatre, &c."[92] Author and poet Josephine Daskam Bacon noted in *American Magazine* that the average household worker seemed to possess "an instinctive distaste for any form of physical culture (except dancing)."[93] One young German woman who worked as a nurse for a series of middle-class families and published her life story in the *Independent* argued, to the probable dismay of many of her middle-class readers, that her employers and their friends did not appreciate Coney Island only because "these high people don't know how to dance. I have to laugh when I see them at their balls and parties. If only I could get out on the floor and show them how—they would be astonished."[94] Annie Marion MacLean's fictional household worker loved to attend the theater, dance halls, and saloons, gushing that she "had the loveliest time" and met some "lovely gentlemen."[95] By 1912, domestics had discovered the movies, and rather than spending time off with family, they enjoyed this new entertainment, which was so cheap that, as one *New York Times* reporter put it, "even a servant can afford it."[96] Domestic workers' participation in the revelry of dance halls, saloons, and theaters marked their working-class identity, and many worried that such revelry would bring moral degradation to the middle-class home.

Along with the idea that domestics were sexually promiscuous, public media barraged middle-class employers with the claim that domestics brought criminal dishonesty from the streets into employers' homes. Some servants did indeed steal from their employers, but many complained that they were unfairly suspected of thievery.[97] Domestics were often the first ones that middle-class employers and the police suspected when property went missing. Middle-class women complained that "thieving servants are sharp thorns in the sides of many a careful housekeeper."[98] Domestics were already morally suspect residents of the middle-class home, and their intimate contact with the middle-class family and its possessions made them criminally suspect as well. Daily newspapers did little to reduce the fear of dishonest household help, reporting in outrageous detail the jewels and dresses that criminal domestics took from their employers.[99] In the minds of public commentators, there was "no doubt about the existence of a great floating criminal class among the people who go out to service."[100] Frances Kellor agreed, blaming intelligence offices for sending domestics into home after home to pilfer and fence middle-class families' possessions.[101] One *New York Tribune* correspondent argued that women who were careful with their shopping bags in public shopping areas should not relax their vigilance at home, since "they ran just as much risk, one would think based on newspaper accounts of dishonest servants, of being robbed in their own homes."[102] To middle-class and elite housewives who read the papers, it was clear that domestic service rendered null the protection of their homes from the criminality of New York City's streets.

In a few unlucky families, newspapers eagerly reported, working-class domestics turned violent. Sensational newspaper reports, such as that of twenty-three-year-old Mary Heany's arrest in Brooklyn for setting on fire the bed in which her employers' children were sleeping, reinforced stereotypes of domestics as not only uncouth but violent.[103] In early 1881, the *New York Times* reported that Mary O'Gorman, in a fit of pique, had thrown a stove-lifter at the Goodwin children, who had just arrived home from school.[104] Kate Goley exacted revenge upon her employers after a reprimand by throwing an expensive Teniers painting to the floor and spearing it with the tip of an umbrella. One journalist suggested that stories like these were commonplace, claiming that by the second day of employment the violently inclined domestic "picks a quarrel under the stimulation of whisky obtained in some mysterious manner; threatens to 'bust up everything'; she does break a few things simply to terrify your wife, gets a week's pay, and takes her bundle and her departure, cursing loudly as she goes and invoking all disaster upon your house and yourself."[105] Grace Eulalie Matthews Ashmore, the prosperous married daughter of a soda water magnate, reported in her diary a fight with her maid that was so intense that Ashmore called the police to physically remove the woman from the house.[106] Middle-class and elite families had their own violence, of course, but working-class women were more likely to engage in public physical confrontations.[107] In these reports, domestic service made the middle-class home, supposedly a haven from urban vice and violence, a venue for class conflict and behavior that was usually enacted on city streets.

Finally, and perhaps most significant, household service disturbed the domestic peace by making the middle-class home a site of the rising tension between labor and capital. Experts worried that there was a fine line between "the servant problem" and the divisive public labor disputes that had arisen in other workplaces at the turn of the century. Pundits predicted the coming of "rebellion that brings the bitterness of labor vs. capital into our kitchens to sour our children's bread and bully us into a state of submission."[108] Others warned that only by recognizing "the relation of the little drama being played out in her kitchen to the great forces of capital and labor" could the household employer avoid "unions and strikes, thus throwing our domestic world into chaos."[109] Lucy Maynard Salmon, also urging reform, agreed that, in order to solve their labor problem, middle-class and wealthy women had to begin to regard domestic service as "part of the great labor question of the day."[110]

As urban historian David Scobey has noted, "The city streets provoked elite anxiety because they were a site of class tension" and "a theater of public disorder."[111] Domestic service, domestic experts and employers alleged, brought this "theater of public disorder," marked by thievery, violence, class conflict, sexual promiscuity, and raucous social gatherings, into the middle-class home. Domestics stood in for a tangle of urban problems that blighted tenement neighborhoods and, through working-class domestics, made their way into middle-class homes. The private home, rather than being a haven from the problems of the urban working class, was in danger of becoming a breeding ground for sexual immorality, labor conflict, dishonesty, and violence.

The Problem with Middle-Class Management

A second strand in the debate over the "servant problem" gradually emerged as observers began to suggest that middle-class women themselves were to blame for what they perceived to be the ill effects of domestic service on the middle-class home. Perhaps the problem was not that domestics could not be refined, observers suggested, but rather that middle-class employers failed to adhere to their own standards of refinement. These critics lamented that in women's dealings with their household employees, "the doctrine of the brotherhood of man is not always applied so as to embrace the sisterhood of women."[112] As one reader more succinctly put it in a letter to a national magazine, "The trouble is not always with the servants. It is the women who employ them."[113] Home economist and social reformer Jane Seymour Klink suggested that incompetent and vice-ridden household workers were "in part the product of inefficient, inconsiderate, and indifferent employers."[114] Frances Kellor also lay some of the blame for the "servant problem" at the feet of employers, arguing that when "supervision is lax, intelligence low, the housekeeping neglected, the employee gradually adopts the standards of sanitation, hygiene, and conversation which she was taught in the crowded tenement."[115] These commentators assumed that domestic service represented the most wholesome and natural of women's occupations. The inability of the middle-class home to uplift domestic workers, they asserted, began with middle-class women's failure to act as patient managers and moral guides.

Most disturbing to these observers was middle-class women's role in allowing domestics to wander sexually astray. By not providing supervised space in their homes for domestics to meet men, critics suggested that female employers contributed to the moral ruin of working-class women.[116] Rheta Childe Dorr, a prolific muckraking journalist concerned with women's labor and a member of New York's Women's Trade Union League, argued that the women who met their lovers on urban park benches were mostly domestic servants. She reminded employers, "You pity them for their immodest behavior in a public place. But most of them have no other place to meet." Employers should supervise meetings between working-class men and women in the middle-class parlor. When domestics had to leave their employers' homes to meet men, Dorr argued, "it is not difficult to comprehend that clandestine appointments in dark corners do not conduce to proper behavior."[117] Citing statistics indicating the presence of a high number of former domestics among women giving birth out of wedlock, Margaret Dreier Robins, the future president of the Women's Trade Union League, called the idea that the middle-class home protected domestics from sexual ruin a "cherished myth."[118] This line of argument persisted into the twentieth century. In 1914, Rose Young published a tract entitled *From Kitchen to Nightcourt*. Young blamed the high numbers of former domestics among the ranks of prostitutes squarely on employers. One reviewer summarized Young's argument with the question, "May not the very fact that we so seldom can or do offer servants a place to entertain callers be just the reason why girls are forced to meet in public places and on the street, and hence are totally without restraint of the presence of others?"[119] It seemed to these critics that the same steps that employers took to protect their homes from sexual vice created the conditions for domestics' moral ruin.

Most of this literature focused on working-class women's encounters with working-class men on park benches and city streets. Although most middle-class women were loathe to admit it, some suggested that middle-class men posed the real sexual danger for household workers.[120] As one employment agent told a reporter, "If the girl is not pretty," young men "think that she is a poor servant."[121] Another employment agent reported that she received frequent calls from men requesting attractive maids and had received one from a female employer asking for a domestic that was neither fat nor pretty since "I don't like fat girls—and my husband does like pretty ones!"[122] Lillian Pettengill, who wrote a muckraking book about her experiences as a domestic in New York, reported that the sexually harassed worker routinely had to "seize her employer's husband by the coat collar and thrust him into the back yard for safe keeping."[123] Kellor also acknowledged the potential for sexually aggressive male employers and recounted the tale of one domestic who, after being sent "as a sort of assistant" to an old man, went to another household where "the two sons forced their attentions upon her" and "she learned to drink and smoke." As was usually the fate of working-class female characters in middle-class reform literature, this morally ruined young woman died in a workhouse within five years.[124] Even the rare depiction of middle-class men as sexual predators damaged the idealized image of domestic service as a refining and wholesome occupation.

Most critics of domestic service, however, preferred to focus on its poor working conditions. When compared to women in other occupations, they pointed out, household workers worked longer hours with fewer predictable tasks. These critics depicted female managers of household labor as capricious and demanding. Even if work in the middle-class home was wholesome, argued a correspondent for the *Ladies' Home Journal*, domestic service's hours were "discouraging, to say the least."[125] Employers should keep in mind, labor reformers like Jane Seymour Klink argued, that "girls are not machines. They cannot keep going from dawn till dark, and always be pleasant, cheerful, and good-natured. They cannot rise above illness or weariness, and be perpetually willing and obliging."[126] The heavy workload of domestic service was unendurable for most women, muckrakers and reformers argued. After all, asked a journalist who had worked undercover as a domestic worker to report on the occupation's conditions, "if your work wears down the constitution of the hearty foreign girl, how could an American endure it?"[127] Critics pointed out that employers' penchant for asking household workers to forgo their day off to attend to "the plans, or even the caprices and thoughtlessness, of her employers," only lengthened the domestic workweek.[128] In other occupations, women could follow their own pursuits on days off, but the domestic worker bowed to "her mistress' convenience, no matter what her own engagements are."[129] In other words, in domestic service, a household worker told Helen Campbell, "you're never sure that your soul's your own."[130] In these embarrassingly public critiques of domestic service, middle-class women did not stand out as refined, Christian managers of their workers but rather as fickle and demanding. Worst of all, they appeared in this literature as employers who were inferior to factory owners and shopkeepers, who at least granted their employees a few short hours off.

In contrast to the much-lauded image of the middle-class home as the most wholesome environment possible for women workers, working conditions failed to meet basic standards. Employers, critics argued, often did not even provide adequate food and shelter. A journalist for the *New York Tribune* described conditions in which domestic workers might consider themselves lucky if they slept four to a small, dirty room. Others had "to sleep in the hallway or kitchen" or on "a mattress that is rolled up in a heap during the day and stretched out on the floor at night."[131] No wonder domestics were hard to find, argued another commentator, if the average household worker's "room is in the garret, if in a house, or a dark, unventilated closet that barely holds a cot, if in an apartment-house." Worse still, some workers ate only "what is sent from the table to the kitchen when the family is through."[132] An employment agent agreed, telling a reporter that "servants don't get enough to eat; often they're half starved; they have to eke out with food bought out of their wages; they come in here looking run down and anemic; and this trouble's worse, if anything, in the wealthiest families."[133] So much, such critics argued, for the middle-class home as "a shelter, which shall be in every sense of the word, a Home" for women workers.[134]

Employers were also notorious for late payment or nonpayment of wages. Reports of middle-class women "forgetting" to pay wages, asking for extra time to come up with the money, or offering secondhand clothing or other gifts in lieu of pay appeared frequently in mass market literature on the "servant question." As one worker declared to a reformer, "I think the meanest thing of all . . . is to be cheated out of your money."[135] Still another complained in *Outlook* magazine that "ladies are sometimes not honest in money matters concerning the girls they employ," and if "the girl has given no written receipt for her wages, she sometimes has no proof of what is due her."[136] In fact, middle-class women regularly appeared in reform literature and the popular press as offering workers neither the moral uplift of the middle-class home nor the predictable working hours, defined tasks, and prompt payment of commercial occupations.

The conclusion that nearly all these critiques drew was that domestic service was out of step with the tenets of free labor. Whereas women in factories sold specific amounts of time at a worktable performing particular tasks, domestic workers' free time was at the mercy of a busy mistress's whim. If household workers put their bodies at the beck and call of others in return for substandard wages and living conditions, critics argued, what differentiated domestic service from slavery? As one journalist explained, domestic service had yet to pass from status to contract in which "persons . . . sell their labor as they would sell potatoes, and owe nothing more to the purchaser."[137] Another writer opined, "Since time immemorial it has been a tradition that certain things should not be given in exchange for money."[138] In spite of such long-held traditions, however, the exploited household worker had "sold her 'liberty.'"[139] I. M. Rubinow compared domestic employment agents to slave traders, arguing that the agent "trades, not in cigars or groceries, as his neighbors do, but in human beings. It is not service that he rents out, but servants. Naturally human goods are more troublesome than live stock or furniture."[140] In short, a worker wrote to the

New York Tribune, a "servant is literally a white slave."[141] The metaphor of slavery ran rampant throughout criticisms of domestic service. One journalist claimed that the "condition of the domestic is scarcely distinguishable from that of a slave." Another argued that the domestic might have the privilege of living in the middle-class or elite home, "but she is not free."[142] Indeed, argued another, "ladies could make domestic service a blessing to the human family of toilers, but alas! As it is now it may truly be called domestic slavery."[143] In these depictions, employers resembled slave drivers more than pious ladies bearing moral uplift. Depictions of the home as the site of wage slavery, as bad as any factory, were particularly damning portrayals of middle-class women's domestic management.[144]

INDEED, BY THE turn of the twentieth century, middle-class women had a problem. Much of the public conversation surrounding domestic service centered on concerns that domestic workers brought behaviors that they had learned in the tenements into middle-class kitchens. Furthermore, it seemed to many employers, reformers, and other observers that hordes of working-class friends and family followed domestics into middle-class homes. These commentators worried that domestic workers, reared amid the filth, vice, and crowds of New York's working-class tenements, could not help but bring moral ruin to middle-class homes. Female employers, who had been overrun by their domestic help, could not provide the gendered and refining influence that reformers and domestic experts attached to the middle-class home. Other critics charged that if middle-class homes were in moral danger, middle-class women had themselves to blame. These observers accused middle-class and elite employers of failing to provide a refined environment for their workers. They pointed to workers who were subjected to unreasonable hours, substandard food and shelter, and inconsistent pay. Critics like I. M. Rubinow argued that instead of moral uplift, employers should promise fair wages and specified hours and tasks. In short, these critics believed, employers in the middle-class and elite home should strive to offer the same benefits as any other workplace.

At the heart of the debate over "the servant problem" was the question of where the middle-class home fit into the turn of the century's public-private divide. Should disputes between household workers and their employers be treated as a private matter, or should the middle-class home be subject to publicly accepted labor standards? Public experts of all stripes agreed that domestic service was in desperate need of reform. They provided two competing narratives about what, precisely, was amiss in middle-class kitchens.

In one, domestics appeared as uncouth, promiscuous, and sometimes vio-lent. In the other, middle-class women promised a good home but deliv-ered only poor wages, long hours, and heavy labor. Middle-class women reformers, some of whom employed workers in their own homes, were left to choose between these two narratives as they designed domestic reform programs. Their decision would highlight the ways in which they imagined the middle-class home as fundamentally different from other workplaces, and, perhaps, as not a workplace at all.

Two
Sticking Together through Good Times and Bad
IMMIGRANT DOMESTIC WORKERS,

ETHNIC COMMUNITIES, AND RESISTANCE

In the late summer of 1893, a small group of Finnish immigrant women, many of whom were current or former domestic workers, traveled to the home of Betty Komula to discuss their plans for a new organization. Komula's home lay not too far from the heart of Brooklyn's growing Finnish community, which spanned the waterfront south of fashionable neighborhoods like Park Slope and Brooklyn Heights.[1] After that first meeting, the women got together regularly in one another's homes to talk about ways to bring economic and social benefits to Finnish domestics. By December the group had named their organization Naisyhdistys Pyrkijä and incorporated its bylaws in the state of New York.[2] In return for an initiation fee of twenty-five to thirty cents and ten cents in dues, Brooklyn's Finnish domestic workers could attend lectures, borrow books from a lending library, and participate in a sewing circle to raise funds for the society. For the convenience of Pyrkijä's members, the sewing circle met on Thursday afternoons, the traditional evening off for domestic workers.[3] Perhaps more important for its working-class membership, Pyrkijä provided both sick benefits and a death benefit. By all accounts, Finnish domestics were eager to participate in the new mutual aid association. By 1916, Pyrkijä boasted 125 members and had outgrown the cramped rooms of the founders' apartments. Instead, the women met in the parlors of the Gloria Dei Evangelical Church, located in the heart of Brooklyn's Finnish enclave.

Although late nineteenth- and early twentieth-century immigrants did not always participate in organizations as formal as this one, they still found ways to build a sense of working-class community even while living and working in middle-class neighborhoods. The conditions of domestic service were often severe, and household employers could be demanding and sometimes even abusive. Domestics developed numerous strategies to help them negotiate these working conditions. Networks of community and support, like those formed by the members of Pyrkijä, were particularly important. Just like class-based networks of industrial workers, domestics' networks rested on a foundation of shared work experience, ethnicity, class, and gender.

Domestics, except for the few with positions on the staffs of large houses, worked in isolation from one another. These young immigrant workers had to create networks that reached between homes employing domestics in middle-class neighborhoods and extended out to tenements that housed working-class family and friends. Middle-class reformers and public observers were right to suggest that domestics brought middle-class homes into contact with communities of working-class people. Working-class friends and family served as vital links to the social support that helped domestics maintain some control over their working conditions. We often think of domestics as trapped in middle-class homes, unable to resist the conditions of domestic labor except through individual acts of insurrection. In fact, domestics built successful networks of collective support among the working-class residents of both tenement districts and middle-class neighborhoods. Looking past the walls of the homes in which individual domestics lived and worked reveals the process by which domestics identified themselves as workers and resisted the harsher conditions of service.

It helped that these young immigrant women, who arrived between the late nineteenth century and the 1920s, were of only a few, usually northern European, nationalities. Even after the turn of the twentieth century, when immigration demographics overwhelmingly shifted toward newcomers from eastern and southern Europe, domestics still tended to be Finnish, Dutch, German, and, especially, Irish.[4] Native-born women and "new" immigrant groups of the late nineteenth and earl twentieth centuries, including Italians and eastern European Jews, generally refused to accept domestic work, making it even more available to women whose native cultures held no such prohibitions.[5] Late nineteenth- and early twentieth-century domestics were also mostly in their teens and early twenties, and most would leave the occupation after marriage. Their relative youth and freedom set them in stark contrast to African American women, who dominated the ranks of domestics in the South and who often worked throughout their lives. Young immigrant domestics were not only demographically similar to one another but they also shared a similar work experience. Domestic service in northern cities like New York before World War I almost always meant living in the employer's home. Live-in service proved particularly attractive to young German, Scandinavian, and Irish women, who often migrated alone, had nobody with whom to share living expenses, and came from cultures that valued women's economic independence.[6] Live-in service also differentiated immigrant domestics in the North from southern African American workers, who generally preferred day work. The maid who appeared once a week to vacuum and dust would not become a fixture in New York apartments until after World War I, when southern African American migrants began to take over the occupation.

A major challenge facing historians who write about these young immigrant workers is the discouraging lack of sources. The few surviving immigrant letters written home to worried family members are so relentlessly upbeat that it is hard to imagine that their writers did not simply omit their most negative work experiences. Evidence left behind by reformers, meanwhile, focuses on the degraded condition of "servant girls," who, reformers claimed, lacked basic hygiene and were more often than not alcoholics and prostitutes. Historians confronted with these wildly different sources have produced a somewhat schizophrenic picture of the average domestic work experience. According to some histories, domestics' long hours, low wages, and atomized work experience engendered a "'peasant' mentality antithetical to collective action."[7] Other scholars argue that domestic service in the United States represented relative freedom and status, especially when compared to conditions for household workers in England, Germany, and Scandinavia.[8] Still other historians argue that domestics' time in middle-class homes Americanized them and instilled a desire for middle-class status, an effect many scholars refer to as "bridging."[9] Uncovering the experience of the average urban domestic worker at the turn of the century is clearly not an easy task. The most fruitful approach seems to consist of reading middle-class and professional writings against the grain in the hope of making working-class women's voices heard over the documents' middle-class style and tone. Combining these sources with oral histories, immigrant letters, and the scant evidence left behind by groups like Pyrkijä yields an analysis that acknowledges the often harsh conditions of domestic service while also demonstrating worker agency. Such an approach also reveals relationships among workers, even those who worked in different houses, rather than focusing narrowly on the unequal power relationship between domestics and their employers.

Another way to solve the problem of sources is to use oral histories. In fact, domestics' strategies for maintaining class networks and resisting employer demands were so entrenched in ethnic working-class communities that workers who immigrated as late as the 1920s recalled experiences similar to those of women who arrived in New York in the late nineteenth and early twentieth centuries.[10] Their working conditions, however, were not the same. These later arrivals landed in New York after federal immigration laws had constricted the flow of new European immigrants to the United States and after most middle-class housewives had turned to African Americans to work in their kitchens. Many of the surviving oral histories of domestic workers who immigrated after 1920 come from workers who were part of large staffs in wealthy households. An employment registry from the upscale A. E. Johnson Agency confirms that, even after African American women outnumbered immigrants in the domestic workforce, wealthy employers almost exclusively employed white immigrant labor.[11] Although they still lived in, working conditions in large homes were substantially better than in homes with single workers. Workers who were part of large staffs benefited from constant companionship, help in completing daily tasks, and more time off. While this chapter focuses on domestics who worked in New York before the 1920s, these later interviews add invaluable first-person accounts of how domestic workers interacted with one another and the wider working-class community.

The working conditions of domestic service could be brutal. Domestics' low wages and isolation, especially for those who were the only worker in a home, often stifled efforts at formal labor organization, closing off one avenue for household workers to participate in labor policy debates with a coherent voice. Although not as brash as industrial workers walking the picket line, household workers still managed to maintain some control over their labor.[12] In public spaces and in private homes, domestics identified themselves as workers and built a gendered sense of ethnic and class identity that persisted even as they lived and worked in middle-class neighborhoods. This sense of community created a vital foundation of support, which many domestics used to negotiate the terms of their labor.

An "Awful Lot of Heavy Work": Domestic Labor in New York City

Domestic service was not the right occupation for workers who lacked endurance and a thick skin. Despite employers' claims that domestic service offered women high wages for easy work, the live-in domestic labor market at the turn of the century demanded ten-to-fifteen-hour days of near-constant labor at very low pay.[13] Because domestics' wages incorporated room and board, their actual cash wages were lower than what they could earn in other occupations, a problem that was especially difficult for workers who used their wages to support their families.[14] In 1872, the average weekly pay for a household worker was a mere $4.76, compared to the relatively queenly sum of $5.96 for shirtmakers.[15] Even this shirtmakers' wage was difficult for working women to live on unless they had other means of support.[16] Hours were long, and domestics traditionally had only Thursday afternoons and every other Sunday to themselves. Aleksandra Rembiénska, a Polish domestic working in Brooklyn in 1911, reported in letters home that "I do well, I have fine food, only I must work from 6 o'clock in the morning to 10 o'clock at night."[17] Rembiénska's day was typical. An anonymous worker wrote to the *Independent*, "This may seem incredible, but . . . from six A.M. to eight P.M. I don't get time to write so much as a postal card."[18] Household workers often rose at six to begin preparing breakfast and did not rest until they had washed the dinner dishes and cleaned the kitchen. In between, workers' days were filled with heavy and repetitive labor. In one position, Rembiénska was responsible for laundering 300 pieces of linen each week. In consequence, four days a week she did "nothing but iron" from six in the morning until eight at night.[19] Putting it more succinctly, one domestic described her work as "work and toil from morning til night for . . . miserable wages."[20] Domestic workers in the 1920s still worked very long hours. Lillian Amundsen, a Finnish immigrant who began working as a domestic while still a teenager, reported that she regularly worked twelve and fourteen hours a day.[21] Aili Howard, another Finn working in New York, recalled having to do an "awful lot of heavy work" in her first job, where she began each day at 4:30 in the morning.[22] Like Rembiénska, she often devoted whole days to ironing. In fact, chief among domestics' primary complaints was that, as one governess put it, "I have no hour in the twenty-four that I am free."[23]

Living conditions for domestic workers in middle-class homes were variable. Some workers enjoyed a private room and nutritious food; others received little more than leftovers to eat and a bed in the hall on which to sleep.[24] Domestics' living conditions were sometimes so poor that, one reformer reported, they had no more than "an ironing-board over a bath-tub offered for a bed, the dining-room table made up as a bed for two."[25] Even if the labor was not too heavy and the living conditions decent, the working relationship between servants and their employers was often fraught. Many household workers resented what they viewed as employers micromanaging their work. One worker disliked feeling that her employer constantly looked over her shoulder while she worked, arguing that "most of us would like a little more independence, and to do our work as we please."[26] Domestic workers also navigated a minefield of conflicting orders from different members of the family. Factory workers had just one manager, but, as one domestic worker told Lucy Salmon, "in housework you receive orders from half a dozen persons."[27] Another frustrated worker agreed: "Girls in housework are bossed too much."[28]

Live-in domestic labor was much more intimate than work in more public venues, and that intimacy created problems for domestics that women working in factories and shops did not face. Although domestics were hardly treated as one of the family, they were privy to many of their employers' private interactions. In return, employers often felt justified in invading their employee's privacy in ways that factory bosses would not. One worker apparently left a place after she discovered that her employer "thought she could go into my room and look through my things whenever she wanted to. I found her reading my letters more than once."[29] Other workers could only entertain guests that their employers had approved. As one domestic complained to Lucy Salmon, "Girls have to . . . comply with whatever rules a mistress may deem necessary."[30] Another domestic reported, "We are bossed eternally, they ask us where we are going, where we have been, and what we did, and who our friends are."[31] Still another added, "Our employer feels, somehow, that she is our guardian and has the right to supervise all incomings and outgoings, to question us about what we do in our leisure, and to be 'mistress' as well as employer."[32] Middle-class employers might have seen such meddling as part of their duty to guide and mold their household employees, but domestic workers viewed these exchanges as an infringement on their personal autonomy, not to mention an invasion of their personal privacy.

In the worst situations, domestic workers fended off sexually aggressive and even sexually predatory male employers. Their perspective on sexual danger on the job was vastly different from that of employers, most of whom refused to admit that harassment ever took place. One "daughter of toil" wrote to the *New York Tribune* in 1886 with the story of "an intimate friend" of her employer's family who "persisted in sly familiarities, and threatened to injure my reputation if I resisted it."[33] Agnes M., the household worker who told her life story to the *Independent* in 1903, reported having been propositioned by a houseguest when he caught her "passing through the parlor when the others were away."[34] Astrid Henning, a Norwegian who worked in New York in the 1920s, remembered that her sister had been working for a wealthy family on Fifth Avenue when one night "she felt somebody get into bed with her." The intruder turned out to be her employer, who told her "not to scream." Henning recounted that the man "got what he wanted, I guess. And then he would come back and she put the chair in front of the door."[35] Henning herself was never raped, but she dealt with frequent sexual harassment. In one home, she trained the family's pet collie to wake her employer in the morning, because "he always wanted to touch me and I didn't like that. . . . I couldn't stand that pinching business."[36] An English friend who worked with her in another house learned that the boss had been watching her undress every night through an open window shade.[37]

Even in the wealthiest homes, workers could not be sure they would not be sexual prey of male family members. As Henning pointed out, newly arrived immigrant domestics were particularly vulnerable to predatory male employers because "we were young and because we couldn't speak very good English and because they figured we were happy to have a good job and frightened enough not to say no."[38] Victimized domestics got no sympathy from their employers. Middle-class women, dependent on their husbands for financial support and intent on protecting the reputation of their households, blamed young working women for any sexual misconduct. Henning reported that "even when the husband was caught, the girls lost the job."[39] Domestic workers quickly learned that middle-class people did not always live up to the values they professed in newspapers and magazines. Although middle-class women proffered themselves as moral guides for their employees, a female employer was unlikely to choose a worker's version of events over her husband's.

BECAUSE DOMESTICS worked long hours, earned low wages, and were separated from one another during working hours, unionization was difficult. The few attempts to organize domestic workers that materialized in late nineteenth-century New York faded away almost before they had begun. In 1899, a group of Brooklyn domestics announced in the *Brooklyn Daily Eagle* that they were forming a union, dedicated to "helping the servants to go fight for their rights."[40] Among their demands were overtime pay for hours worked before 6:30 A.M. or after 8 P.M. and time off on Sundays for religious worship. Their hope, organizers explained, was that "stingy housekeepers when they have to pay more wages will not be so domineering and sassy."[41] "It is," they proclaimed, "high time to stop the slavery."[42] Despite the excitement of the initial announcement, however, the Brooklyn union almost immediately petered out. Whispers of another organizing attempt appeared a year later, in the last months of 1900, when a journalist reported that Mrs. St. Justin Beale, a member of New York's Social Reform Club, planned to "organize a servants' 'protective union.'"[43] St. Justin Beale's vision included defined tasks and hours, overtime pay, and two half days off per week, as well as a training program, rooms in which to receive visitors, a restaurant, and a library.[44] But like the proposed Brooklyn domestics' union, St. Justin Beale's union had disappeared by mid-1901. Attempts to organize domestic workers in other cities were equally unsuccessful, although their initial promise demonstrates domestics' willingness to publicly express dissatisfaction with the conditions of service.[45]

Domestic workers were eager for ways to combat employer power, but they faced opposition to unionizing on all sides. Much to the chagrin of St. Justin Beale, for example, the American Federation of Labor refused to affiliate with her union because it "did not consider that domestic servants came within the category of people who could establish a fixed rate of wages or fix the hours of labor, as servants are part of a household."[46] Employers vehemently opposed domestic worker organizing, and labor leaders expressed skepticism about organizing household workers in the first place. Domestics' meager cash earnings also made paying union dues difficult. Paying dues may also have seemed futile to workers who worked such long hours that they could rarely attend meetings. Uniting with women industrial workers with more organizing experience also presented obstacles. Most working women's clubs expressly excluded household workers, and women industrial workers generally avoided both domestic service and its workers.[47] Considering union leaders' reluctance to see domestic service as "work" that could be organized, inattention from middle-class women labor reformers, and scorn from women industrial workers, domestics had little incentive to see organizing a union as holding out much promise of better working conditions or wages. Domestics would have to find other ways to express their discontent.

"Many a Servant Is Working for People Far beneath Them": Working-Class Networks and Class Conflict

Without unions and without even a factory floor on which to unionize, domestics faced special challenges in building a working-class support system. Industrial workers could make friends over shared work tables, but domestics had to maintain friendships and support networks on a citywide scale. One way for domestic workers to stay connected to working-class friends and family was to insist on working nearby. Before the advent of the subway in the 1890s, New York City had already developed a world-class public transportation system, consisting of elevated trains and horse-drawn omnibus and railcar lines. These systems were, however, overcrowded and too slow for commuting over long distances.[48] Workers therefore carefully chose their employers based on their proximity to family and friends. Despite the flocks of young female immigrants arriving in New York's ports, domestic workers were hard to find for employers who lived out of reach of the city's public transportation system. In 1884, one journalist claimed that the great estates of the Hudson Valley, even though they offered higher pay and better working conditions, could not attract a full staff of domestic workers because of Irish women's reluctance to leave the city.[49] Another reporter observed that many household workers even insisted on working in specific neighborhoods. "They let the very best places go because they are outside their limits," an employer complained. "'Oh, I never go above Fifty-ninth Street.' Says one; another won't go 'beyond Seventieth Street.' And so on."[50] Perhaps as important as wages or working conditions to many immigrant domestic workers was a location close to friends and relatives and to the multiple support structures they found there. Domestics' social lives connected middle-class homes not to working-class communities in general but to those close by and filled with families and friends.

New York's mass transit system grew exponentially between the late nineteenth century and the 1920s. At the turn of the century, New York opened its first subway line, which sped middle-class commuters from offices in Lower Manhattan to newly developed, well-to-do neighborhoods like the Upper West Side. By 1913, additional subway lines reliably moved

New York City residents between Manhattan and the outer boroughs of Queens, Staten Island, Brooklyn, and the Bronx. These subway lines had been built by businessmen and real estate developers who hoped to grow wealthy from middle-class commuters, but the middle classes were not the only ones riding the trains. The low subway fare made public transportation accessible to even the poorest household worker.[51]

These new transportation networks served to broaden the area in which live-in domestics were willing to work. Even in the 1920s, however, many workers still refused jobs in the suburbs because of having to spend most of their Thursday afternoons and every other Sunday off commuting back to New York City. Lillian Amundsen, a Finnish immigrant, recalled that she "didn't stay too long" at her first job in the Long Island suburbs "just for the simple reason, it was too far for me to travel." She quit this job soon after starting and "found myself a job in New York City."[52] Mary Heany, an Irish immigrant, also quit her first job, in the upper Bronx, because it was "too far up" and "by the time I get down and meet the girls and we go to Tuxedo Park . . . or we go to any of the Irish dance halls . . . it would be too late."[53] Astrid Henning, who emigrated from Finland in the 1920s, explained that it "was very monotonous to live that far out if you didn't have friends out there."[54] After spending a summer working at her employer's vacation house, Irish immigrant Mary Condon realized that "I was lonesome and I was glad to get back to the city where my sister was. . . . I decided that we were going to stay together; that we wouldn't do that again." She then got a job closer to her sister.[55] Proximity to friends, and the support and recreation they provided, was especially important to domestic workers, who lived most of their time away from that community in middle-class and wealthy neighborhoods.

On afternoons off, domestic workers made special trips out of middle-class neighborhoods to attend dances. In the late nineteenth century, commercial dance halls sprang up in cities all over the country to cater to working-class young people's newfound obsession with dancing. If young people could not find an official dance hall, they attended dances in local saloons, in amusement park pavilions, or at ethnic halls. Young women eagerly looked forward to weekend dances, dressing in their best party dresses and heading out to dances in groups. Once there, they met young men who had also come to mingle and dance. Dance halls were places where young women could avoid the watchful eyes of their parents or employers, and they tended to behave in ways those older generations, and certainly their middle-class employers, would not have approved of. They drank. They smoked. They pulled their dance partners close, in dances with names like the Dip, the Charlie Chaplin Wiggle, the Bunny Hug, and the Turkey Trot. Sometimes, they did more than just dance with the men they met.[56] By the turn of the century, dances had become a staple of working-class youth culture, providing young women of all ethnicities with an opportunity for autonomy and cultural, physical, and sexual expression.[57]

No less than other working-class women their age, domestic workers loved to dance, and despite workers' long hours, revelry often lasted into the early morning hours. Wilhelmine Wiebusch, a German immigrant who arrived in New York in 1885, eagerly described the dances she and her friend Anna Beckermann attended in New York in her letters home. On November 26, 1886, she wrote Marie Kallmeyer, who had stayed behind in Germany, "We are both invited to a ball, harrah! Then we'll get to dance again and have a swig from the bottle as well, we're looking forward to it very much."[58] Agnes M., the young German nursemaid who told her story to the *Independent* magazine, declared that she was "very fond of dancing."[59] Agnes took boat trips to popular dance halls on Coney Island and Far Rockaway Beach and danced "all the way there and all the way back, and . . . nearly all the time we are there."[60] Another maid, Anna, did not return for several days after heading to a dance in Hoboken with a friend on a Sunday, forcing her employers to begin the tedious process of finding a new maid.[61] To employers like Anna's, domestics' regular attendance at dances represented an inconvenience at best and, at worst, a conduit for working-class vice to make its way into middle-class homes. But for household workers, dances were a chance to carouse with one another, maintain social relationships, and, not least, meet eligible young men, far away from the watchful eyes of their employers. Workers like Anna insisted on their right to participate, regardless of their employers' complaints. Dancing, then, represented not just domestics' participation in working-class culture (although it was that too) but also a point of conflict and negotiation between middle-class women and their employees over workers' autonomy. It was a battle that dancing domestics largely won.

Domestic workers who emigrated after World War I still danced the night away. Dances provided a chance to forge ties between immigrant domestics living in middle-class homes and a wider ethnic community. Mary Heany remembered the Irish dance hall she used to visit, with "fiddlers and accordion players and all kinds of things they had there, here from Ireland." Heany recalled taking taxis with four or five friends "and coming home" to her employers' house "at three and four o'clock in the morning.

I was up dancing all night."[62] Ann Kelly Craven, also Irish, remembered dances as a way to keep up with Irish friends. She frequently went to "our country dance, you know, you go and you meet all the people from home with you and have like a reunion."[63] Maintaining this ethnic connection was often more than symbolic. Lillian Amundsen met her first husband in a Finnish dance hall, where "all the Finns they used to go dancing."[64] Dancing simultaneously allowed domestics to participate in the same culture as other young working women and renew connections to their ethnic communities. These connections would, in turn, provide support long after household workers stopped dancing and traveled back to their jobs in middle-class neighborhoods.

The camaraderie that domestics shared with one another was an important building block in the formation of working-class networks. This camaraderie took place among domestics working in the same home and among domestics who worked in several homes in the same neighborhoods. Domestics' links of friendship and support thus spanned the boundaries of individual homes and yards. Wilhelmine Wiebusch bragged to her friend Marie that she and Anna Beckermann had "had the dumb luck of both getting a job together in a very fine private house in Brooklyn. . . . Anna is the scullery maid and I'm the cook, we each get 12 dollars a month (50 marks)."[65] Later, after Beckermann and Wiebusch got jobs in separate houses, Wiebusch reported that they continued to "stick together through good times and bad" and that they traveled to meet one another on their days off.[66] Household workers could and did socialize with domestics living nearby.[67] In 1910, for instance, Margaret Gilmartin, a twenty-year-old Irish immigrant who had arrived at Our Lady of the Rosary Home for Irish Immigrant Girls in 1907, was working for Joseph and Leah Neise at 125 East Eighty-first Street.[68] A young Hungarian woman was also in the Neises' employ, but if Gilmartin yearned for the company of her countrywomen, she had only to visit with Mary Haner, who worked for the Neises' next-door neighbors. She could also have traveled a few doors down to visit Mary Riordan, Annie Rialand, and Margaret Fayne, Irish women in their twenties who worked at 121 East Eighty-first Street.[69] Although private middle-class homes did not offer the kind of work-site community enjoyed by factory workers, neither were domestic workers living in middle-class neighborhoods completely isolated from one another. Working-class networks could be, and were, maintained even within middle-class communities.

If domestics were unhappy with the social options they found around them, they often invited friends and family to visit them in middle-class homes. Bertha Schade, a German immigrant working as a cook in the 1880s, frequently entertained her sister, Matilda, and her brother in her employer's house. Sometimes her brother even helped Bertha with the cleaning.[70] Later in the twentieth century, Lillian Amundsen visited with a Finnish maid who lived nearby.[71] Astrid Henning, meanwhile, learned how to swear and play cards from the Irish maids who lived next door. "I never heard such swearing in my life," she remembered. Then, after a long night of playing poker, to Henning's astonishment, "they went to mass in the morning. Swore to Dickens and played cards and went to mass early in the morning."[72] This visiting contributed to a distinct working-class culture among domestics in middle-class neighborhoods and between immigrant domestic workers and the ethnic working-class community that lay outside its boundaries. A social reformer investigating domestic service who tried to infiltrate household workers' social circles confessed, "We tried to dress like employees and become acquainted, but they held aloof until we had learned their language and habits, and could talk in up-to-date slang about places and mistresses."[73] Employers frequently complained about working-class riffraff streaming into their kitchens. Domestics, on the other hand, viewed visiting as an important way to participate in working-class culture.

Employers might have preferred that their employees be the only working-class members of their household, but workers continued to visit and socialize in middle-class kitchens. Indeed, the kitchen was a space of both labor and sociability for household workers. Nineteenth-century architects acknowledged this fact by building kitchens in basements or back rooms, as far as possible from the middle-class and elite family's more refined living quarters.[74] The parlor was a showroom for middle-class visitors and the master bedroom was an intimate space for middle-class homeowners, but many domestics claimed the kitchen as their own. Kitchens were hardly elegant spaces, but they did afford domestics some autonomy. As the "Servant Girls of Cambridge Place" put it in a letter to the *Brooklyn Eagle*, "Some ladies go into the kitchen and stick their noses in the pots and pans to see what is going on. Such a lady as that is not fit to live with."[75] Employers continually complained about the "present ruler of our kitchen," and cartoonists depicted cowering mistresses confronting furious domestic workers at the kitchen door.[76] One magazine writer described having to "slink half-apologetically into the kitchen, to have a finger, so to speak, in the pie."[77] Claiming the kitchen for themselves did not change domestics' low wages, long hours, or the fact that both employers and workers understood that, in the end, the kitchen, like the rest of the home, belonged to the employer. It did, however, allow domestics to carve out some symbolic autonomy, while also carving out an actual space in which to meet their friends and family. It also demonstrated domestics' view of the middle-class home, or at least its kitchen, as a place of work where they should be the acknowledged experts. In domestics' view, middle-class notions of domestic privacy and benevolent maternal guidance just did not apply there.

Just as visiting provided a point of conflict between workers and employers, domestics' consumption of the latest fashion trends also irked their employers, who did not look favorably upon their employees' avid attention to style. Journalists and middle-class employers wished that household workers would dress plainly and accused them of mimicking their employers' dresses, but in cheaper fabrics and with gaudy finishes. One employer spoke for many, arguing that dress was domestics' "foible and curse. They ape their mistresses and make shows of themselves."[78] Another employer added that "the 'doormat fringe' over the forehead does not exactly add to their natural charms."[79] Yet another observer chimed in that it was "out of taste" for domestics "to ape the costumes of their mistresses."[80] A journalist who visited an employment agency also wrote disparagingly of domestics' costumes, commenting on the assortment of "hats, many of them battered, weather worn and drooping as to the brim" but adorned with "artificial flowers."[81] He added that "jewelry—of a certain character—was everywhere in evidence."[82] A Catholic minister, Rev. George Deshon, meanwhile, chastised young Catholic women who spent their money on colorful dresses, "perhaps in a lilac silk, with a pink satin bonnet, and an ostrich feather sticking out at the top of it," instead of paying the "small sum for a seat in the house of God."[83] Deshon's rancor on the subject suggests that more than a few young Catholic domestics had what Deshon would have characterized as a sinful reverence for fashion.

Domestic workers, in contrast to their middle-class critics, viewed dressing well as a way to denote working-class respectability. One domestic worker wrote to the *New York Tribune*, "We must for our own credit dress decently and a little in accordance with the fashion of the age in which we live."[84] Domestics certainly took pride in their appearance. A *New York Times* reporter made special note of the "servants and cooks, dressed in their best finery," who "walked proudly toward their homes after their 'Sunday out.'"[85] Those who could not keep up with the latest trends keenly felt their deficiency. Aleksandra Rembiénska wrote home from Brooklyn in 1911 that, although she had "spent more than 50 rubles on myself for the coming winter," she still was "not so beautifully dressed as all the others."[86] Her cousin, by contrast, "buys herself a new dress every week. . . . She thinks only how to dress and says she does not need to think about anything more."[87] This focus on dress occurred within a distinctly gendered and classed context. Far from "aping" middle-class fashion trends, historian Nan Enstad argues, elaborately dressed working-class women "staged a carnivalesque class inversion that undermined middle-class efforts to control the definition of 'lady.'"[88] Or, as one domestic worker put it, "it is all nonsense to say that as a class that we imitate our mistresses. They put more money in a single dress than I earn in one year."[89] Domestics readily understood their class position in the middle-class household, but through consuming the latest fashions, they sought to claim respectability and taste for themselves. They did so in the face of tremendous employer disapproval and in a place—the middle-class home—that their employers imagined would display their own class-based conceptions of refinement. Through dress, household workers rejected middle-class efforts to control workers' personal appearance. Instead, they insisted on their right to wear styles that visibly identified them as workers living and laboring in middle-class neighborhoods and homes.

IN ADDITION to participating in working-class activities like dancing, shopping, and frequent socialization, domestics also dedicated significant financial resources to supporting ethnic institutions. Domestics created formal organizations designed to provide mutual aid to household workers. Scandinavian women, and particularly Finns, proved particularly adept at finding ways to pool resources and establish self-help organizations.[90] In addition to the Pyrkijä society, a group of New York Finnish women established the Finnish Woman's Cooperative Home in 1910 to give Finnish live-in domestics a place to relax and entertain male callers and other guests.[91] The Finnish Home was a place where household workers could set their own rules of behavior. The establishment also opened an employment society, which was "kept busy with housewives in search of domestic workers."[92] The Finnish Home proved popular among its clientele. By 1920, it had opened a residence for domestic workers and had won the support of 400 working-class shareholders.[93] Mutual aid associations run by and for domestic workers were widespread. In 1917, in Englewood, New Jersey, a group of Finnish household workers established the Finnish Bethel Congregational Church and Home for Women, where domestics might go for fellowship on their days and afternoons off.[94] In Brooklyn in 1891, Swedish immigrant women started a women's society called Freja, whose name was "derived from a

Scandinavian goddess—the wife of Thor, the mother of Jupitor [sic]."[95] Although Swedish and Finnish women seemed most likely to organize formal societies, Irish women were heavily involved in various Irish Catholic church groups and affiliated themselves with many Irish organizations that grew up around the city.[96] Ann Kelley Craven remembered that there were so many Irish organizations in New York in the 1920s that "I wasn't lonesome, you know, I wasn't homesick."[97]

Where domestics could not join an ethnic community already in existence, they created their own. Domestics not only sent money home to aged parents and younger siblings, but they used their wages to bring their sisters to the United States to work alongside them. In fact, approximately 75 percent of young Irish women immigrating to the United States at the turn of the twentieth century had their ticket paid for by a sister already in America, many of whom worked as domestic workers.[98] Through judicious use of the wages they earned in middle-class homes, domestics supported and enlarged the ethnic community. They also used their resources to support the institutions that anchored that community. Our Lady of the Rosary Home for Immigrant Girls, run by the Catholic Church and championed by women reformers, was one such beneficiary of domestics' largesse. Just before Christmas, in 1899, Margaret Shea wrote to Father Henry, the home's director, thanking him for his help to "a little greenhorn girl" whose "horns were so long and green at that time I did not know whom to thank for the great kindness."[99] She asked for a book of raffle tickets, which she promised to "trot around" and sell to her friends.[100] The tickets were modestly priced at ten cents each. The winners would be announced later at the Church Fair, a fixture in the Irish immigrant community, usually organized and run by young Irish women.[101] Church fairs were an excellent opportunity for household workers to meet one another while also financially supporting ethnic churches. Through small contributions from young Irish immigrant women and the patronage of the Irish community at their church fairs, Our Lady of the Rosary paid off the home's $10,000 mortgage in 1887.[102] Although their Protestant employers would have been horrified, domestic workers essentially created a direct flow of money from middle-class homes into working-class and often Catholic institutions.

In some cases, domestics resorted to illegally funneling middle-class resources and possessions to the ethnic community. Although most immigrant women working in middle-class homes were honest, some believed themselves to be in a unique position to help poor family members and friends. This redistribution of middle-class resources might range from the misappropriation of a few kitchen supplies to outright theft. Mary Frances Cusack, an Irish nun and prolific author, warned Irish women against thinking that a bit of graft in the service of friends and family was morally sound. She argued that it was the devil who tempted the household worker, "anxious to do all she can for her parents," to take money, clothing, or food, under the rationale "that her parents want it, and that the person that she takes it from does not miss it."[103] The Reverend Deshon agreed, writing that young Catholic women should avoid thinking they were doing right by giving "away to poor people something that wouldn't amount to much" or small amounts of food "that wouldn't be missed."[104]

Such behavior was not just a myth of prescriptive literature. Annie Kane admitted to taking seventy-five dollars in cash from her employer, fifty dollars of which she sent to her mother in Ireland.[105] Matilda Schade, a German immigrant, reported that her sister, Bertha, a cook in a private home, regularly visited her with "goods consisting of pieces of china ware and other small articles of small value and presented them to me." Matilda later discovered that these items had been stolen. When Anna quit her position in the Hunt household, she sent her trunk to Matilda's house. Upon opening the trunk, Matilda, and later the police and the Hunts, found an assortment of the Hunts' possessions, including china, glassware, utensils, wine, cigars, Prince Albert coats, sheets, pillowcases, towels, ten dresses, a set of corals, a necklace, and earrings. To the dismay of Mr. Hunt, when he visited Matilda's house in search of his purloined possessions, he also found "all of his winter and some of his summer underclothing" and "his best black silk socks, with the heals [sic] all worn off, lying soiled in the bath tub."[106] In smaller doses than the case of Bertha Schade, this expropriation of middle-class resources was part of the network of mutual assistance in which immigrant domestics were firmly embedded.[107]

Domestics given responsibility for ordering food or other items for the household sometimes enriched themselves and service industry workers at their employers' expense. One historian calls this kind of behavior "honest graft," which usually took the form of "padding accounts and . . . getting rebates from merchants."[108] She cites the example of a cook who acknowledged that "one could make a lot on the side," including up to "$100 a month, counting what she got off tradespeople."[109] Mary Frances Cusack warned that domestic workers who "take inferior articles, or articles that are under weight from the stores, and then take a bribe from the person they were buying from" were nothing more than thieves.[110] It is difficult to know how widespread the practice was of defrauding employers or, for that matter, of outright pilfering of employers' possessions. Few domestics admitted to fraud or thievery in print or in oral histories. Those who did viewed the act quite differently than did employers, who viewed this activity as theft. Some domestics, however, believed they had a right to middle-class goods as a form of compensation. Some, like Ellen Gilroy, a New York maid who stole from her employer after she "had been unable to obtain four months' wages due her," viewed stealing as taking what was rightfully theirs.[111] As Mr. Hunt, who had lost even his socks and underwear, would attest, theft not only brought vice into middle-class homes but also directed middle-class goods and resources into working-class homes and communities.

Class conflict over dances, dress, and, sometimes, stealing allowed live-in workers to express a sense of class identity and to exert authority over their leisure hours and recreation. Household workers continually identified employers not as the refined, pious ladies that middle-class women often imagined themselves to be but rather as self-indulgent layabouts who asked their workers to perform tasks that they refused to do themselves. Wilhelmine Wiebusch wrote to her friend Marie Kallmeyer that "the *Ladys* [sic] don't pay much attention to the household, they don't do anything but dress up themselves 3–4 times a day and go out."[112] The "Servant Girls of Cambridge Place," writing to the *Brooklyn Daily Eagle*, inverted the lady-servant relationship, declaring that "many a servant is working for people far beneath them."[113] Later in the twentieth century, Astrid Henning recalled that she did not enjoy her brief stint as a ladies' maid because she had to render personal service, such as helping her employer in and out of her corset. "She had to lay on the bed and I had to pull it on," she remembered. She pronounced the experience "disgusting." "For goodness sakes," she argued, "that they should do themselves."[114] When her friends visited Henning after she married, Henning reported that they talked avidly about politics and during the Depression voted Democratic. Household workers, Henning recalled, "figured the rich people were Republicans and that was no good so they became Democrats."[115] Domestics viewed their relationship with middle-class women in a class framework and identified themselves as different, and maybe better, than the women for whom they worked.

Negotiations and Resistance

The networks that domestics built and maintained, while not necessarily political in and of themselves, helped workers to mitigate the occupation's harshest conditions. Much of this resistance occurred in places where domestics gathered, places that could be quite alienating to middle-class visitors. For example, as part of her investigation of New York's employment agencies, Progressive social reformer Frances Kellor and her investigators (whose work will be discussed more fully in chapter 3) dressed up as prospective employees and visited tenement agencies in person. What they found when they got there appalled these refined, middle-class women, who had lived their lives by a specific set of class-based rules for social interaction. An investigator visiting an employment agency that offered its patrons lodging while they looked for work described a scene at dinner that was, in her estimation, full of "disgusting conversation and familiarity."[116] The women (there were no men present) shared their food and used their fingers, all behavior that the investigator could barely tolerate. She reported, "One would 'toss over' a boiled potato for a piece of meat, or a carrot for a cake, and so it went on with constant 'jollying.'"[117] When it came time to go to bed in the agency's tight quarters, the prospect of sharing her bed with the others proved too much for Kellor's investigator. At "ten o'clock," reported Kellor, "she had enough and could not stay."[118]

For Kellor and her cohorts, these interactions demonstrated the disorganization and fraud of tenement agencies. But read another way, employment agencies emerge as an important site of domestic worker organizing and resistance. Most employment agents specialized in a specific nationality and spoke the language of their working-class clientele, making them perhaps more partial to domestics than to employers. Tenement agencies also set up shop in the heart of the ethnic community. In the 1890s, for example, Atlantic Avenue in Brooklyn played host to nearly twenty Swedish employment bureaus.[119] Sometimes the proprietor was a personal friend or neighbor of the prospective domestic's family. One New York City official reported that many neighborhood "women who acquire an acquaintance with the relatives of immigrant girls find opportunities to place them in positions, and a little success in this work at the beginning soon develops their business."[120] Indeed, one tenement employment agent left Frances Kellor to entertain his children while he scoured "the neighboring tenements for help."[121] Tenement agents turned their offices into social centers, introduced workers to one another, and even hired handsome clerks to appeal to young working-class women.[122] Many may also have been former domestic workers themselves. Kellor reported that the vast majority of employment agents were women.[123]

In the interest of attracting prospective workers in a tight labor market, employment agents strove to create an atmosphere of camaraderie. A disapproving Kellor noted "the familiarity and the ease with which girls make each other's acquaintance, and how readily they rely upon each other."[124] A New York City official called the employment agency a "social headquarters" for domestics.[125] Prospective domestics did indeed make fast friends with their fellow workers in employment agency waiting rooms. Helen Paness, a Hungarian cook and general houseworker, met Kate Hordi, a Polish domestic, while waiting in Schultz and Freyer's intelligence office on 117th Street in Manhattan. Hordi asked Paness if she would help her buy a suit by translating with the sales clerks. Paness agreed, and after their shopping trip Hordi and Paness went off to Hordi's nearby apartment with the intention of "going to have some fun."[126] Later in the twentieth century, Astrid Henning recalled that when she went to an employment agency to change jobs she knew she "would meet up with some of my friends there in the office." Sometimes she might even bump into "a friend of mine from my own home town."[127]

Domestic workers who patronized these agencies found working women with whom they could exchange information about wages and conditions. In employment agencies, the networks that household workers had so painstakingly built also provided support as workers negotiated with employers. Kellor claimed that in the waiting rooms of employment offices new domestics learned from older workers "how to get ahead of the employer, how to shirk their work, receive, break contracts, extract higher wages and unreasonable concessions."[128] Of course, Kellor and household workers probably would have disagreed about which concessions were "unreasonable." Negotiations with employers over wages and working conditions also took place in these waiting rooms in front of a group of, as Kellor put it, "many curious, critical, and often railing listeners."[129] A worker's resolve to work only for the highest wages was hardened by the knowledge that, at the merest suggestion of a faltering will, her "listening 'pals' will guy her, or accuse her of having a 'weak back' or 'broken spirit.'"[130] An employer, stuck with the task of negotiating wages under such conditions, predictably complained about this kind of solidarity, grousing that "if you can only pay moderate wages, you are snubbed."[131]

Some employment agents also supported domestics' attempts to get the highest wage and set basic working conditions. As one employer complained to the *New York Tribune*, "My experience with the agencies leads me to believe that they are not trying to help the mistress secure a good girl, but are trying to place the girls in good paying positions."[132] Kellor reported that employment agents routinely advised her investigators, posing as domestics, not to apply for general housework jobs but instead to try for specialized and higher-paying jobs such as waitress or maid, regardless of their professed training or experience.[133] Later in the twentieth century, Della McGovern, an Irish maid, remembered that if she wanted higher wages than an agent initially offered, she simply demanded more. "Whatever I asked for," she recalled, "I got."[134] McGovern must have been extremely lucky, because the average wage remained low throughout the late nineteenth and early twentieth centuries. Nevertheless, her experience testifies to the fact that, in the waiting rooms of employment agencies, the ethnic networks that domestics had gone to great lengths to maintain helped them to command decent wages and hours.

Workers who did not want to use an employment agent also relied on friends to find jobs with acceptable working conditions. According to Father Henry, the young immigrant charges arriving at the Our Lady of the Rosary Home often declined the services of its employment office, choosing to find work through friends.[135] This information network among domestics was a subject of much trouble for employers, who regarded their labor relations as a private household matter. One employer claimed that her household worker "would be contented and happy in her work were it not for her relatives and friends, who have been in this country some time" and who "urge her to get another place with higher wages."[136] The city's commissioner of licenses, who was responsible for regulating domestic employment agencies, agreed that working-class immigrant domestics relied on each other for information about the best places to work. "For instance," he recounted, "one servant may meet another employed elsewhere" and one might tell the other "about a family where the work is not so hard or the hours so long. The first servant, thinking to better her condition, leaves her present place and goes to the other."[137] Catherine Leddie, who emigrated from Ireland in 1907, recalled a nearly identical situation. She reported that once in a while "I'd hear of something better, something with more money." For instance, she might "meet a friend" who would tell her about "a vacancy in their house, you know, and they would speak for you."[138] Later in the twentieth century, these networks were still in working order. Sarah Gillespie, Ann Walsh, and Elizabeth Horan Schmid, who emigrated from Ireland in 1910, 1922, and 1926, respectively, all reported that they found their first jobs in a house through a relative who already worked there.[139] Achieving decent wages and humane hours in domestic service, especially in the absence of protective labor legislation or formal unions, was often a matter of whom you knew.

Domestics not only helped each other find employment, they also gave each other information on where not to work. Employers and public observers often dismissed this kind of information sharing as an irritating form of gossip.[140] One employer overheard domestics discussing their experiences in different homes and more accurately summed up the situation. "In short," she explained, "the girls were seeing if their would-be mistress could furnish suitable recommendations—rather a reversal of the usual status of affairs" in which employers evaluated household workers.[141] Being part of an information network could mean the difference between working with decent pay and reasonable working conditions and finding oneself in a home with poor accommodations and food, low wages, heavy work, or, worse, a predatory male employer. Of course, even the best information network could not entirely shield domestics from poor working conditions or sexual harassment on the job. But gossip networks did provide domestics with some information on the homes of potential employers, which might allow them to steer clear of abusive employers or exhausting hours.

On the job, some domestic workers tried to set commonly accepted standards defining the tasks they would and would not perform. These standards might be set among workers in a single household or they might be passed along by word of mouth to workers in various households across the city. This task was made easier by the fact that domestics often worked in the same neighborhoods, if not the same households, as someone they knew. Thus, the same networks that helped domestics find jobs also helped them to set standards once they started working.

Domestics framed the tasks they were willing and unwilling to perform in strongly gendered and classed language. One Irish domestic wrote to the *Brooklyn Daily Eagle*, in 1897, to defend her countrywomen, whom she argued were hardworking but unwilling to "do such slavish work as others may do, and they are right not to do a man's work."[142] Another Irish worker chimed in, arguing that household employers should not expect Irish women "to do men's work."[143] Domestics lucky enough to work together in the same house helped one another to enforce these standards on the job. Lisa Nelson, an eighteen-year-old Swedish immigrant, began work as a kitchen maid in a private home. Her employer, seeing she was unoccupied, asked her to wash the ceiling. When Nelson climbed up on a chair to begin the task, a more experienced German waitress "came and pulled me off. She said, 'Man will do that, man will do that.'"[144] Employers certainly might have preferred employees who were uniformly obedient, but workers defined among themselves the tasks that were appropriate for respectable working women. Some domestics were willing to enforce these standards even at the risk of their own jobs. When Rachel Ellison, Annie O'Donnell's employer, refused to pay her after O'Donnell had given notice, O'Donnell went to the Legal Aid Society, a charitable organization that provided workers and the poor with legal services. Ellison claimed that O'Donnell had left without notice. The Legal Aid Society informed Ellison that there was "a witness, namely your cook who . . . is still in your employ" who would "testify to the fact that there was not an abrupt leaving, but that due notice was given."[145] Working-class networks, both within employers' homes and between homes in middle-class neighborhoods, gave domestics a firm foundation on which to negotiate the terms of their labor.

Family and friends also provided crucial support for household workers who had been dismissed or who had quit a job with working conditions they found unendurable. One employer complained to the *New York Tribune* that she was unable to find inexpensive domestic workers because "girls will go home and live on their parents or friends rather than work for less than the usual rates."[146] Other evidence also suggests that workers used this strategy to survive between jobs. After Anna, a maid in a wealthy household, missed several days of work and lost her job, she stayed with the janitor in her employers' apartment building.[147] If household workers did not stay with friends they might stay in rooms owned by ethnic organizations. For instance, Helen Paness regularly stayed at the Hungarian Society when she was out of work or between jobs.[148] Having somewhere to stay when out of work, especially somewhere that did not incur rent, was a useful tool in the arsenal of domestic workers fighting to establish basic on-the-job standards. In this context, domestics' loyalty to ethnic clubs and churches represents more than just ethnic loyalty or religious piety. Without such connections, attempts to exert even this limited control over their working conditions would have been virtually impossible.

"I Did Not Like to Work for Nothing": Quitting and Legal Aid

On October 6, 1885, Bella McKeown arrived at her new job in the Richards household. She had not arrived until "after lunch," but she "left before dinner" because she did not "like the kitchen accommodations."[149] Over the next year, the Richards family would experience this kind of abandonment again and again. In that single year, Henrietta MacLauren Richards, a prosperous New York City housewife, had six different cooks and numerous nannies join and then abruptly leave her employ. Twenty years later, another maid woke Grace Eulalie Ashmore, the soda water magnate's daughter, and her husband in the morning with the announcement that "she didn't think the place would suit her and that she was going."[150] The Ashmores begged the woman to make breakfast before she left. After that, Ashmore watched a parade of household employees move in and out of her kitchen. A terse note in her diary, "Dinner was late," almost always signaled that the following morning her cook would inform her that "she was going."[151] Desertion by a cook created a special problem for the Ashmore family, who were dependent on their staff for all manner of household chores. Grace Ashmore did not even learn how to make coffee until after she was married, and her culinary skills were limited to Welsh rarebit, glorified cheese on toast. Without someone to work the stove, the Ashmores relied on the kindness of friends and family for most meals and dined frequently at Delmonico's.

Quitting was the easiest and most often-used way for domestic workers to deal with working conditions that they did not like. Many historians have seen quitting as evidence of domestics' lack of power, a personalized form of resistance and their only meager alternative in the absence of unions or federal and state labor laws.[152] Although quitting did not give domestics the political clout enjoyed by unionized factory workers, it was hardly an individual act. Most domestic workers who quit relied on friends and family to find a new position, provide accommodations, and lend financial support. Workers with a place to stay could take their time to look for just the right position. Quitting also allowed household workers to punish their employers, perhaps by leaving with little or no notice or, better, just before a dinner party.[153] Furthermore, because domestic workers changed jobs so often, their most consistent social ties were with other domestics and working-class friends and family, rather than with the disparate middle-class women for whom they worked. Rather than being an alternative to the working-class identity exhibited by union members, then, quitting reinforced domestics' self-identity as workers. It was an individual act of resistance, but it relied on the existence of a wider working-class network.

Domestics chose which jobs to keep and which to leave based on strictly rational criteria of wages and working conditions. As Aleksandra Rembién-ska, the Polish domestic living in Brooklyn in 1911, put it, she left one place because "I did not like to work for nothing" and "they wouldn't pay me more than $12."[154] In 1916, Aili Howard, a Finnish immigrant, left her first position after tiring of its long hours and heavy labor. Her next position was no better, since it involved cleaning out the coal furnace, which "used to shoot dust and dirt."[155] So, after learning what she could, Howard moved on, finding "very nice jobs after that."[156] Like Howard, Astrid Henning would not stay at a job where she was mistreated, recalling that if "you weren't happy in a household you would get another job."[157] New York City official George Bell observed that "servants are at this time extremely independent and leave positions that do not satisfy them with but little ceremony."[158] Wilhelmine Wiebusch saw quitting as a right of her new American citizenship. Writing home about her frequent address changes, she observed, "Today I am here but I can be gone by tomorrow if I don't like it anymore, that's what the land of freedom means."[159] Quitting, as Wiebusch observed, offered dissatisfied domestic workers immediate results, more immediate than those of any union, even if it could not offer them a coherent political voice.

The most public protest a domestic could make, however, was to seek redress through the court system. This course of action generally required the help of an attorney, most often from the Legal Aid Society, which was initially founded in 1876 as an arm of the German Society of New York, an organization dedicated to protecting German immigrants from exploitation. Arthur von Briesen, a German immigrant, Civil War veteran, and distinguished patent attorney, became president in 1890 and set to work expanding the organization's reach and mission. Soon after assuming the society's highest office, von Briesen doubled its membership and devoted its resources to seeking justice for the poor through the court system. In 1896, the organization officially changed its name from Der Deutsche Rechtsschutz Verein to the Legal Aid Society. The society continued to expand, and by 1900, it had opened at least eight offices throughout the city, including a Woman's Branch at Fourth Avenue and Twenty-second Street, offering legal services to the poor of all nationalities. As the twentieth century progressed, Legal Aid also offered an increasing range of services to its clientele, providing, for example, legal advice in divorces and in a range of civil and criminal matters. Legal Aid attorneys charged their clients as little as ten cents for their services, a fee that could be waived for the truly indigent.[160] The Legal Aid Society, which would not receive public funding until after World War II, was unable to handle every case that would-be clients brought to its offices, but in the late nineteenth and early twentieth centuries its lawyers offered the poor access to the court system that they would not otherwise have had.[161]

Domestic servants found these services particularly useful. In 1903, Rosalie Leow Whitney, Legal Aid's attorney in chief, estimated that household workers made up as much as a quarter of all its cases related to wages.[162]

By 1908, these complaints were so ubiquitous that the Legal Aid Society released a booklet that clearly described the rights and responsibilities of both domestic workers and their employers.[163] Despite frequent complaints from household employers that they were being unfairly targeted, Legal Aid attorneys felt bound to take the side of their domestic worker clients. "We must in the final analysis," explained Phillip McCook, a Legal Aid lawyer and future justice of the Supreme Court of New York, "take our client's word and enforce her rights, if the truth is reasonably in doubt."[164] The court system offered New York domestic workers a formal means by which to challenge their employers. With backing from Legal Aid lawyers, moreover, workers' wage claims were often successful. In 1911, Fannie Maki and Minnie Salo sued their employer, former New York City mayor Thomas F. Gilroy, for payment of back wages. The Legal Aid Society pressed the case, over the considerable objections of the Gilroy family. Despite the Gilroys' political power, the workers received their money. Similarly, when Priska Sillanpaa and Hilma Weikkala's employer sought to "teach them a lesson" by refusing to pay their wages after they abruptly quit early one Friday morning before breakfast, the women sought the help of the Legal Aid Society. The workers eventually received their earnings.[165]

Many domestic workers, part of the legions of New York's working poor, could not afford to go without the small wages they had earned, and the monetary amounts that workers sought to recover were often quite small. Emergencies like illness or unemployment exacerbated this financial need. Sarah Mehler wrote to von Briesen in 1905 asking him to help her claim a judgment of $5.10 she had received against her employer since she was now sick and needed the money.[166] A worker's trunk, which stored all of her worldly possessions and which she lugged from job to job, was also precious to her. When one domestic refused to open her trunk for her employer to inspect for stolen goods as she left the house, her employer took custody of both her trunk and her pay. Society lawyers gave her a letter to show her employer, and "within half a day she returned to the office with the news that she had her trunk and pay in full."[167] On the one hand, domestics' need to turn to the Legal Aid Society in such large numbers highlights the frequent abuse that they suffered at the hands of middle-class employers with infinitely more political and economic power. On the other hand, in seeking the help of the Legal Aid Society, domestics demonstrated their belief in basic standards for their work and their willingness to publicly demand what they viewed as their right.

The society was so effective in pressing cases against delinquent employers that one employer compared it to a "Black Hand" or "a bug-a-boo to women of refinement who, rather than go into a court-room to fight, allow themselves to be mulct of unjust claims."[168] Another employer agreed, urging that the "over zeal of some of your legal employees in these servant girl cases may be restrained" and went on to complain that the "servant question in New York is bad enough without having the Legal Aid Society lend itself to the oppression of the employers who resist the unjust claims of their servants."[169] Despite middle-class women's objections, the court system sometimes gave domestic workers leverage over obstinate and abusive employers.

The Legal Aid Society was not, however, a consistently reliable way to pursue meaningful change for workers or to exact retribution from neglectful or abusive employers. The professional, even if charitable, lawyers who took workers' complaints did not always welcome their clientele with open arms. One sympathetic employer presented Arthur von Briesen with the case of his employee, Ida Busch, who had been cheated out of ten dollars by a previous employer. She went to the Brooklyn Branch of the Legal Aid Society with her aunt, only to be "very roughly spoken to by the attorney in charge."[170] Similarly, when a young Irish domestic's sister complained to her Legal Aid lawyers that the settlement they had negotiated was inadequate, the lawyer in charge of the case did not back down. Instead, he declared that her criticism had only confirmed "the opinion I formed after hearing the defendant's story. Her impudence, independence and unwillingness to perform her regular duties were only some of the reasons why the applicant is no longer working for the defendant."[171] In 1910, seeking a middle ground between employer outrage over suits by former servants and the responsibility it felt to enforce the law, the society passed an internal rule that it would no longer accept cases from domestic workers who left without notice. Quitting without notice was one of the few means of leverage that workers wielded over employers, and there was no law that said household workers had to announce in advance their plans to quit. But in 1912, the society's attorney in chief expressed his opinion that "the fault is often with the employees in these cases, as they are undisciplined and irresponsible."[172] Of course, when employers fired household workers without notice, the workers had no legal recourse. In addition to having the courage to press a legal case against an angry employer, domestic workers who used the services of Legal Aid also had to answer questions about their own behavior from men and a few women who were predisposed to disapprove. More traditional methods of resistance, maintained through ethnic and community networks, probably seemed to many workers to be less degrading and more potentially successful. Furthermore, a well-negotiated wage and a carefully selected employer provided better protection against exploitation than the inconsistent sympathy of Legal Aid lawyers. Domestics' willingness to seek help from Legal Aid in the first place, however, belies the notion that they were passive workers, unable or unwilling to publicly protest their working conditions.

THE NETWORKS THAT workers maintained with one another and with a wider ethnic community provided myriad ways for household workers to resist employer demands. Domestics who worked together looked out for each other's interests on the job, often by adhering to a set of tasks that they deemed appropriate for women workers in the home. In employment agencies and on the street, domestics shared information about desirable (and not so desirable) employers and lent solidarity to workers who negotiated the terms of their employment in public. When one worker lost or quit her job, another might tip her off to a job opening in her own workplace or pass along information she had heard about open positions. Friends and family in a worker's ethnic community might direct her to a reputable employment agent. Sometimes that agent was a friend of the family in one of the fly-by-night operations that dotted the city's Lower East Side. Sometimes merely visiting a household worker in her employer's home served to preserve a worker's right to company while on the job. Friends and family who welcomed unemployed domestics into their homes also helped to preserve the freedom to quit, ultimately the most efficient and effective weapon in domestics' arsenals. Although the conditions of domestic service were always hard, and sometimes brutal, domestics were neither entirely isolated nor doomed to suffer at their employers' every whim. In fact, workers frequently reached beyond employers' households for help in negotiating the conditions of work in middle-class homes. When necessary, many domestics, like those who besieged the offices of the Legal Aid Society to demand back wages or others who sent angry letters to the city's newspapers, gave voice to their discontent.

Middle-class employers decried a tide of working-class vice moving freely between tenement neighborhoods and middle-class homes, but domestics recognized this as a vital network that allowed them to retain some power in an unequal labor relationship. When employers derided domestic workers as uncouth, it was probably because domestics identified more with other workers than they did with their employers. From the point of view of household workers, then, the "servant problem" actually represented a form of class conflict, made up of skirmishes over wages, hours, and workers' personal autonomy. Domestics found support for those battles in the networks they had built in ethnic aid societies and dance halls and on the street corners and in the kitchens of middle-class neighborhoods.

AT THE TURN OF THE CENTURY, however, middle-class reformers began to think about domestic service as a political problem, one that could be solved through organized reform and public policy. At the same time, other reformers were beginning to formulate policies that gave basic labor protections to women working in industry. Because domestics did not have a formal political organization, such as a union, to speak for them, they were unable to join the public political debate about "the servant problem" or protective legislation for women workers. Neither women reformers nor male union leaders viewed the middle-class home as a public workplace, and few reformers were likely to advocate for household workers. Instead, their efforts to maintain a sense of autonomy on the job indirectly shaped the terms of the political debate, as reformers repackaged the class conflict in middle-class homes as a social problem in need of reform. Thus, while domestic workers' efforts to resist employers' demands gave shape to the public debate over domestic service, they could not by themselves create lasting change.

Three
Encouraging the Good, Weeding Out the Bad, and Teaching the Ignorant

WOMEN'S ORGANIZATIONS AND DOMESTIC

WORKERS IN NEW YORK CITY, 1870–1915

The stakes for middle-class women in the public debate over domestic service were high. Unless and until female employers confronted the labor problem festering in their kitchens, experts and public observers agreed, they had no business committing themselves to other benevolent reform missions. Inez Godman, a muckraking journalist who disguised herself as a domestic for a series of investigative magazine articles, pointed to the hypocrisy of a National Consumers' League member signing petitions demanding chairs for store clerks "when her own maid is on her feet for at least 11 hours a day out of a working day of 14."[1] Home economist and social worker Jane Seymour Klink sympathetically described the suffering of one domestic who was never allowed to go to church, although her "employer subscribes liberally to foreign missions."[2] Accusations that middle-class housewives more closely resembled slave drivers than pious ladies and depictions in the popular press of the middle-class home as the site of immigrant domestics' carousing, papist idolatry, and immodest sexuality threatened to undermine women's moral authority to promote social change.[3] Not only that, as many commentators asked, but how could elite and middle-class women be entrusted with the vote when they could not even manage the politics of their kitchens? Julia Everts Robb argued that before demanding suffrage women should ask themselves whether they handled matters in their own households in "a manner to show executive ability that justifies the widening of our sphere?"[4]

Such arguments were not lost on women engaged in Gilded Age and Progressive Era social reform. Muckraking journalist Ida Tarbell called for the "vast machinery of the Federation of Woman's Clubs" to be "turned to this problem of the democratization of domestic service."[5] A New York housewife echoed this sentiment, writing the *New York Tribune* to ask "the noble sisterhood" of women's clubs to take up the task of solving the domestic problem that lingered "near at hand, at the very door, nay, inside the door."[6] Lucy Maynard Salmon warned employers that "reforms begin at the top, revolutions at the bottom," and called upon "men and women of the so-called upper classes" to find "a satisfactory solution of the vexed question of domestic service."[7] Rather than seeing domestic service as a series of personal conflicts between middle-class women and their employees, reformers saw a political and social problem in need of reform. As Margaret Dreier (later Margaret Dreier Robins) argued in 1904, "This entire question touches every home in our city." Domestic service was a vital project for organized women, she added, because "the home is the bulwark of a nation" and "we women have had entrusted to us its sanctity."[8] As keepers of the home, women had a special interest in maintaining its place as a moral haven from urban problems. The need for some solution to the domestic labor problem seemed especially clear to middle-class women reformers, who justified their place in public by pointing to their ability to bring domestic morality to urban politics. On a more practical level, of course, many middle-class women who wished to engage in moral reform needed someone at home to do the dirty work.

Women's domestic service reforms between 1870 and 1915, which included immigrant girls' homes, training programs, employment societies, and servants' clubs, represented a direct response to the public and increasingly political debate over "the servant problem." As this long list of reforms demonstrates, reform organizations were hardly reluctant to apply their Progressive ideas and, later, the power of government to the problems they viewed as plaguing domestic service. Domestic workers were not left out of Gilded Age and Progressive reform. Instead, reformers created a different set of reforms than those aimed at industrial women workers. In effect, domestic service reform programs separated household workers from the tenement's working-class and ethnic community, consolidated middle-class control over the hiring process, and inculcated manners and behavior that reformers deemed appropriate for workers in private homes. Although they expressed sympathy for the labor concerns of domestic workers, middle-class women's reform programs failed to address the hours, wages, and working conditions that made domestic service so unappealing to many women workers in the first place. Other middle-class women's organizations created working-girls clubs for factory workers or lobbied for protective labor legislation, but reformers of domestic service focused instead on protecting middle-class homes from what they viewed as ill-behaved and incompetent workers.

These reformers put the middle-class home at the center of the Gilded Age and Progressive Era debate about urban public policy. Organized women believed that poverty, poor housing, and urban vice had direct and negative consequences for families who employed domestic help. They did not, however, see a connection between these urban problems and domestics' low wages and poor working conditions in the same clear way. Even reformers like Frances Kellor, who most plainly articulated the connection between the city's public problems and middle-class families' allegedly private labor concerns, did little to address working conditions in middle-class homes.

There were differences between the reformers discussed in this chapter. Late nineteenth-century charitable organizations sought to transform domestic servants into refined workers and entice industrial workers into jobs in middle-class homes. These reformers tended not to have graduate degrees, and their reforms tended to be local programs, unconnected to national organizations. After the turn of the century, women's organizations embraced Progressivism by bringing state authority to reforming domestic work. These reformers, led by women like Frances Kellor, had graduate degrees in fields like sociology. They hoped to use their expertise to cast the "servant problem" in a new, more modern, and more scientific light. In the process, they reimagined working women as victims of urban vice rather than merely as purveyors of it. The domestic service reforms that organized women pursued throughout this period were diverse, drawing on the resources of both government and private agencies. But domestic service reform took a different path than labor reform for industrial and retail workers, one that did not include an organized campaign by middle-class women for regulated hours and wages or improved working conditions.[9]

The Diverging Paths of Domestic
and Industrial Labor Reform

In the last years of the nineteenth century, middle-class women reformers and members of various, and often interrelated, organizations began to create a reform agenda to improve the conditions for women laboring in factories and retail stores. New York City, one of the country's largest industrial metropolises, was the epicenter of this reform movement. Women labor reformers believed that they shared a gendered sympathy for working-class women and that they were uniquely positioned to speak on their behalf. They also viewed women workers as a particularly vulnerable group, not least because they were all but ignored by male union leaders. Women's organizations pointed out that women worked long hours at wages that were sometimes less than half of what men earned. Furthermore, as the deaths of 146 women workers in the 1911 Triangle Shirtwaist Factory fire so horrifically demonstrated, women workers often labored under extremely dangerous, and sometimes even deadly, conditions. On the front lines of this new middle-class women's reform movement stood two organizations, the Women's Trade Union League (WTUL) and the National Consumers' League. These organizations led the way in setting the agenda for women's labor reform and, later, state and federal labor laws. Along the way they formed connections with other organizations that shared their commitment to reaching out to working-class women and children.

Women's labor reform groups initially used just the power of their membership to create change for workers in factories and stores. Florence Kelley, a former resident of Jane Addams's Hull House, worked with the National Consumers' League to persuade factory owners and retail establishments to pay their workers fair wages and to provide healthful working conditions and reasonable hours. Women of the National Consumers' League promised to buy only clothing bearing the group's "white label," which indicated that the factory it came from did not sweat its workers. By using women's consumption habits to create social change, the National Consumers' League linked women's traditional role in middle-class homes with women's organizations' burgeoning reform agenda. The WTUL, on the other hand, took a different approach, seeking to create coalitions between working-class and middle-class women. The WTUL welcomed working-class women into the organization and employed full-time organizers to help women workers in various industries form unions. Middle-class members also used their class status to protect striking women workers, walking picket lines in the hope that the presence of middle-class and wealthy women would prevent violent strikebreakers from assaulting strikers. As these two groups grew, the National Consumers' League and the WTUL became the acknowledged experts on women's labor.[10]

The National Consumers' League and the WTUL were not, however, the only groups engaged in cross-class reform at the turn of the twentieth century. The Young Women's Christian Association (YWCA) considered itself a cross-class organization from its beginnings in 1858, seeking to provide for the "welfare of young women who are dependent on their own exertions for support."[11] The YWCA provided a wide array of services for working-class women in towns and cities across the country, including libraries, job training, employment services, gyms, subsidized restaurants, and meeting rooms.[12] By 1904, its industrial program had solidified and YWCA leaders were supporting a variety of efforts to ameliorate women's working conditions, including protective labor legislation. Grace Dodge, a prominent New York philanthropist and social reformer, also made an effort to reach out to working women. In 1876, she began holding discussions with women working in the silk industry, an effort that eventually grew into a series of Working-Girls Societies.[13] These societies offered working-class women meeting places, educational classes, and health services. The National Consumers' League and the WTUL were therefore not isolated examples of women's labor reform efforts. Rather, they were part of a vibrant network of middle-class women reformers interested in providing services and pursuing social change for working-class women and children.

Like other Progressive reformers in the early twentieth century, women labor reformers began to look to the power of government to enact broad social change. The major focus of this reform agenda was to pass state labor laws, including hours restrictions and a minimum wage. Although activists at the heads of organizations like the WTUL and the National Consumers' League hoped to include male as well as female workers in state labor protections, the courts repeatedly struck down efforts to enact hours restrictions or minimum wage laws for men. The door on protecting male labor finally slammed shut with the 1905 case *Lochner v. New York*, in which the Supreme Court declared unconstitutional a law limiting the hours of male bakers to ten per day. According to the Court, protective labor laws abridged men's constitutional right to freedom of contract, which granted them full independence to negotiate whatever terms they liked with their employers. As it became clear that courts would not uphold protective labor legislation for male workers, labor reformers, and women activists in particular, began to craft labor laws for female workers alone. They hoped this approach would create an "entering wedge" for labor legislation affecting workers of both sexes, but they also saw women workers as being particularly vulnerable to labor exploitation and particularly in need of state protection.[14]

States passed women's labor laws, including bans on night work and hour restrictions, in rapid succession. Women's groups, led by the National Consumers' League and the WTUL, also pursued a minimum wage, although reformers had a harder time convincing legislators to enact laws with so direct an effect on industrial profits. In 1908, the Supreme Court finally articulated a legal rationale for women's protective legislation that differentiated it from protective legislation for male workers. In *Muller v. Oregon*, the Supreme Court upheld an Oregon law that limited women's workday to ten hours. The Court's decision was guided by the brief submitted by Louis Brandeis, which had been assembled with research by the National Consumers' League. The Brandeis brief cataloged a list of maladies that might befall women who were forced to work too many hours under harsh factory conditions, ranging from varicose veins to lung disease to "displacement of the uterus."[15] Women were more vulnerable to these conditions because of their "special physical organization," and it was, Brandeis argued and the Court agreed, in society's interest to protect the health of mothers of future generations by limiting their hours.[16] Men had the freedom to negotiate their working hours directly with their employers, but women needed state protection. Although the decision seemed to confirm a disturbing array of gender stereotypes, the Supreme Court had opened a space, however small, for state regulation of labor.

The *Muller v. Oregon* decision has received criticism from all corners, from early twentieth-century feminists to contemporary historians. These critics argue that the Court's rationale for women's protective legislation ghettoized women workers by encouraging sex segregation in the labor market, hampered women's ability to compete with men, who had no limits on their working hours, and enshrined in law women's status as mothers and wives first and workers second.[17] There is no question, however, that domestic workers would have benefited from some form of labor protection. Working hours for household workers, especially for the majority who lived with their employers, were interminably long. Many could not even find respite at night, when employers often asked them to sleep in children's rooms and remain on call through the wee hours. Moreover, domestics were usually paid by the week, not by the hour, and so as they worked longer days, their hourly pay fell proportionally. Finally, domestic work was firmly sex segregated. Hours laws, however restrictive they were for other women workers, would only have improved domestics' quality of life.

Although neither *Muller* nor the slew of women's hour restrictions that followed mentioned domestics, the decision highlighted domestic work's place in labor, law, and culture at the turn of the twentieth century. As the Brandeis brief and the Supreme Court's ruling made clear, "work" took place in factories and shops and not in private homes. The *Muller* decision essentialized women's role in the home while casting work in factories as wreaking havoc on the bodies and minds of women workers. Reformers and other observers frequently referred to domestic service as the most healthful occupation for women workers—and just as frequently tried to induce women workers to leave factories and shops for domestic service.[18] The unequal value placed on work in homes and work in factories and shops was important to women's labor reform ideology. Acknowledging that real "work" took place in the home would have undermined the careful rationale that labor reformers had developed in order to push labor laws past judicial scrutiny. Women deserved special protections, Brandeis argued, because work was hazardous to their health. But it was factory work, not housework, that broke down women's bodies. In order to protect women, Brandeis and his allies in the National Consumers' League argued, the state had the right to limit their "working" hours. Perhaps because they too accepted the different values that law and culture assigned to domestic work and to factory work, the largest women's reform organizations did not include domestics in their labor agenda at the turn of the century.

Given reformers' and journalists' near-constant calls for domestic labor relations to be put, as one domestic reform group put it, "on a sound business basis," the political exclusion of domestic workers is difficult to understand.[19] Mary White Ovington, one of the founders of the National Association for the Advancement of Colored People, noted that the "study of the household employment question to-day continually brings out the need of more business-like relations between the employer and the employee."[20] A reporter for the *New York Tribune* claimed that the "servant problem" could be attributed almost entirely to a "singular defect in what we may call the business organization of women."[21] Home economists also got into the act, offering detailed schedules and kitchen layouts modeled on the principles of Taylorism, which were being used in factories, all designed to allow paid household labor to proceed at its utmost efficiency.[22] This rhetoric was so ubiquitous in turn-of-the-century reform literature and mass media that historians have often hailed reformers' intentions to bring the relationship between mistresses and servants into line with the employer-employee relationship that prevailed in public industry.[23]

Despite these abundant calls for the home to be run more like a business, however, home economists, sociologists, and other public experts recognized a fundamental difference between the home and a commercial enterprise and between domestic service and other forms of paid labor. The home was a place of nurturance, not a profit-driven factory, and reformers believed that the hours and wages of the home could not be regulated with the standards that state and local governments increasingly applied to retail and industry. As one housewife wrote to the editor of the *New York Tribune*, "The woman who does housework for board and wages should understand that a household cannot be inflexible as a business house, if it were, it would not be a home."[24] Middle-class women debating the "servant problem" at a club meeting claimed that domestic labor could not be "wedged into an eight hour system any more than a mother can or any useful working member of a family."[25] Outraged at the mere suggestion of an eight-hour day for domestics, another club member argued that "no possible mode of domestic service can be laid upon this bed of Procrustes."[26] Although she supported employer efforts to limit domestics' hours, home economist C. H. Stone warned that state regulation of an eight-hour day would only "bring chaos to all but the most independent housekeeper."[27] Domestic labor, these women argued, was attuned to the rhythms of household and family and could not be put on a uniform schedule, especially if it meant standardizing workers' hours and wages.

Plans for the limitation of domestics' hours almost always relied on self-regulation by employers and usually involved workers being on the premises for twelve or more hours a day. In one schedule approved by Inez Godman, for example, the domestic rose at 6 A.M., prepared breakfast, and washed dishes. She then prepared a light lunch and took care of some morning cleaning until eleven A.M. After resting in her room for a few hours, she went back to work from four until eight in the evening.[28] For turn-of-the-century reformers and experts, commercial labor management techniques might be incorporated ad hoc into the housewives' administrative style, but putting the home on a "business basis" did not mean state regulation of hours and wages.

Middle-class reformers' approach to domestic service reform therefore differed markedly from their approach to other sorts of women's labor. In the nineteenth century, household workers were explicitly excluded from many of the services that middle-class clubwomen offered to other working women. Although it later opened a training school and employment society for African American domestic workers at its Harlem branch, the New York City YWCA initially found positions only for women whose skills fit them for something other than domestic service. Domestics, they argued, could "be better aided by sister societies, whose aim is to supply this great household want."[29] The Brooklyn YWCA was no more inclusive, placing workers in "almost every occupation in which women are engaged, except that of domestic service."[30] The employment arm of the Working Women's Protective Union similarly catered only to "women who obtain a livelihood by employments other than common household service."[31] The Alliance Employment Bureau, affiliated with the New York Association of Working Girls' Societies, occasionally placed day workers but generally tried to exclude "applicants for domestic service, who are referred to the proper agencies."[32] Working-girls clubs also excluded domestic workers. Even the term "working girl" was generally understood to mean factory and department store workers.[33] After the turn of the twentieth century, few if any domestic service reform agendas included calls for an eight-hour day or a minimum wage, and as we have seen, domestics were not included in any of the protective labor laws that women reformers brought to women workers in industry.

In the view of middle-class labor reformers, women's labor in factories and stores and women's paid domestic labor could not be reformed in one broad stroke. Labor that took place in private middle-class homes was different than labor that took place in commercial enterprises. Domestic service required a reform program of its own, and the program that emerged was not at all like the one labor reformers created for women who worked in factories and shops. Domestic service reform focused not on protecting domestics from labor exploitation in middle-class homes but on fostering the home's essential morality. Legislation, middle-class women activists argued, should assist, rather than regulate, middle-class employers' management of household help. Rather than addressing the poor wages and long hours that prevailed in many homes, labor reformers sought to exclude dishonest or sexually promiscuous domestics from the labor pool and separate the others from what they viewed as the degrading influence of the working-class communities.

Training Programs

Although larger women's reform organizations like the National Consumers' League and the WTUL occasionally weighed in on the domestic labor problem, late nineteenth-century reforms were left almost entirely to smaller organizations, which hoped to do their small part to solve what they referred to as "the servant problem." These groups were often local organizations, and they did not generally rely on social scientific expertise or the regulating power of government as reformers would after the turn of the twentieth century. The domestic service reform that these organizations and their public supporters advocated most, by far, was training programs. Social reformers argued that training schools would make domestic service a skilled trade, encouraging employers to pay more for skilled workers and attracting more women to the occupation.[34] The women who administered the Christian Aid to Employment Society thought that the occupation's problems might be solved when "a systematic training school, embracing all kinds of domestic employment, is opened, upon a sufficiently liberal basis to insure admission to the poorest seeker of knowledge."[35] Mary Allen West, an educator and a Woman's Christian Temperance Union member, wrote that nothing seemed "more needed" than training schools for domestics.[36] Household adviser Mary Bancroft Smith agreed, lauding training programs as the best remedy for "the masses of untrained girls crowding New York's intelligence offices."[37] To middle-class employers—and to reformers who hoped to solve their household labor problems—training programs offered the best hope for increasing the pool of willing and well-trained help.

Training programs sprang up around New York City with almost as much frequency as middle-class reformers and public experts called for them. The Sisters of Charity of the Holy Communion hoped that work in middle-class and elite homes might one day offer both moral protection and a good wage to the young orphans they trained to become "capable and respectable servants."[38] The Society for Befriending Working Girls, meanwhile, hoped to convince working women to "take positions as domestics, rather than the equally menial and less remunerative positions in factories or stores."[39] The Brearly League Industrial Evening School harbored a similar plan, outfitting a bedroom and a dining room in which they hoped to train disaffected factory workers to become domestics. Brearly administrators spoke proudly of each student, who they claimed "loves to scrub and into that work puts all her superabundant energy," to the detriment of "the floor and the paint."[40] The German Housewives' League, of which the wife of Legal Aid Society founder and president Arthur von Briesen was a proud member, took a similarly practical approach to training domestics. In a furnished kitchen and dining room, the league hoped to train "greenhorns" to cook and serve meals.[41] In 1908, meanwhile, the New York chapter of the WTUL planned simultaneously to end unemployment and to put "household industries" on a "basis of regular hours and good wages" by organizing a training program in cooking and serving for unemployed factory workers at Hartley settlement house.[42] Very little evidence of these programs still exists, but it is clear that training programs were a frequently proposed, and frequently enacted, reform program for domestic service.

The Wilson Industrial School for Girls has left behind enough material for a more detailed analysis. Like the Sisters of the Holy Communion, the Wilson School focused its domestic training efforts on the young. In "Kitchen-Garden" classes, teachers provided poor girls from six to fourteen years of age with "toy table-cloths, napkins, dishes, tubs, scrubbing-brushes & c & c," to help them to "become very skillful little workers" and prepare them for positions in "domestic service in good families."[43] These lessons were eventually compiled into a volume, "Little Lessons for Little Housekeepers."[44] Should the little housekeepers need extra practice, volunteer teachers sometimes took "the children to their homes and allowed them to make beds, set the table and wash dishes, thus putting in practice the lessons they have received."[45] Administrators hoped that the young girls would one day choose domestic service over factory work, thereby giving "the School the honor of doing something toward solving the vexed and perplexed servant question in New York."[46]

The Wilson Industrial School for Girls did not, however, stop at teaching practical housekeeping skills. When not practicing with their toy scrubbing brushes, Wilson schoolgirls studied Bible verses and struggled "amid the temptations which surrounded them."[47] Class-based religious differences also provided a target for Wilson School lessons, and administrators claimed to have had great success in "christianizing" young girls.[48] One young Catholic scholar supposedly grew up to be "a communicant in the Episcopal Church, lady-like in manner, and occupying a position of trust" as a domestic in a middle-class home. Another young woman allegedly worked as a domestic in a family for nine years and ultimately joined her employers' church.[49] A reporter for the *New York Times* emphasized the importance of the Wilson School's work in training young women for domestic service, observing that it was "irrational to expect that a girl who has spent her early life in an Irish cabin, or a negro's, or in a shanty on the rocks of the upper part of this City, should be expected to be either gentle-spoken or deft-handed, or neat in dress and habits, or scarcely anything else that the house-servant of a respectable family should be."[50] Perhaps most significant, in the reporter's view, was the question of how else a working-class young

A drawing included in the Wilson Industrial School for Girls' 1884 annual report. (Courtesy of Goddard-Riverside Community Center Collection, Rare Book and Manuscript Library, Columbia University)

woman could learn "to be civil either in language or behavior, when her rude wit and coarse language has always been encouraged by the laughing approval, or perhaps the brutal treatment, of men ruder and coarser than she."[51] Inculcating middle-class standards of morality and behavior was thus a vital part of training women to work in middle-class homes. Administrators hoped that newly trained and newly Protestant young working-class women and girls might be purged of their ethnic and class behaviors and become accustomed to female middle-class guardianship.

Workers who had secured positions in factories and shops were not eager to become household workers, and domestics generally failed to enroll in training courses. Robert Erskine Ely, in a speech to the Household Economics Association, rejected a member's suggestion of training programs as a solution to household labor problems by pointing to one school in Boston "which practically had to go out of business for want of pupils."[52] Training programs offered few guarantees of fair wages, normal hours, or decent working conditions. Furthermore, given housewives' constant demand for domestic workers, working women felt little need for a training certificate before going to work in private homes. In 1912, the New York City commissioner of licenses reported that training programs did not solve "the servant

Students at the Wilson Industrial School for Girls, ca. 1900.
(Courtesy of Goddard-Riverside Community Center Collection,
Rare Book and Manuscript Library, Columbia University)

problem in a direct manner because servants do not attend them."[53] One housewife, who had visited several training programs in New York, complained that "in every instance we have been informed either that there were no girls then in the establishment who would suit our purpose" or, more frequently, that "parents would not allow their children to accept such positions."[54] Training programs could not survive if they could not attract students or even convince the ones they had to take domestic service positions. Both tasks proved insurmountable for many programs.

For the Wilson Industrial School, problems cropped up early on. As early as 1876, only 166 of the 397 students enrolled at the school attended daily.

That same year, administrators admitted, one young woman who had been a student for some years abruptly transferred to a public school, "giving as a reason that she had but one more year to go to school and wanted an opportunity to study without being interrupted by sewing or housework."[55] As the years rolled by, domestic training at the Wilson School lost its focus on training women for employment. In 1895, although Wilson administrators still hoped to train a few domestic workers, their larger goal was to teach their pupils how to "help mother at home, and make father more comfortable."[56] By 1910, the "Kitchen-Garden" had become a regular kindergarten and the Wilson School's administrators had dropped all pretense of training women for domestic service. Instead, they offered evening cooking classes to young married women as a sort of marital therapy, "for we all know that the way to a man's heart is through his stomach."[57] Four years later, administrators admitted that students in domestic training courses were mostly "Stenographers, Telephone girls, Clerks, and some young married women."[58] Although training programs might have supplied a solution to an ideological and material problem for female middle-class organizers—how to hire a working-class woman for domestic labor without bringing the problems of the working-class into one's home—they failed to solve "the servant problem."

Immigrant Homes

While training programs sought to entice factory workers to domestic service, other reformers reached out to women who were more likely to take up paid housework. Because western European immigrants made up the vast majority of domestic workers in turn-of-the-century New York, homes for immigrant women represented an important tool for reformers seeking to address domestic labor. In New York City, such homes were numerous, with four different institutions serving immigrant Catholic women alone.[59] Immigrant homes provided young women who had just landed at Ellis Island and Castle Garden with a place to stay and usually steered those looking for work into domestic service. Home administrators saw themselves as immigrants' protectors and shared reformers' view of the middle-class home as the best possible place for long-term guardianship of young working-class women. In fact, many immigrant homes organized their outreach programs around filling middle-class housewives' constant demand for domestics. For instance, the supervisor of one home run by Methodists reported that she never had a problem finding domestic work for "respectable women who are willing to work," and that, in fact, employers often expressed "a prefer-ence for immigrants newly landed."[60] The administrators of another home agreed that "the demand for 'green girls' greatly exceeds the supply, and for every one that lands there is no end of available positions."[61] In addition to lodging and employment, many homes, like the Immigrant Girls' Home and the Home Co-operative Society, offered residents domestic service training programs and employment societies.[62] Others, like the Mathews Woman's Home Missionary Society, provided a meeting place for former residents who had found work as domestics to meet their friends on their "days out."[63] The Mathews Home was also a regular stop for middle-class employers making the rounds in search of new domestic workers. Middle-class women knocked on the Mathews Home's door so often that on the frequent occasion that it ran out of immigrant domestics looking for work, administrators hung out a large block-lettered sign reading, "No girls for household service to-day."[64]

Reformers of domestic service, therefore, saw immigrant homes as an important piece of the equation in any solution to "the servant problem." Those homes with training programs taught not only domestic skills but also manners and behavior appropriate for a worker in a middle-class home. In doing so, administrators hoped to counteract the vice and bad habits that they believed young women immigrants learned among working-class friends and family and then brought with them into their employers' homes. Miss J. Corbin, supervisor of the Immigrant Girls' Home, expressed her dis-may at "how almost uncivilized in their table manners some of these girls are." Corbin explained that it was "no unusual thing" for a new resident to take a bite of bread and "then lay the rest of the slice in her lap until she is ready to finish," adding resignedly, "We do what we can while they remain with us."[65] Fulfilling a purpose that was much more important to reformers than table manners, homes for immigrant women separated prospective do-mestic employees from the vice that was endemic to New York City streets. Future WTUL leader Margaret Dreier believed that, above and beyond their usefulness to immigrant women, immigrant homes held a "distinct advan-tage" for housewives, who could have "some knowledge" that their employ-ees had come from homes that were "clean and wholesome and not from the dens they now frequent for lack of a better place."[66] Venila S. Burr-ington, a researcher for Frances Kellor's Inter-Municipal Council on House-hold Research, agreed, arguing that immigrant homes saved the potential domestic from moral degradation "resulting from the evil environment into which she is often thrust unwittingly from lack of proper shielding or guidance."[67] By protecting the young immigrant from contact with the tenement or its residents, experts and reformers believed that immigrant homes also protected the private home from working-class corruption. Under the watchful eye of middle-class administrators, working-class women might also learn the good manners and good morals necessary for paid domestic labor.

The Mission of Our Lady of the Rosary for the Protection of Irish Immigrant Girls, founded in 1886 by Charlotte Grace O'Brien, was one of New York's first immigrant homes. O'Brien, daughter of well-known Irish revolutionary William Smith O'Brien, worried over the moral danger that young, single, Irish immigrant women faced when they arrived in New York's harbor. In order to investigate these conditions for herself, O'Brien traveled to New York under an assumed name, surveying the steerage conditions aboard ship. After landing in New York, she researched the lodging options for newly arrived single women. She was appalled at what she found. Decrying the "perils to which" women immigrants "were exposed," O'Brien established the Mission of Our Lady of the Rosary on State Street near the Battery.[68] She died before she could witness the success of her project, but the mission continued under the auspices of the Catholic Church. The home thrived, housing over 5,000 women in its first year and managing to increase the size of the home and pay off the $10,000 mortgage.

The Catholic priests and other administrators who ran Our Lady of the Rosary made no bones about their view of the city as a dangerous place for newly arrived young women. As Father Henry, the mission's director, argued, his institution protected many "young maidens," who escaped "the perils of the sea" only to "become a prey to the land sharks that infest" New York City streets. These "land sharks," he argued, were "more cruel and voracious than the monsters of the deep, for they seek to rob these innocent and confiding women . . . of that which is more precious to them than life itself—their faith, the jewel of purity, for which the Irish maiden all the world over is so conspicuous."[69] The original plan for the mission had been to send young immigrant women to existing reputable boardinghouses. But as Father Riordan, Father Henry's predecessor, reported, this plan allowed too much contact between young immigrant women and the working-class denizens of even the best lodging houses. It had been, he asserted, "impossible to exercise the thorough surveillance necessary for the protection of the girls under this system."[70] Young immigrant women, Father Riordan, Father Henry, and domestic service reformers made clear, entered New York harbor free of the moral taint that inevitably came with contact with working-class New York. The trick was to reach young female immigrants before tenement employment agents and lodging house runners did.

Immigrant homes, Our Lady of the Rosary among them, employed various strategies to do just that. Its address, so far downtown, put Our Lady of the Rosary in a particularly favorable place to catch young Irish immigrant women before they went astray. Each day, as was typical of many immigrant homes, Our Lady of the Rosary sent workers to the docks at Castle Island to intercept new immigrant women before they had time to fall prey to the urban land sharks prowling Father Henry's imagined city. As part of this effort, Our Lady of the Rosary agents printed a leaflet, which they distributed to newcomers, warning them of the moral peril that lay outside the gates of Castle Garden. Disembarking female passengers, Our Lady of the Rosary administrators admonished, should "on no account venture out into the City to seek employment." The leaflet informed women that they could purchase train tickets, buy food, and exchange money "without leaving Castle Garden" and that those meeting friends should not under any circumstances "leave Castle Garden until they come for you." For good measure, the leaflet's authors repeated that there was "no necessity for going out into the streets of the City, and you must not allow idle curiosity to tempt you into doing so."[71]

Our Lady of the Rosary could not lodge immigrant women indefinitely. Administrators hoped that the women in their care would find long-term protection in "suitable positions with good families."[72] Middle-class employers, they clearly believed, would exert a more positive influence on new immigrant women than would their working-class friends. Administrators urged immigrant women to "take a situation, and when here for some time then look up your friends."[73] For reformers of domestic service, like Venila S. Burrington and Margaret Dreier, as well as for the directors of Our Lady of the Rosary, protection of both immigrant women and the middle-class home necessitated isolating young immigrant women, as much as possible, from the working-class and ethnic communities of tenement districts.

The Clara de Hirsch Immigrant Home, founded by Jewish philanthropists Oscar and Susan Straus and the home's namesake, the Baroness Clara de Hirsch, offered similar protection and occupational guidance to Jewish immigrant women. The Immigrant Home had two facilities: a home for working women, which trained live-in boarders and day students for domestic service, and a separate home, which boarded young Jewish immigrant women and placed them in domestic service. The Clara de Hirsch home hoped to channel the increasing surge of eastern European Jewish immigrants away from factory work and toward domestic service, despite the fact that eastern European Jews, like Italians, generally refused to take domestic work. Like Our Lady of the Rosary, the Clara de Hirsch Home sent a representative to the docks. Mrs. Meirowitz, working on behalf of both the Clara de Hirsch Immigrant Home and the National Council of Jewish Women, patrolled the docks at Ellis Island and Castle Garden looking for Jewish immigrant women in need of aid.[74] Boarders and day students at the Clara de Hirsch Home, meanwhile, took classes in "General, Advanced, Fancy and Invalid cooking; all kinds of Laundry work from the use of soaps, starch and washing fluids, to the laundry of the finest laces and embroideries, a complete course in Waiting; Household Science; Marketing and Hygiene and Emergencies."[75] Like Our Lady of the Rosary, the Clara de Hirsch Home was also known to middle-class employers as a potential source of domestic workers. In 1905, Frances Kellor's Inter-Municipal Committee on Household Research reported that even though the Clara de Hirsch Home had already managed to place 118 women at service, the placements fell far short of demand.[76] By 1910, it was still receiving an average of twenty-five inquiries a week from domestic service employers.[77]

Preparing immigrant women for what directors hoped would be a future in domestic service required more than just practical domestic training. Young women from eastern Europe, like working-class women everywhere else, exhibited a variety of ethnic and class-based behaviors that made them unfit for middle-class homes. To remedy this problem, the board hired Rose Sommerfeld to supervise the Clara de Hirsch Home so that "by precept and example" she might wield "the most beneficial influence over her charges."[78] Administrators encouraged young women to pay a small fee in return for the services rendered, so as "to instil [sic] in the girl's mind, at her very arrival in this country, that she must pay for what she receives."[79] Thus, board members hoped to do away with any notion that young immigrant women might get along without working, trade sex for money, or steal what they should earn. In addition to inoculating young women against working-class immorality, these homes also fought the diseases that residents had contracted in "poverty stricken" homes, where they had fallen "below the average physical development."[80] After a series of doctor's visits and curative tonics, the women at the helm of the Clara de Hirsch Home hoped to send residents "into the world" and into middle-class homes both morally and "physically strong."[81] Not only would these moral lessons and physical care make residents more "independent," they would also make them more fit for household service.[82]

The Clara de Hirsch Home did not initially include plans for a residence—administrators intended only to help new immigrants find friends and reach their final destinations. But they soon felt pressed to make more complicated arrangements. The directors felt they could not allow immigrant women "to go to some of the addresses given, on account of [the] number of lodgers kept, or because there were inside bedrooms, or rooms behind restaurants, cellar housing, etc."[83] Board members, like other immigrant home administrators, saw physical separation from the tenement and its residents as a vital part of protecting immigrant women, especially those whom they hoped to mold into domestics. Clara de Hirsch Home agents met women at Ellis Island and took them directly to the facility. Once there, residents would not be released into the care of friends "without an agent personally visiting and inspecting the prospective living quarters."[84] Although some immigrant women protested such supervision, administrators stood firm, arguing that "those who were most insistent, were those whose accommodations were inadequate," "filled to overflowing with children or lodgers."[85] It was so important to directors that residents live separately from working-class neighborhoods that the Home for Working Girls was situated uptown on Sixty-third Street, a location that was, as one historian has argued, "a safe distance from the 'solid block of Europe' that was the Lower East Side."[86] By keeping young immigrant women away from working-class and ethnic communities, immigrant home administrators hoped to save potential domestics from tenement corruption.

White and ethnic immigrants, although they made up the bulk of women bound for domestic service at the turn of the century, were not the only travelers to experience moral uplift in resident homes before going to work as domestics. Located at various times in and around Harlem, the White Rose Mission served a different clientele than either the Clara de Hirsch Home or Our Lady of the Rosary. The White Rose billed itself as the only home "managed by Colored women for Colored women" since its founding by former slave and prominent African American social reformer Victoria Earle Matthews in 1897. The White Rose Mission offered shelter and employment to the "eager, earnest working girl," finding her way "to the great city in search of work."[87] The White Rose Mission opened its doors long before African Americans began to migrate en masse to northern cities and long before African American women made up anywhere near the majority of domestic workers in New York. Still, the mission never wanted for clients. Few other New York charitable institutions accepted African Americans, and the White Rose Mission hosted women from as far afield as the American South, Honolulu, Bermuda, and Brazil.[88] Like the Clara de Hirsch Home, the White Rose Mission not only helped to place women in domestic service positions but also trained them for various domestic jobs, including "Housekeeping, Cooking, Expert Waiting, Sewing, Laundering and all home occupations."[89] The White Rose Mission also offered a "clean, respectable" parlor for domestics to meet friends on their afternoons off.[90] The mission's success was immediate. Administrators reported that so many women needed aid that "cots, lounges and even the floor have been used as beds."[91] White Rose administrators also met some success in finding women employment in domestic service, placing fifty women in 1906 and receiving "not less than twenty" reports from employers attesting to the "reliability and industry of White Rose Girls."[92] Like immigrant homes and training programs, the White Rose Mission promised middle-class employers a well-stocked source for well-trained domestic employees.

But the White Rose Mission differed from other immigrant homes in a few important respects. First, rather than positioning itself near the Battery or in another neighborhood far away from the community it hoped to serve, the mission set up shop in the heart of the African American community. In fact, over time it moved to be closer to New York's black community. The first quarters were located in the "crowded colored section of East 97th Street."[93] By 1918, the mission had moved to 262 West 136th Street, at the center of "the populous Harlem colored district."[94] The White Rose Mission also followed a settlement house model. Black New Yorkers could take advantage of a wide array of programs, ranging from a Penny Provident Bank to classes in child rearing, physical culture, and thrift.[95] The black women who ran the White Rose Mission thus provided to the African American community services that they could not get from city welfare agencies or from other charitable organizations.[96] Few other travelers' services accepted African American residents. In 1918, the mission reported that of the scant seventy-five beds open to African American women in philanthropic homes, the White Rose Mission held fourteen.[97] Thus, rather than simply training women for domestic service, the White Rose Mission sought to bring social services to a neglected community.

Second, White Rose administrators' choice to train women for domestic service reflected a harsh racial and economic reality. In turn-of-the-century New York City, white workers found jobs much more easily than did African Americans, even in low-status fields like domestic service. There were still plenty of immigrants arriving on New York's shores, and given the choice, most middle-class household employers preferred to hire white immigrants, even the hated Irish, over African Americans. By offering domestic service training, the administrators of the White Rose Mission hoped to change the perception of African American women as workers and as women. Historians have found that many late nineteenth- and early twentieth-century middle-class black women activists embraced a "politics of respectability," which encouraged women to practice industry, sexual chastity, and good manners. The politics of respectability was not an imitation of white cultural norms but rather a way to combat racist stereotypes of black women as lazy and sexually promiscuous.[98] Like these other African American activists, White Rose administrators emphasized "self-help and right-living" in their ministry to young African American migrants.[99] But administrators also encouraged racial pride, providing a class and a comprehensive library on African American history. The library included works by black authors such as Booker T. Washington, Charles Chesnutt, Paul Laurence Dunbar, Phillis Wheatley, and Harriet Jacobs. Other immigrant homes tried to assimilate young immigrant women into white, Protestant, middle-class, and mainstream culture by ridding them of behaviors that marked them as members of their native ethnic communities. The White Rose Mission did not ask African American women to shed their racial and ethnic identity but rather expected them to embody its most respectable and ladylike version. Through training and education, the White Rose Mission hoped to provide its residents with a livelihood as well as to mold them into "respectable" African American women.

Nevertheless, administrators at the White Rose Mission agreed with their counterparts at Our Lady of the Rosary and the Clara de Hirsch Home about the moral peril faced by newly arrived women in New York City. Perhaps even their own neighborhood held danger. They described their surroundings in "The Hollow" as ones in which the "most depraved Negroes lived side by side with those who were striving to live respectable lives."[100] White Rose administrators worried that black migrants might fall victim to agents who were bent on taking "advantage of that class of travelers who seem bewildered."[101] The rhetoric that White Rose administrators used to describe the danger to African American migrants mirrored their counterparts' rhetoric about unaccompanied white immigrants. The White Rose program included not just lodging and domestic service training but also "Protection from City Evils," and White Rose administrators worried over the fate of the young woman who "is ready to go with the first man or woman who says a kind word to her—ready to go, too often, alas, to degradation and shame."[102] Recalling the case of a girl who was "lured away" before a White Rose agent could meet her ship, Victoria Earle Matthews stressed the importance of being "vigilant" in meeting and guiding the young women disembarking in New York, lest they "go astray."[103] Although the White Rose Mission represented more than just a venue for training and lodging potential domestics, leaders shared with the administrators of other immigrant women's homes worries about the temptations that a new arrival might encounter alone in the city. They did not exhibit much worry about the perils young black women might encounter in white homes, especially in the form of predator male employers. In general, the White Rose Mission, like its white counterparts, saw the middle-class home as a place that would continue to guard the sexual and moral purity of the city's young female new arrivals. Judging by the praise the mission received from white women's groups, white middle-class reformers saw the mission's efforts as part of their larger objective to ensure that such urban evils did not find their way into middle-class kitchens.[104]

The long-term relative success of immigrant homes in helping to solve the "servant problem" depended on changing demographic patterns and the cultural attitudes of different ethnic groups toward domestic service. Given Irish women's long-standing willingness to accept domestic jobs, perhaps it is no surprise that quite a few of the residents of Our Lady of the Rosary took positions as domestic workers in private families. As the tide of Irish immigration gave way to waves of new immigrants from eastern and southern Europe, however, the supply of Irish immigrants for domestic service ebbed. In addition, it is not at all clear that Irish women wanted the care of Our Lady of the Rosary. In 1902, Father Henry admitted to the *New York Tribune* that most Irish immigrant women had "friends or relatives somewhere in the country to whom they are going. If it is their ultimate intention to go out to service they almost invariably prefer to wait until they have consulted their friends." In consequence, he acknowledged, "we are flooded with applications for girls which we cannot supply."[105]

The Clara de Hirsch Home had even bigger problems. Jewish immigrant women overwhelmingly refused domestic work.[106] Between 1904 and 1910, only 14 percent of the 3,400 immigrants taken in by the Clara de Hirsch Home went into service.[107] As Rose Sommerfeld put it, despite her best efforts to make domestic service attractive to Clara de Hirsch Home residents, "Jewish girls do not go into service."[108] Thus, even with the influx of eastern European immigrants to the United States, middle-class housewives would have to rely on the dwindling supply of immigrants from northern Europe for domestic help, a situation that only exacerbated the "servant problem."

African American women, in contrast, generally did not have the luxury of choosing an occupation other than domestic service, and training gave them a small advantage in competition with white workers. The White Rose Mission offered shelter and lodging to poor women who could not get help elsewhere. As African American migration from the South to New York City increased around World War I, the mission had more than enough residents to fill its beds. By 1920, White Rose Mission administrators reported that the mission was "overcrowded" and that they were unable "to take care of all the girls who applied for admission."[109] The success of the White Rose Mission notwithstanding, immigrant homes could not hope to provide New York housewives with enough well-trained and respectable domestics to fill their kitchens. And because immigrant women's homes did not help working women to negotiate a good wage or limited hours, the homes had little to offer women workers.

When they successfully placed workers in middle-class homes, however, immigrant homes claimed to offer employers well-trained and respectable household help. Immigrant homes uniformly preached to residents the virtues of sexual chastity, honesty, efficiency, hard work, and refined manners. They all tried to intercept young women before they could join working-class or ethnic communities and attempted to physically isolate their residents from those who shared their ethnicity or class status. It is certainly true that newly arrived young women were vulnerable to con artists and sexual predators, especially in their first days in a new city. Immigrant homes were conscious of this threat and were well-intentioned in their efforts to protect young women from the dangers they believed lurked in tenement districts.[110] But immigrant home administrators consistently located the source of corruption, vice, and disease in working-class and ethnic communities. Few worried about the very real possibility that domestics might encounter a sexual predator or two among the male members of New York's households. What was most important to immigrant home administrators, and to domestic employers, was that domestics did not have a chance to bring the vice and dangers associated with the city streets to work with them.

Employment Societies and Servants' Clubs

Turn-of-the-century employment societies and servants' clubs also contributed to the efforts of immigrant homes and training programs to place well-trained, refined young women in household service. Employment societies, organized by groups of women who tried to match trustworthy domestics with employers, seemed especially promising to late nineteenth-century women reformers. The Ladies' Protective Union, for instance, hoped that its employment society would cause a "steady improvement" in the available pool of domestics, by "encouraging the good, weeding out the bad and teaching the ignorant."[111] The Christian Aid Association, meanwhile, hoped to "command the confidence of those seeking employment, and of those requiring their services, as to secure the most favorable relations between employers and the employed."[112]

By taking over the business of supplying domestics, reformers hoped to control the kinds of women sent into private homes. Margaret Dreier suggested a model employment society whose workers would "study the employees and mingle with the employers" in order to make better matches, rather than "the two thrown together haphazard."[113] The Ladies' Protective Union, meanwhile, hoped to improve the pool of available domestics by strictly requiring employer references. The administrators tersely directed domestics who could not procure such references to "seek employment elsewhere."[114] Administrators of the Christian Aid to Employment Society harbored a similar plan, only to find that it could not meet domestic employers' needs because the supply of household workers was short on "such persons as we are able to *recommend*."[115] By carefully choosing the workers they placed in middle-class homes, domestic service reformers sought to protect themselves and their clientele from immoral, dishonest, unreliable, and unruly domestics. Few of these proposals had anything to say about protecting domestics from exploitative employers.

Servants' clubs also seemed a promising way for middle-class reformers to create a pool of trustworthy workers. Rather than rejecting domestics who did not meet their standards, middle-class servants' club leaders worked to uplift domestics to become industrious and moral. The women at the helm of the Innovation Club in Brooklyn also ran an employment society that stood "for fair dealings between employer and employee, and for helpful and friendly service to household workers."[116] Despite its emphasis on "fair dealings," the program tended to focus more on refining domestics than on reforming domestic service. Servants' clubs, both organized and supervised by middle-class women, worked to channel working-class women's leisure hours into activities that employers might deem respectable. Innovation programs allowed middle-class women both to monitor domestic workers' social contacts and to move troublesome social gatherings of working-class men and women out of employers' kitchens. Administrators also hoped that holding club meetings on Thursday nights, domestics' traditional evening out, would provide appropriate leisure activities for working women and "promote a pleasant social life."[117] The leaders of the Golden Rule Club aspired to similar goals. They hoped their club would encourage "a helpful spirit" among domestics and "a friendly spirit between employers and employees."[118] Home economist and social worker Jane Seymour Klink helped the domestics attending the Golden Rule Club to plan their first event. The workers voted for a dance, to which, they eagerly proposed, they should each invite six men. Klink stepped in, steering them as gently as possible toward a more respectable reception, with flowers, music, ice cream, cake, and printed invitations. She added that after the reception the workers might hold "a little quiet dance, if you like. . . . That would be dignified and I think all our friends would be glad enough to receive an invitation."[119] Servants' clubs, then, were more than simply a space for domestics to meet friends. Middle-class women hoped to intervene in the social relationships of young working-class women, which many felt made them unfit for work in middle-class homes.

Studying Domestics "Impartially and Thoroughly": The State and Domestic Reform

In 1904, Frances Kellor created a new model, born out of the Progressive Era shift toward research, education, and legislation, to reform domestic service. Kellor was one of the first reformers in New York with connections to larger women's organizations to take on reforming domestic service. Perhaps Kellor had a special vantage point on "the servant problem" because her mother had taken in laundry for families in Coldwater, Michigan, where Kellor had spent part of her childhood.[120] Whatever her motivation, after getting a degree in sociology from the University of Chicago, Kellor moved to New York City, where she turned her skill and attention to the plight of female domestic workers. Like other ambitious and educated young women building a career in social reform, Kellor brought her experience in research and fieldwork to pinpointing the exact nature of the domestic labor problem. Over the course of a two-year investigation, Kellor and members of the College Settlement Association disguised themselves both as prospective employers and as domestics looking for work and visited every intelligence office in New York City, as well as some in Boston, Chicago, and Philadelphia. Kellor's research, and the influential study, *Out of Work*, that resulted from it, were models of Progressive Era reform, which sought to bring the

Sociologist and reformer Frances Kellor, ca. 1900–1915. (Courtesy of
The Schlesinger Library, Radcliffe Institute, Harvard University)

insights of science to curing urban social ills. Although immigrant homes,
employment societies, and servants' clubs often persisted into the twentieth century, they were the remnants of old ideas. Kellor, on the other hand,
represented a new generation of Progressive reformers, many of whom had
earned graduate degrees and who looked to use the power of government
to solve social problems. Her work, then, marked a shift away from private
solutions to the "servant problem" and toward solutions that used the insights of modern scientific research and expertise — and, most important,
the regulatory power of the state.

Before pursuing legislation, Kellor made inroads into the networks of
women's organizations interested in issues of city governance and labor
reform. Kellor began with the Woman's Municipal League, allying herself
with Margaret Dreier, who had considerable experience and skill in lobbying city and state government. Dreier was the eldest daughter of Dorothea
and Theodor Dreier, successful businessman and civic leader. In her teens,
Dreier became involved in social reform, beginning many years of work
on behalf of the poor and working classes. When she met Kellor, Margaret Dreier was working with the Woman's Municipal League, which had

transformed itself from a narrowly defined women's civic league to a wide-ranging social reform group interested in municipal government, labor, and welfare reform. Margaret Dreier, who became Margaret Dreier Robins after marrying Raymond Robins in 1905, would ascend to the presidency of the WTUL in 1907. Through Margaret Dreier, Kellor met Margaret's sister, Mary Dreier, and the two began a lifelong personal and professional partnership. Kellor's relationship with the Dreiers was significant, because of her long-term romantic relationship with Mary and because the three shared a deep commitment to labor reform. In fact, perhaps owing to Kellor's influence, Mary Dreier would be a lifelong advocate for domestic workers.

Kellor easily persuaded Margaret Dreier and the Woman's Municipal League to pursue legislation to address the urban vice in New York's employment agencies. The legislation they produced, however, is revealing. At the helm of a political coalition that included political figures, larger employment agents, and other women's organizations, Dreier and Kellor authored and successfully passed an employment agency law through the New York State legislature in 1904. This law applied to every city in New York with a population over 50,000, which in 1900 included New York City, Albany, Buffalo, Rochester, Syracuse, Troy, and Utica.[121] In each of these cities, the law created the Office of Commissioner of Licenses, to be run by local governments. In New York City, this office oversaw the licensing of all employment agencies and agents and conducted biannual inspections of every agency in its jurisdiction. The law required employment agencies to keep careful employment records, to investigate and keep on file all employee references, and to refund fees to both domestics and employers if they could not provide a placement.[122] It also regulated office conditions, outlawing so-called living room agencies, in which an employment office operated out of the agent's living quarters. Finally, the law mandated that employment agencies could not share the premises with a business that sold alcohol.[123] Kellor hoped that the New York legislation would serve as a model for other large cities, including Chicago, Boston, and Philadelphia. Kellor's work did indeed receive national attention from Progressive politicians. In 1906, President Theodore Roosevelt, to whom Kellor became a close adviser, wrote to Kellor praising her new book, *Out of Work*, and expressing his "wish that it could be distributed as a tract among just about four fifths of those who hire household servants!"[124]

Kellor did not stop work after the law had passed. In 1904, she met with various women's organizations, including the Clara de Hirsch Home and outlying branches of the Woman's Municipal League, urging them to investigate the conditions of employment agencies in their areas.[125] Determined to rout out tenement agency conditions, which they believed corrupted domestic workers, Kellor and members of the Woman's Municipal League made themselves thorns in the side of the new commissioner of licenses. They accused him of refusing to punish employment agency violations to the full extent of the law and hired a lawyer to bring violations to the attention of the mayor. Although the outraged commissioner claimed that the charges were "without foundation in fact" and impugned the reputation of her investigators, the rogue employment agents exposed by Kellor's inspectors eventually lost their licenses.[126]

Kellor also gathered a group of prominent women reformers and philanthropists, including Grace Dodge, Lucy Maynard Salmon, WTUL leader and labor organizer Leonora O'Reilly, Rose Sommerfeld, settlement house leader Lillian Wald, National Consumers' League president Maude Nathan, and philanthropist Mrs. Russell Sage, to form the New York Association for Household Research. The New York Association then joined with the Women's Educational and Industrial Association in Boston and the Housekeeper's Alliance and Civic Club in Philadelphia to form the Inter-Municipal Committee on Household Research.[127] Kellor and her compatriots, like other Progressives, had faith that social scientific research could create a foundation for social change. Headquartered in New York, the committee set out "to study impartially and thoroughly the conditions which attend household work" and to provide the results of that research to employers and employees.[128] Between 1904 and 1906, when it was absorbed into the Woman's Municipal League, the committee studied such diverse subjects as immigration, African American migration, employment agencies, and household working conditions and published a monthly bulletin describing its findings. Kellor and other committee members also took speaking engagements to publicize their research to middle-class employers across the country.

Kellor's reform of New York City's employment law marked a significant departure from middle-class women's previous handling of domestic service reform. Kellor moved the focus of domestic service reform away from reforming the behavior of domestics to addressing what she saw as the larger forces that shaped working-class women's development. Kellor and her associates connected such public political issues as tenement reform, immigration, and public health to the problems that middle-class women faced in their relationship with domestics in the private home. The Inter-Municipal Committee announced that it would study such "apparently alien subjects as immigration and working girls' homes" because of their "direct bearing" on the question of women's paid household labor.[129] Immigration, tenement conditions, and issues such as working women's "standard of living . . . how she is treated, how housed, how trained, and with what associates she is thrown," the committee argued, were the very factors that would "determine whether she shall be a desirable, efficient worker, of good moral character, temperate, faithful and honest."[130] If reformers did not step in to change the conditions in tenement employment agencies, Kellor argued, middle-class employers would be left with "incompetents" or, worse, a "class of diseased, paupers, criminals, and degenerates."[131] Kellor and her followers believed that the private middle-class home was at the center of urban political debate and public policy. Domestics, they argued, created a direct link between middle-class homes and urban problems.

Kellor also had a different understanding of the vulnerability of working women than did the women who created immigrant homes, training programs, servants' clubs, and employment societies. In Kellor's view, domestics were victims of working-class exploitation before they became agents of corruption in middle-class homes. Kellor attacked employment agents, whom she believed defrauded women looking for work, many of them immigrants, by charging fees without providing positions and exploited them by sending them to work in brothels and "disorderly houses."[132] African American women seemed to Kellor to be particularly vulnerable to such fraud. Kellor argued that agents in southern ports enticed African American women to migrate to the city, offering to pay their fare. Upon arrival, however, these women often found themselves in debt to agents for the trip, sometimes forced to repay three or four times the actual fare. The commissioner of licenses reported that agents often took possession of migrants' trunks and refused to return them until the exorbitant fee had been paid. Employers and agents then withheld black domestics' wages to exact further repayment. The commissioner stated that "the girls were practically held in servitude" until the fraudulent claims were paid.[133] The employment law outlawed this practice, standardized the fee that employees paid to agents when looking for work, and mandated that agents return fees to employees for whom they could not find positions. Kellor depicted African American women, along with the European immigrants who made up the majority of domestics in early twentieth-century New York, as victims of urban vice rather than agents of it.[134] Like other Progressives interested in urban reform, Kellor argued that working-class women were not innately bad but rather the products of an immoral, unsafe, and corrupt environment.[135] Although not free of racial stereotypes, Kellor's work was the first foray by middle-class reformers into reforming domestic service rather than focusing solely on reforming domestics.

Kellor's work also gave middle-class women and domestics a public, state-sponsored forum in which to arbitrate their disputes with employment agents. In addition to enforcing the employment agency law, the commissioner of licenses presided over hearings held in his city offices to mediate disputes among domestics, employers, and employment agents. In 1909, the commissioner held approximately 600 of these hearings and ordered many of the agencies to return fees to both domestics and employers.[136] Such hearings allowed domestics, as well as employers, to bring claims against employment agents and to air their complaints in a public setting. When Katie Kossat complained that agent Bernat Deutsch had sent her to work in disorderly houses "on two different occasions," the commissioner's office revoked Deutsch's license.[137] Sophie J. Laux, Janie and Tillie Regan, Margaret Jones, and Nellie Johnson all received refunds of agents' fees in hearings at the commissioner's office.[138] Indeed, in 1906, as in most years, the commissioner reported that workers recovered more money in fees from employment agents than did employers, receiving $2,130 of the total $2,815 of the fees refunded that year.[139]

The commissioner also responded to employer complaints about corrupt agents and unfaithful domestics, although he acknowledged that determining blame was often difficult. Employers often accused agents of repeatedly sending workers who quit after only a few days—and then refusing to return the fee. The commissioner explained that the agent usually claimed "that the fault lies with the employer, who either works the girl too hard, gives her unfit food, or imposes tasks which she said nothing about when hiring." The commissioner then investigated, ruling on "dozens of such complaints" each week.[140] Sometimes the commissioner revoked an agent's license, as in the case of agent Pauline Neinchil, who sent Mollie Posner to four different employers in the space of six weeks, collecting a fee from each of them.[141] At other times, the commissioner sided with the agent, refunding, for instance, only half of employer Joseph Stubin's fee because the agent, Alexander Gorlitzer, claimed he could prove that the worker he sent had stayed with Stubin for more than one day. The commissioner made his ruling despite Stubin's threat to the commissioner that "I will see that you give me justice or out you go."[142] Before the creation of the Office of Commissioner of Licenses, these employers might have argued with domestics who quit after only a few days or might have complained privately to friends and family about the fickleness of household help. Instead, the commissioner's office offered a public venue for labor disputes that would otherwise have been dealt with in private.

Kellor's employment law clearly had positive results for some aggrieved domestics and employers, but her reforms also shared the agenda of previous domestic service reform efforts. First, although she saw state authority as a useful tool to regulate domestic employment practices, she did not pursue regulation of domestics' hours, wages, or working conditions. Kellor was not blind to the exploitation that sometimes occurred in middle-class homes. She cataloged a list of abuses that domestics suffered, including sexual exploitation, long hours, and poor accommodations. But she located the source of the servant problem far away from the middle-class home. Kellor focused her reforms on employment agents, who, she charged, cheated working women and exposed them to sexual vice and criminality, rather than on middle-class employers who paid low wages, demanded long hours, and provided inferior accommodations. In doing so, Kellor acknowledged the poor conditions of domestic service without openly criticizing middle-class women employers.

Second, like employment societies, immigrant homes, and training programs, the employment agency law gave employers more control over the hiring process and tended to favor larger employment agencies run by middle-class managers. Although Margaret Dreier heartily supported the fifty-dollar licensing fee as "a fair estimate to place on a man's business," for many agents, who had previously operated informally out of their rooms on the Lower East Side, the fee was back-breaking.[143] Agent Ernest L. Williams, for instance, wrote a letter to Margaret Chanler of the Woman's Municipal League, chastising her for her support for doubling the employment agency licensing fee to fifty dollars. Williams and his wife ran an employment agency for black women and complained that if the measure passed they would have to abandon his tenement office, in which they also lived. Williams insisted that he had never defrauded working women or their employers.[144] A *New York Times* reporter corroborated Williams's complaint with a story about an impoverished elderly couple who had run a domestic service employment agency out of two rooms on a back street on the Lower East Side. Their income had been meager, but it had been, the reporter related, "just enough to keep the couple out of the poorhouse."[145] The new regulations and fees enacted by Kellor's employment agency law put the couple out of business. By forcing placement services out of the tenements, Kellor and her supporters demonstrated their view that the working-class men and women who ran tenement agencies were not appropriate supervisors for potential household workers.[146] Like servants' clubs, immigrant homes, and training programs, then, Kellor's reforms separated young domestics from the working-class and ethnic community of the tenements and pushed them into the arms of middle-class guardians. Kellor also benefited more tangibly from the law. Among the eighteen inspectors hired by the commissioner of licenses, three were women. One of those women was Jane Seymour Klink, who worked with Kellor on the Inter-Municipal Committee on Household Research and was a prominent reformer in her own right.[147] By focusing on tenement employment agents, Kellor found a way to reform domestic service without challenging middle-class women's dominion over their homes.

The employment agency law also undermined the individual bargaining power of domestic workers. In the social atmosphere of tenement agencies, where young working women knew one another and the agent, all sorts of working-class subversion might go on, including blackballing undesirable employers from that agency and those nearby.[148] Closing tenement agencies and pushing the employment agency trade to large, impersonal agents had a dampening effect on such behavior. Luckily for employers, the commissioner reported, "by forcing the agents to conduct their places in a business-like way, even at the expense of making them less popular with the servants, all these rather objectionable social features have been abolished."[149] Furthermore, by compelling agencies to check references, the law forced employment agents to do what training programs, employment societies, and immigrant homes had only attempted to do: protect the middle-class home from infiltration by corrupt, dishonest, or incompetent workers. Kellor was proud of these reforms, even if they came at the cost of domestics' bargaining power with employers. No longer, argued Kellor, could "thieves, street walkers and intemperates" be "dumped without regard into the household."[150] Using the tools of Progressive reform, Kellor sought to rationalize a system of supervision that middle-class women's reform groups had been trying to achieve on an ad hoc basis for decades.

The employment agency law's ban on "living room agencies"—those run out of owners' living quarters—highlights Kellor's belief that the intimacy of tenement life could have a perilous influence on young working women and, by extension, on the middle-class home. Far from "technical and trivial," Kellor argued, the living-room clause was vital to destroying tenement employment agencies' "cloak for immorality."[151] In her investigations, both before and after the employment agency law passed, Kellor expressed her feeling that merely being in the presence of tenement living conditions was enough to taint a young domestic irrevocably. She recounted with horror employment interviews taking place in agents' kitchens. In one, a "man was lying on the couch" and in another domestics and employers waited while the proprietor did the laundry. An appalled Kellor described their discussion of "'servants' and 'places' to the time of a rhythmic 'rub, rub,' through clouds of steam and soapy vapor, with an occasional flap of wet cloth for variation."[152] Such intimate contact between tenement residents and future domestics, Kellor believed, could not but be dangerous to both domestics and employers. By forcing employment agencies to be more "business-like," Kellor and her supporters sought to enforce divisions between private and public in employment agencies. In doing so, Kellor hoped to erect more barriers between denizens of the tenements and the middle-class home. Middle-class families were, after all, only once removed from intimate contact between potential domestics and working-class employment agents.

The most intimate and, as Kellor would have argued, most corrupting species of tenement agencies were the ones that offered patrons lodging as well as help in finding employment. Dreier worried that lodging houses in tenement employment agencies "indiscriminately mixed" the "young and old, moral and immoral, temperate and intemperate." In these conditions, she wondered, was there "any escape" for domestics "from the disreputable house?"[153] Lodging houses in tenement agencies, reformers worried, might serve as unsupervised "meeting places for servant girls and male companions" or merely as a place for a domestic to leave her things while she went to "a saloon, dance hall, or other undesirable place."[154] Even if domestics managed to avoid these nightly perils, by morning "proprietors and lodgers are in all stages of dressing for the day, beds are upturned, meals are being prepared, and altogether it is a most unbusiness-like place."[155] In Kellor's view, domestics who were not kept from such intimate contact with tenement residents and boarders could only too easily carry immoral conditions into middle-class homes. Through research, political lobbying, and legislation, Kellor hoped to protect both working-class women and the private middle-class home from the corruption of the tenements.

Frances Kellor, along with most of the reformers discussed here, made her career as a passionate advocate for working women. Kellor would have described herself as pro-union, and she ended her career as the first vice president and a founder of the American Arbitration Association, which resolved labor disputes using expert arbitrators.[156] As a committed Progressive, Kellor believed that an unregulated market disproportionately harmed poor working women and children. Similarly, Mary Dreier and Margaret Dreier held leadership positions in the WTUL and dedicated their careers to unionizing women workers and lobbying for protective labor legislation. Throughout this period, women reformers successfully crusaded for state-level legislation to limit the hours of women in factories and shops, set a minimum wage, and mandate basic working conditions. Domestic workers, however, were excluded from all such legislation, just as they were excluded from many of the working women's employment societies that reformers established at the turn of the twentieth century. But the story of domestic service at the turn of the century is not one of total exclusion from all legislation or reform. Reformers created a separate program of reform for domestic workers, including immigrant homes, training programs, domestic service employment societies, and servants' clubs. Domestic service reformers reiterated that their goal was to protect working women while also providing them with a wholesome way to make a living. Not coincidentally, however, these programs worked to separate domestics from what many middle-class women and public experts believed to be the corrupt influence of tenement neighborhoods and working-class communities.

Frances Kellor, however, changed the way that reformers thought about the problem of domestic service. Kellor put the home at the center of urban debate and sought to protect working women and middle-class employers by bringing order to the hiring process. Kellor hoped that the strength of the state could shift the balance of power from employment agents to middle-class employers and protect domestics from the immoral influence of tenement living conditions and exploitation by agents. Kellor did not, however, bring state authority to regulating working conditions in middle-class homes, which she herself admitted were grim. Although criticism of the working conditions in middle-class homes was as much a part of the debate over the "servant problem" as concern over tenement vice, Kellor and her contemporaries did not act with any urgency to reform private homes. Kellor and other Progressive reformers cast the "servant problem" as a problem of municipal management and urban reform rather than as a labor problem. By introducing the state into reform of domestic service, however, Kellor created a new ideological quandary for would-be reformers of domestic service. Whether and how much the state should be involved in the private affairs of the middle-class home was a question that middle-class employers and reformers would continue to struggle with through 1940.

Four

The "Enlightened Majority"
versus the "Die-Hard Fringe"

THE STATE AND REFORM OF

DOMESTIC SERVICE, 1915–1940

In January 1938, approximately 150 members of the Women's City Club met to discuss bills pending in the New York State legislature that would provide domestic workers with a sixty-hour week, minimum wage, and inclusion in workers' compensation laws. First, the would-be reformers made their pitch. Emily Sims Marconnier, chair of the Women's City Club's own Committee on Labor and Industry and associate general secretary of the National Consumers' League; Blanche Freedman, a New York Women's Trade Union League (WTUL) lobbyist; and Dora Jones, president of the newly formed American Federation of Labor–affiliated Domestic Workers Union, each rose to make a case for the legislation. The organizers could not have expected what came next. The room exploded in outrage. A journalist in the audience reported that the Women's City Club members "appeared unable to distinguish between legislation and unionization."[1] An observer from the *New York Times* agreed with this assessment, reporting that even though Marconnier "pointed out that enlightened housewives" had nothing to fear from either the legislation or the union, speakers from the floor conjured images "of union inspectors grilling them on hours their help spent with the baby or the vacuum cleaner."[2] Members stood up, "one after another," to voice their concerns that legislation and unionization would bring public labor disputes into their private homes. One woman declared that "no union was going to regulate" her "home routine," while another complained that her "husband has enough troubles with unions in his business without having union trouble at home."[3] Government regulation and union agitation seemed of a piece to Women's City Club members. The Domestic Workers Union seemed to them only a precursor to state regulation of middle-class homes. Audience members insisted that they would not allow their homes to become subject to state mandates or union demands.

This meeting was merely the explosive conclusion to a long-running and increasingly tense conversation among women activists about the role of the state in regulating domestic service. Despite the insistence of middle-class women that government stay out of their kitchens, New York's progressive women reformers, in concert with state and local officials, devised various plans between 1915 and the 1930s to apply the power of government to the labor problems of domestics. Many progressive women's organizations demanded that their homes remain free from state labor laws but also felt that government had every right to invade the privacy of household workers when they believed that doing so would protect the middle-class home. In addition to battling among themselves over labor regulations, middle-class women reformers considered legislative bills requiring health examinations for household workers and joined a New York City commission to suppress street-corner domestic employment markets. The Works Progress Administration (WPA), guided in part by women activists on its advisory board, developed training and placement programs for domestic workers on relief. All of these programs existed in the context of a domestic labor market that had shifted inexorably after World War I toward African American day workers and a family ideal that focused increasingly on the isolated suburban home. A careful examination of these debates and of the state's role in regulating, and not regulating, the lives, bodies, and working conditions of domestic workers reveals that domestic service posed a problem for those who believed the private home to be a world apart from the public realm of work, labor conflict, and public politics.

In the years after World War I, middle-class women reformers continued to pursue a gendered reform program focused on working-class women and children. As time went by and their political influence grew, these women became key participants in the creation of New Deal social policies. The idea that cultural values about race and gender influenced their policy designs is nothing new. Historians have long argued that women crafted social programs that reinforced racial and gender hierarchies because they looked at the world through a racial and gendered lens that prioritized women's roles as wives and mothers over their roles as workers and imagined program recipients as white women.[4] Middle-class and elite women white reformers promoted policies that encouraged full-time motherhood for working-class women. They worked to outlaw homework and to push paid labor out of the working-class home. Many also pursued a welfare system to sustain single mothers and fought for decent wages and humane working conditions for women workers.[5] When working-class women came to work in middle-class homes, however, many reformers found themselves more concerned with protecting their homes from labor regulations and from allegedly sexualized and unqualified workers than with protecting household workers from labor exploitation. Debates among labor reformers over state power and domestic service throughout the interwar years highlight the careful distinction that progressive women's groups drew between public and private in the application of government power.

Women Reformers after World War I

This disconnect between progressive women's private labor relations and their public politics can, in part, be traced to how gender roles shaped women reformers' view of domestic service and the possibilities for reform. Throughout the 1920s and 1930s, the position of progressive women's groups in American politics changed drastically. The most obvious change was that women could vote. New York granted women voting rights in 1917, and in 1920 the Nineteenth Amendment guaranteed all American women the right to vote. Many women left the suffrage movement after 1920 to pursue a broad political agenda, lobbying for specific causes like labor regulation, education, and birth control or working in the peace movement. In the years after 1920, the number and membership of women's organizations grew exponentially.[6] Some women also embraced a more direct politics, running for office or accepting government appointments.[7]

The years after 1920 were difficult ones, however, for reformers concerned about the problems of working women. In 1923, the Supreme Court ruled against a minimum wage just for women, in *Adkins v. Children's Hospital*. The National Consumers' League had authored the legal brief for *Adkins* in favor of the minimum wage. But the league watched in horror as the Supreme Court decided that, now that women could vote, they no longer needed the state to protect their wages. Women labor reformers in the National Consumers' League and the WTUL, along with their allies in a host of other progressive women's organizations, redoubled their efforts in pursuit of protective labor legislation. These organizations continued to support women's maximum hours laws and desperately sought state-level minimum wage legislation that would be acceptable to the courts. Progressive activists made New York a testing ground for labor reforms, and the state eventually became an epicenter for battles over the minimum wage.[8]

The issue of protective labor legislation caused even more trouble for women's politics when former suffragist Alice Paul and the National Woman's Party sent the Equal Rights Amendment (ERA) to Congress in 1923. Had it passed, the ERA would have amended the U.S. Constitution to strike down laws that discriminated against women on the basis of sex. Paul and the National Woman's Party believed that laws that distinguished between the sexes were inherently discriminatory.

Progressive women's organizations, the Young Women's Christian Association (YWCA), the WTUL, the Women's City Club, the National Consumers' League, and many members of the League of Women Voters among them, held a more complicated view. These groups had been prosuffrage and they supported equal rights, but they also believed there were real differences between the sexes. More important, they worried that the ERA would endanger what was left of women's protective labor legislation, a cause for which many women activists had worked for decades. In 1927, for example, Nellie Swartz, writing for the Women's City Club, attacked the ERA and insisted that the state had a responsibility to "give thousands of women who are young and unskilled, many of them foreign born, not only greater capacity for work but to protect them against the danger of exploitation."[9] In their view, women industrial and retail workers were particularly disadvantaged in the labor market. They earned far less than men did for the same jobs, and most labor unions excluded them from membership. Progressive women reformers reasoned that women workers needed labor legislation more than men did. This conflict between protective labor legislation and the ERA would therefore cause a major rift in the women's movement. Progressive women's groups, including those that appear in this chapter, championed the positive effect that protective labor legislation had on women's working conditions and vehemently opposed the ERA.[10] They met opposition, however, from early feminists, who called for absolute gender equality under the law, and conservative women's groups, who generally resisted state intervention in the marketplace.[11]

While the debate over the ERA raged on, the leaders of women's labor reform organizations began to move into policy-making positions. The avenues for women's participation in government ran primarily through state and federal departments of labor. At the federal level, the Children's Bureau and the Women's Bureau, housed in the Department of Labor, brought women from labor and welfare reform organizations into government. The Children's Bureau, established in 1912, attracted settlement house leaders and prominent activists like Florence Kelley, Julia Lathrop, and Lillian Wald and focused most of its energies on establishing welfare programs for poor women and children and abolishing child labor. The Women's Bureau, begun six years later in 1918, became a governmental home for women interested in labor legislation, filling many of its positions with the leadership of the WTUL.[12] From the beginning, female policy makers staffed and ran both bureaus, even though they were largely excluded from other government offices. In fact, the director of the Women's Bureau was Mary Anderson, a former boot maker with a long membership in the Chicago WTUL.

In New York, progressive women activists followed similar paths to state power. In 1938 Governor Herbert Lehman made Frieda Miller, a former secretary for the Philadelphia WTUL, his industrial commissioner in the New York Department of Labor. New York Department of Labor positions could also become pathways to federal jobs. In 1944, Miller succeeded Mary Anderson as director of the Women's Bureau. Frances Perkins, who would become Roosevelt's secretary of labor, began her government career in New York, where she was appointed the first woman on New York's Industrial Commission. Government jobs gave women more than just personal power. As women activists took top positions in state and federal government, they offered women's organizations a new and powerful way to influence the policy-making process. Indeed, New York's organized women had built so much political capital by the late 1930s that, one historian quips, "the New York WTUL had for all intents and purposes *become* the New York State Department of Labor."[13]

Progressive women based their success in achieving positions of government power and a voice in policy on the idea that middle-class women reformers were particularly suited to advocate on behalf of impoverished women and children. Although the separation of public and private spheres no longer strictly ordered women's lives in the mid-twentieth century, women's voices in policy making were firmly rooted in a gendered understanding of women's politics. Politically active and progressively minded women continually referenced the idea that women practiced a different kind of politics than men. Women who ran for office repeatedly cited their domestic roles as their primary qualification, regardless of how many years they had competed in the rough-and-tumble world of politics.[14] Women in nonpartisan organizations also cast their activism in gendered terms. In 1938, Mary Duryee, president of the Women's City Club, argued that "because all of us are women" the club could bring about a "practical improvement in the functioning of city government." Women's politics sprang from a gendered nonpartisanship or, as Duryee put it, from "something that is stronger than political loyalty."[15] Middle-class activists argued that women, unlike male politicians, could engage in politics without being corrupted by it and were therefore more inclined than men to work in the best interests of society as a whole. For example, a National Consumers' League activist argued that women avoided involving themselves in "dirty state politics, which unfortunately, even though we dabble in, we can't control; we are just not slimy enough."[16] It is perhaps no surprise, then, that so many women activists were reluctant to support wage and hour legislation for domestic workers. Most obvious, many middle-class activists, though not all, relied on household workers to perform domestic chores while they pursued careers in government or reform. Equally important, however, was that the idea that middle-class women had to be prohibited by statute from abusing their domestic help undermined their claims that they, by virtue of their racial, gender, and class position, were particularly sympathetic to the needs of disadvantaged women.

Political influence and government jobs, however, did not always add up to policy-making success. Even those progressive women who had achieved the most prestigious positions in state and federal government struggled to put their policy ideas into action. They were often stymied in their efforts by male legislators and conservative interest groups. Sometimes progressive women's organizations and female New Dealers lost policy battles entirely. Other times, women activists won legislation they sought, but not in the form that they had intended. For example, organizations like the National Consumers' League doggedly lobbied Congress to pass the federal Fair Labor Standards Act (FLSA) in 1938, which guaranteed workers a minimum wage and overtime pay and abolished most forms of child labor. The FLSA passed, but progressive women's groups were devastated to find that it left four-fifths of workers uncovered. The FLSA applied only to workers involved in interstate commerce and explicitly excluded both domestic and agricultural workers. Although subsequent amendments to the FLSA gradually brought more workers under wage and hour protections, women workers remained disproportionately left out of coverage.[17] Progressive women's organizations did not have the power to order labor relations as they saw fit. Nevertheless, they were the acknowledged experts on women's labor policy and central participants in the construction of the New Deal social safety net.

Suburban Domesticity and Domestic
Service Reform before 1929

Complaints about the difficulty of finding good "help" date to the Civil War, but after World War I and the passage of the first federal immigration restrictions, American housewives faced real domestic shortages. World War I made leaving Europe nearly impossible, and U.S. government policy made it increasingly difficult for new immigrants to enter the country. During and after the war, Congress passed a raft of legislation that excluded immigrants, for reasons ranging from political radicalism to illiteracy to disease to criminal history. Household employers collectively shuddered as they watched the pool of immigrant domestics begin to shrink. With the Immigration Act of 1924, Congress finished the job that World War I had begun. The 1924 act set quotas for immigration derived from the 1890 census, which severely constricted the flow of European immigrants to American shores. After 1920, immigration began to decline, a process that would not reverse itself until after 1970.[18]

As the supply of household workers dried up, progressive women's organizations renewed their efforts to categorize domestic service as a labor problem. In the 1910s and 1920s, major women's labor reform groups began to think seriously about how to lure more women to the occupation. This reform took place in the context of changing notions about the family and the home and women's role in both. Certainly the association between middle-class white women and the home became less strict as the twentieth century wore on. More respectable white middle-class women worked for a living, at least until they were married. In the first two decades of the twentieth century, the number of women in professional schools multiplied, and by 1922, nearly every woman college graduate planned to find a job. There were 1,000 trained social workers in 1890; by 1920, there were almost 30,000. Teaching and nursing, both feminized professions, grew exponentially in this period, and women's numbers in the fields of medicine, law, and science increased as well.[19] Women also voted, ran for office, joined political parties, and lobbied local, state, and federal governments.

As women's gendered political rhetoric demonstrates, however, ideas about gendered domesticity changed in the 1910s and 1920s but did not disappear. The cultural connection between women and domesticity remained ideologically and practically powerful in the lives of women reformers and domestics and their employers. In fact, the ideal of familial privacy itself only became more entrenched as families, thanks to cheap construction, a booming economy, and easy financing, could afford suburban, single-family homes. Suburbanization, a process that really began in the 1920s, offered families more separation from their neighbors than a city apartment ever could. Indeed, the appeal of the suburbs was the separation it provided to white middle-class families from the city's vice, crime, and working-class residents. Journalists, home economists, and other advice-givers portrayed the suburbs as a place where white middle-class families could raise their children away from the corrupting influence of the cities. As the 1920s wore on, separation between urban vice and the middle-class family came to mean a physical separation of several miles of commuter rail.[20]

As ideas about domesticity shifted in the 1920s and became focused on the privacy of the suburban single-family home, domestic service as an occupation underwent a revolution of its own. Most significant, African Americans began to fill the vast majority of domestic service positions. Of course, African American women had long worked as domestics in New York City, and African Americans who migrated to New York at the turn of the twentieth century, like those who would follow in even greater numbers during the Great Migration, were no strangers to domestic work either. According to sociologist and National Urban League cofounder George Edmund Haynes, 89.3 percent of employed African American women in New York in 1905 worked in domestic service.[21] But middle-class white housewives, when given the choice, almost always chose white ethnic immigrants over African American migrants to live and work in their homes. This choice was made easier because foreign-born women outnumbered black women in New York City 423,869 to 21,216 in 1900.[22] Most African American women who lived in New York at the turn of the century sought some sort of domestic work, but they often could not find jobs because of competition from immigrant workers. When they did find work, mostly as cooks, laundresses, and general houseworkers, they almost always performed the heaviest and lowest-status domestic tasks. Researcher Isabel Eaton noted that African American migrants to Philadelphia had such trouble finding domestic work that many with light skin tried to pass as white. When their employers discovered even "the slight tincture of African blood," however, these migrants almost immediately lost their jobs.[23] The occupational options for African American women, hamstrung by race and sex, were already mostly limited to domestic service, and at the turn of the twentieth century, new migrants could not even count on that.

As European immigration slowed to a trickle in the 1910s and 1920s, African American women were finally able to gain a foothold in the domestic labor market. Suddenly, housewives who wanted domestic workers no longer had a choice. The few remaining western European immigrants, who might once have cleaned and cared for white middle-class families, easily found places on the staffs of large houses or in industry, leaving low-status and low-paid housework to black women. This demographic shift coincided with a tremendous influx of southern African American migrants seeking racial freedom and economic opportunity during the Great Migration. Between 1910 and 1940, 1.5 million African Americans moved from the South to the North, often settling in places like Harlem in New York City.[24] Women often came north with their husbands and children, but even when men found industrial jobs, black families found they could not survive without the financial contribution of women and girls. Other times, southern families sent their daughters north to help support the families they left behind, many of whom were drowning in a never-ending cycle of debt on tenant farms.[25] Domestic work, after all, was easy to come by for black women, and, indeed, most of the women who arrived in New York City during these years found work in domestic service. Although African American women made up only 3 percent of the population in New York City in 1920, they represented 58 percent of women working as laundresses and servants.[26] Mary Ovington, a founding member of the National Association for the Advancement of Colored People (NAACP) and a white racial liberal, described flotillas of "boats from Charleston and Norfolk and the British West Indies" bringing "scores and hundreds of Negro women from country districts, from cities where they have spent a short time at service, girls with and girls without experience, all seeking better wages in a new land."[27] Declining immigration and the rush of black migrants elevated black women's numbers in the domestic labor force. By 1930, the proportion of black domestics in Manhattan was rising five times faster than that of their white counterparts.[28] The domestic employment agency industry exploded around this expanding workforce. In 1922, the commissioner of licenses reported that, although there had once been only a few employment agencies specializing in African American domestic workers, there were now more than sixty.[29]

African American women brought their own ideas about domestic service to their new positions in northern homes. In fact, African American domestic workers differed from European immigrants in important ways. African American women, unlike young Irish women in New York at the turn of the century, usually continued to work after marriage in order to supplement their husbands' poor earning power. Women's wages were vital to both the majority of black women living in New York State in 1930 who were married and to the approximately 41 percent of women over fifteen years of age who were either widowed or single.[30] But because stores and factories rarely hired them, domestic service was often their only occupational option. African American domestics also tended to be older than earlier generations of immigrant workers, and they tended to have families of their own. Black migrant women therefore often refused to accept live-in domestic service positions. The transition from live-in to live-out work occurred gradually over the course of the 1910s, as newly arrived southern migrants increasingly demanded the autonomy and independence of day work. By the 1920s, this transition was all but complete. Day work fundamentally changed paid housework, forcing employers to give domestics a set of defined tasks instead of insisting that they serve at their beck and call. Day work also offered married women workers family lives of their own, allowing them to live with their families and perform their own domestic chores at home at the end of the workday.[31]

As these changes took place, however, race became increasingly salient in discussions of domestic service. Concerns about domestics' ethnicity had always been present in debates over domestic service, but in the 1910s and 1920s, race influenced the relationship between domestics and their employers as well as housework in general in new ways. Home economists sang the praises of newfangled household appliances—vacuum cleaners, gas stoves, electric irons, washing machines, and refrigerators—which promised to make housework easier and more efficient. Middle-class families, however, did not give up their domestic help. Indeed, in a 1920s study of one hundred married professional women, only nine did not hire domestic workers.[32] In households that employed domestic workers, new appliances simply allowed employers to pack more tasks into the worker's day, especially as standards of cleanliness rose.[33] Newly professionalized home economists, meanwhile, carved out a managerial role for middle-class housewives, leaving the heaviest household labor for working-class domestics, who were, by then, likely women of color. Indeed, housework itself had become racialized in many white middle-class homes.[34] Although the emotional labor of nurturing a family was reserved for employers, the physical chores of housework were left to African American workers.

This trend persisted into the 1930s. Domestics in modest homes often no longer waited at table or announced callers. Instead, they regularly found themselves performing heavy manual labor. A worker on Long Island, for instance, wrote to the Women's Bureau in 1933 to complain that her work was "a drudgery," requiring her to spend "all day going, cooking and serving, cleaning, wax floors, wash windows inside and out, oftimes [sic] expected to wash walls, scrub porch," and in "winter attend furnace."[35] The move to the suburbs offered middle-class families more privacy, but it also gave domestic workers more rooms to clean. One New Jersey worker reported that she worked two days a week when she "scrub[bed] clean [a] house of eight rooms, [including the] cellar [and] front porch."[36] Another worker cleaned a house of ten rooms and two bathrooms each day while cooking and cleaning for a family of five. In addition, she reported she had to "Scrub. Sweep, dust. Do some washing and ironing. . . . Prepare all fresh vegetables. Bake." All of this required her to "work 84 hours a week."[37] A group of workers wrote to Eleanor Roosevelt four years later that they were each responsible for "most of the heavy washing, all the windows to clean, ironing, taking care of the children and practically all cooking and all the dish washing."[38] Day work may have offered African American workers defined tasks and personal autonomy, but the work itself only got more onerous.

White Women's Organizations and the "Servant Problem"

As this transition between white ethnic workers and black migrants, begun in the 1910s, played out, household employers struggled with what they viewed as a dearth of willing household workers (particularly, one suspects, of willing white household workers). Two organizations, the YWCA and the WTUL, stepped into the breach on either side of World War I, offering wildly different solutions to the problem of domestic service. Their divergent approaches set the stage for later conflicts over protective labor legislation for domestic workers and other government measures.

In some ways, the two organizations could not have been more different. The WTUL, focused on unionizing women workers, was significantly more radical than the YWCA, which sought to improve women's working conditions through legislation and reform. Despite these differences, however, the two groups often found common ground on the issue of labor legislation for women industrial workers. Both groups put terrific energy into lobbying state and federal governments for women's wage and hour legislation. Both also generally believed they had a duty to advocate for poorer women. The YWCA's organizational mission was devoted to creating relationships between working-class and middle-class women. Although the YWCA was staffed and run by middle-class women, it maintained an active program in industrial and labor relations and increasingly incorporated the views of its working-class membership into its activism.[39] The YWCA invited workers to its industrial clubs, where they enjoyed social interaction and some discussion of labor standards. The WTUL went much further, explicitly endorsing unionism for women workers and providing many fledgling industrial unions with direct financial and organizing support.

The YWCA was the first organization to come up with a plan to repopulate the kitchens of America's middle class. In 1915, the YWCA convened its first Commission on Household Employment, which sought to examine domestic service in "its larger sociological and economic aspects."[40] In a sense, Frances Kellor's call to bring the full power of progressive women's organizations to investigating and reforming domestic service was finally heeded. The YWCA's hope was that through its efforts more women might be convinced to enter domestic service and "household employment will be able to compete successfully with the store and factory."[41] The conference participants settled on a program of training and professionalization for domestics and education for employers, all aimed at doing away with the "social stigma" that they felt shadowed the occupation and made it unappealing to competent and efficient working-class women.[42] The YWCA's success in convincing industrial and retail workers to become domestics is dubious at best. One worker reported to conference attendees, "A domestic seems to be [a] sort of slave to her employer, while the factory girl's time is her own after a certain hour."[43] Another added, "A factory girl is not a drudge, as she is not at the beck and call of the whole family."[44]

With the conclusion of the 1915 conference, the YWCA dug into the project of educating employers and household workers about the problems of domestic service. Leaders held several more conferences in New York City, convened a subcommittee on household employment to recruit domestic workers for YWCA programs, and investigated local conditions for household service around the country. This effort eventually grew so large that it gave birth, in 1928, to the National Council on Household Employment (NCHE), which dedicated itself to being a "clearing house" for research on domestic service.[45] The NCHE continued the YWCA's educational work, with conferences on household employment held in New York City in 1928 and again in 1931, and published a monthly bulletin. It also hired a full-time researcher to coordinate its investigative efforts.[46]

The YWCA's Industrial Department, meanwhile, sponsored club meetings for domestic employees, at which workers discussed occupational problems and came up with solutions. The YWCA, like its offspring, the NCHE, believed that there was a natural harmony between household employers and their employees. With education, both groups hoped, employers and domestics might find a willingness to compromise. The clubs may have brought working-class women together to talk about their problems, but they were emphatically not unions. Although one group pledged to "maintain the right" of domestic workers to collectively bargain, its "Code of Ethics" focused mostly on how workers could do all in their power to "maintain the highest standards of home life" through such efforts as caring for their personal appearance, conserving food and household supplies, guarding their "habits in order to maintain good health and to enjoy wholesome recreation," and considering "relationships with [their] employer and her family confidential, refraining at all times from gossip."[47] Indeed, the YWCA National Board went out of its way to reassure suspicious employers that the clubs were not unions in disguise and that they actually "benefit the employer" because they encouraged domestics "to act more ethically."[48] The NCHE shared the YWCA's wariness of domestic unionization. When a domestic wrote to its chair, Columbia University home economist Benjamin Andrews, asking for information on unions in 1936, Dr. Andrews responded with the experience of a failed California unionist, who had found "a fighting organization" ineffectual. Much more useful, Andrews argued, would be "a welfare type of organization which carried with it the sympathy and support of employers as well as employees."[49]

Just four years after the YWCA's 1915 conference, the WTUL passed its own very different resolution to reform domestic service. This resolution favored "exactly the same standards of hours, wages and working conditions for domestic workers as for workers in any other occupation."[50] Significantly, the WTUL coupled this resolution with one that sought a "general and national recognition of the social and economic value of the work of women in the home and appreciation of the fact that the millions of women so occupied are a very important part of the labor world."[51] The difference between the WTUL's view of domestic service and that of the NCHE is staggering. While the YWCA hoped to better housewives' chances of finding willing and competent workers, the WTUL tied the poor working conditions of paid domestic workers to the low status of women's domestic labor in general. In the WTUL's view, housewives and domestic workers suffered a shared oppression. Perhaps most significant, the WTUL's resolution categorized housework, alongside industrial labor, as real work. For the WTUL, the only way to raise the status of household workers, and women workers in general, was to ensure that domestic service was valued, well-paid, and protected by labor laws. Rather than seeking common ground between domestic employers and employees, the WTUL sided wholeheartedly with workers and asserted that an equitable solution for workers demanded better pay, better hours, and other legal protections.[52] These insights would not become clear to other white middle-class activists until the feminist revolution of the 1970s.[53]

These different views on domestic service can, in part, be attributed to the subtle class differences that separated the two groups. These class differences created a gulf of experience and belief between the WTUL and almost all other progressive women's organizations, including the National Consumers' League, the Women's City Club, and the League of Women Voters.[54] Many of the leaders of the New York WTUL, including Elisabeth Christman and Rose Schneiderman, had themselves once worked for a living. In contrast, the YWCA's leadership, as well as that of many other women's organizations, had more often been born into middle-class or elite families. These differences in membership and in purpose had tangible results in the attitudes of the WTUL and of other women's organizations toward domestic service. As a frustrated Anna Arnold Hedgeman, then a worker at the African American YWCA branches in Brooklyn and Harlem, pointed out, many "of the prominent YWCA members did not believe in trade unions" and many "of these same employers gave large contributions to the support of the YWCA!"[55] Although some YWCA committee members and working-class industrial club members felt differently, the YWCA was institutionally disinclined toward unionization.[56] Class status also gave groups like the YWCA a bigger stake in protecting the privacy of the middle-class home. They and other progressive women's organizations were therefore less likely to insist that wage and hour regulation accompany the other proposed government interventions in domestic service.

To be fair, the WTUL was hardly perfect in this regard. Although the WTUL continued to unionize nondomestic workers, helping to form a successful laundry workers' union in the early 1930s, the organization failed to devote comparable resources to organizing domestics.[57] For instance, when

WTUL leader Cara Cook suggested working with domestics as a project for organizers in training, the organizing committee rejected the idea on the grounds that domestics' problems were too "different" from those of other women workers and that "the next job to be done" for domestics was "primarily an educational one."[58] The Domestic Workers Union, independently organized and affiliated with the American Federation of Labor, also repeatedly asked the WTUL for organizing help, only to be turned away because of lack of funds.[59] Its pleas of poverty, however, reflected real money problems. The group's membership fell sharply in the 1930s, and branches outside of New York and Chicago all but disintegrated. It got so bad that in some months Eleanor Roosevelt contributed $300 of her own money just to help the organization keep the lights on. WTUL leaders likely weighed these financial concerns heavily when they considered the seemingly insurmountable task of organizing large numbers of household workers.

Still, the WTUL remained at least ideologically committed to the idea of unionization for domestics. A newly organized and largely African American Domestic Workers Union eventually became part of the WTUL. WTUL leaders also included the Domestic Workers Union in its decision making on the issue of domestic service by the late 1930s.[60] Thus, when WTUL leader Elisabeth Christman received a letter in 1936 like the one that NCHE president Benjamin Andrews had received that same year from a union-hungry domestic, her response was very different. Lula Jane Cotter wrote for help organizing a union "for the poor unfortunate women who work from 7 A.M. to 12 P.M. many a day for $10 to $15 a month." Cotter criticized middle-class employers who underpaid their workers, arguing that "if one is able to pay for domestic service, they are able to pay a living wage."[61] The NCHE's Benjamin Andrews had advised union-seekers to found a "welfare type organization," but Christman wrote that, as "a trade unionist" herself, she believed that "the only effective way to establish an employer-employee relationship is through a trade union."[62] The progressive women's groups in this chapter represented a broad range of constituencies and agendas, but all supported protective labor legislation for industrial women workers. Among the women's organizations that weighed in on domestic service legislation, however, the WTUL stands out, not only for its passionate support for protective labor legislation for all women workers, but also for its willingness to put working-class women in positions of power.[63] Leaders of other women's organizations championed the cause of labor legislation in public, but the membership of these organizations had trouble reconciling these humane ideals with the reality in their kitchens.

The Bronx "Slave Markets"

As the government found new ways to assert itself during the New Deal, it also inserted itself in new ways into the middle-class home. In many ways the New Deal was the apotheosis of the progressive impulse that had guided American reformers since the late nineteenth century. Labor reformers, municipal reformers, welfare reformers, and settlement house workers had worked for decades on the state and local levels to knit together a social safety net for American workers, the poor, and single mothers. Throughout these years, Progressive Era reformers ran up against conservative politicians who accused them of socialism, conservative judges who declared their reforms unconstitutional, and an American public that was unwilling to provide enough support to make Progressive reforms law. The crisis of the Great Depression, however, changed everything. Conservatives of all stripes fell silent in the face of an unprecedented economic meltdown. Many New Deal liberals were in fact old school Progressives with new government power in the Roosevelt administration. As they began to cast about for solutions to the crisis, they fell on reforms that Progressives had been working to enact on the local level years before. These reforms were fully and carefully thought out, making them all the more appealing to government planners looking for quick solutions to the crisis. New Deal reforms, including labor laws, financial regulation, Social Security, welfare, and other social programs, tended to reflect Progressives' focus on using government to help workers and the poor compete in an often unfair capitalist economy.[64]

The new strength of government exhibited in New Deal programs forced women reformers to reconsider the problems of domestic workers, who still represented the largest category of women workers in the United States. The Depression wreaked havoc on workers in all industries, but domestics, as members of the lowest status, least paid, and least regulated occupation, suffered particularly acutely. The Great Depression, in fact, hit domestic workers doubly hard. As low-waged workers, they had been poor before the Depression, and they became even more desperate after the market crashed. But the Depression was an economic crisis so mighty that it did not just devastate poor families. Middle-class Americans had spent the 1920s building their savings or, more likely, buying new consumer goods on credit. Suddenly in the 1930s, they found themselves in the jaws of economic catastrophe. When factories and offices closed their doors, middle-class breadwinners could no longer pay their mortgages. Doctors and lawyers lost nearly half of their yearly incomes. To cope with the crisis, extended families pooled their resources and moved in together. Happy couples put off having children, and unhappy ones delayed expensive divorce proceedings. The marriage rate dropped to new lows as men and women chose to remain single so that they could help support their parents and siblings. Mothers and children looked for work; fathers and husbands negotiated with debt collectors and applied for more loans to tide the family over.[65]

This financial crisis for the middle-class family meant a labor crisis for its domestic workers. Many workers lost their jobs or took pay cuts as families tried to make ends meet. Other workers experienced domestic speed-ups when employers fired all of their other paid workers and piled all the household tasks onto just one worker. Firing some, but not all, of their domestic workers was a common way for middle-class and wealthy families to economize during hard times. In many homes, domestics found themselves, as one worker reported, "doing the work of 3 persons and some places hardly getting enough to eat."[66] Another angry worker wrote that in many households "one or two women" carried "on where once a staff of servants performed the household duties."[67] Although the work got harder, wages did not rise. Anna Cose, working in Brooklyn, argued that, although the Depression had undoubtedly affected middle-class finances, "their only economy seems to be the servants wages."[68] By 1938, domestic service had become, as the WTUL put it, the "immense court of last resort" for "displaced workers."[69] The YWCA reported in the mid-1930s that "hours have been greatly lengthened and that low wages are the rule, rather than the exception."[70] Mary Anderson, of the Women's Bureau, agreed, noting that domestics were "shockingly underpaid," with some women working "merely for food and shelter."[71]

Household labor standards also took a precipitous dive. Letters poured into the Women's Bureau detailing the hardships that Depression-era domestics faced. One northern New Jersey maid reported, "My pay is so small that [I] cannot buy the things I need," and begged Frances Perkins, the secretary of labor, to "please do something for us. Please crack your whip for us."[72] A New Yorker wrote that many domestics had "to work so hard that many of them can't stand the hardships and others are so desperate from wory [sic] without any work for months. Hours are fraighful [sic] . . . so that [a] person can't enjoy neither eat nor sleep from being overworked."[73] Julia Mauer added from Brooklyn, "God only knows that sometimes I am so tired, I'm just ready to drop."[74] Desperate workers endured abuse for the sake of having a job. Cora Coker, a migrant from a small Louisiana town, remembered being asked by one employer to eat out of the dog's dish when the family ran out of plates at dinner.[75] In another home in which she had a live-in position, Coker had to sleep on a camping cot in the basement.[76] Bessie O'Banyon recalled going to work for one woman, only to find out that "they were taking my money out of my pocketbook and they were paying me with my own money."[77] Other women described being asked to scrub floors on their hands and knees instead of being given a mop.[78]

In the Depression's cut-throat competitive labor market, black women were left with the lowest paid and least stable jobs in this already low-status occupation. For many black female domestics in New York City, that meant standing in line in one of the 200 "slave markets" that appeared on street corners throughout the five boroughs, but particularly in the Bronx.[79] Here, mostly African American women waited for housewives to stop and offer them a few hours work, sometimes for wages as low as ten or fifteen cents an hour.[80] Indeed, the image of black women waiting for domestic work on public street corners became, in the words of one historian, "an alternative symbol" of the economic crisis of the Great Depression.[81] Employers' racism and greed, along with the workers' obvious desperation, made street-market workers particularly vulnerable to abuse. Employers were notorious for lengthening workdays by secretly turning back their clocks or claiming a domestics' work was undeserving of pay.[82]

The Bronx street markets also presented middle-class women's organizations with an opportunity to address the low wages and long hours of domestic service, when New York City mayor Fiorello LaGuardia established a commission to solve what he saw as an urban blight. Their response to the markets underscored the conflict between women's gender ideology and their reform ideals when it came to domestic service.

In truth, it was the publicity surrounding the "slave markets," rather than the markets themselves, that made them an item for study among New York's women reformers and a target of government reform. Only one year before she joined Mayor LaGuardia's Committee on Street Corner Markets, WTUL leader Rose Schneiderman claimed, "I really don't think there are such places."[83] Such ignorance or indifference would not last. The markets came to light most famously in an article written by Ella Baker and Marvel Cooke in a 1935 issue of *Crisis*.[84] A persistent stream of critical articles in publications, from the African American weekly *Amsterdam News* to the national magazine the *Nation*, documented the continued exploitation of these workers by New York housewives over the next several years.[85] Constant media attention made the markets and their middle-class patrons' exploitation of household workers visible not only to passersby but to the city and the nation at large.

Initially, Mayor LaGuardia's office was reluctant to do anything about the markets. As late as 1937, LaGuardia felt that it was not up to city officials to "regulate hours, rates of pay or collection of wages."[86] And, after all, his office had received "few complaints" of the women obstructing the sidewalk.[87] The persistent image, however, in New York's newspapers and in national magazines of African American women, "thin, tattered, haggard, sitting on soap boxes or leaning against lamp posts," waiting for work in so public a venue, not to mention the "hundreds of complaints" the mayor's office received from the workers and their advocates in the NAACP and the National Urban League, proved too much for the mayor to ignore.[88] After some interdepartmental wrangling, LaGuardia and New York State labor commissioner Frieda Miller brought together a committee in 1939 to investigate the markets. The committee included representatives from various city departments and, tellingly, from the nongovernmental groups widely acknowledged as experts on women's labor, namely women's organizations. Among those who attended meetings of the Committee on Street Corner Markets were Cecelia Cabaniss Saunders of the YWCA's Harlem branch, Cara Cook and Pauline Newman of the WTUL, and representatives of the Women's City Club. Rose Schneiderman, former WTUL president, was also present, representing the New York State Department of Labor.[89]

From the start, it was clear that the public abuse of domestic workers was particularly shocking to the men and women on the committee. Committee members and other investigators acknowledged the workers' starvation wages and poor labor conditions, but they focused much of their attention on the fact that the women's exploitation began on the street. Charlotte Carr, the director of the city's Emergency Relief Bureau, the former Pennsylvania secretary of labor, and a reformer in her own right, admitted, "There is something so dramatic and scandalous about this situation, from our point of view."[90] Particularly dramatic and scandalous, according to the committee's report, was that, in addition to labor abuses, women were "subject to the degrading process of hanging around public streets waiting to be approached."[91] Women's Bureau director Mary Anderson's main concern about the markets was her strong feeling that domestics "should go to the employment office instead of the corner."[92] Labor exploitation was rampant during the Depression, but the abuse of domestics by middle-class women on public streets seemed especially degrading.

And if women were willing to sit out in the elements for the promise of wages as low as ten or fifteen cents an hour, many committee members wondered, what else were they willing to do? How could housewives tell the difference between domestics and prostitutes, if both plied their trades in public space? Race is key to understanding the committee's concern here. Since slavery, American culture and literature had portrayed black women as sexually and morally loose. These ideas, still powerful in the 1930s, may have made it hard for some committee members to discern the difference between street-market domestics and prostitutes. Although they found little evidence of sexual commerce on Bronx street corners, the city's committee asserted that the workers suffered the "undeserved stigma" of prostitution.[93] Undeserved or not, committee members were suspicious of the workers' sexual morality. After they opened domestic employment offices in the Bronx, the committee hinted that those who persisted in standing on the corner of 170th Street "during the late afternoon and evening hours" were, in fact, "not interested in housework jobs."[94]

Media reports on the Bronx markets echoed this reasoning, suggesting that sexual commerce occurred alongside labor exploitation. Some writers presented the women as victims of sexual harassment. One journalist described "girls fresh from the backwoods South standing around on street corners day after day receiving what are euphemistically called *immoral advances*."[95] Marvel Cooke, writing for the *Amsterdam News* and the NAACP's *Crisis*, was among the first to break the news of the markets. She wrote that the workers constantly fielded "indecent proposals" from male passersby. Cooke argued that, except for the fact that "most of the girls themselves are actually interested in finding gainful employment," the Bronx street corners would almost certainly "degenerate from a 'slave market' to a red light district."[96] Other journalists doubted the workers' sexual virtue, warning that the young women had "a hard time turning down 'man after man trying to jibe you with an easy dollar.'"[97] Bargaining for women's household labor on public streets bore disturbing similarities in the minds of some journalists and committee members to bargaining for women's sexual labor.

The committee's solution for New York's street-corner markets also reflected its members' prevailing concern, which was their public venue. In line with "their primary purpose of getting girls off the street corners," the committee opened two employment offices, one on Simpson Street and one on Elliot Place, both near the epicenter of the Bronx markets. There, under the protection of a roof provided by the New York State Employment Service (NYSES), they invited household workers and employers to bargain for day work. There would be no mandated minimum wage or limit on hours.

Instead, wages and hours could be settled between employers and employees "as informally as possible at whatever rates the parties will agree on."[98] The committee felt that this arrangement was the only one that might attract housewives to the agencies instead of the street-corner markets. The initial wage rate must have been low, since it was not until 1941 that the Simpson Street office reported that they noticed "an increasing number of employers paying 40¢ per hour," the minimum wage for workers who fell under the FLSA in 1938.[99]

The new domestic employment bureaus thus offered a remedy for what committee members saw as one of the most objectionable elements of the markets: that they took place in public. The employment centers begged, "Please — Don't Hire your Houseworkers from the street corner" and advertised "No fees" and "No red tape."[100] Domestics, meanwhile, could "Enjoy Protection From Rain, Heat, Cold."[101] The centers' insistence that these negotiations take place indoors was highlighted when the Simpson Street office decided that it would discontinue the practice of placing household workers on a first-come, first-served basis, "even if a different procedure has to be imposed upon the workers against their wishes."[102] The problem was that a line began forming on the sidewalk as early as 3:45 in the morning. The office matron complained that on one morning as many as twenty-five workers had begun standing in line by 7:15, and over the next fifteen minutes, twenty more joined the throng. The matron declared the resulting crowd "a neighborhood nuisance," and the only solution was to find another way of distributing job placements. Domestic workers, the committee determined, could not continue selling their labor on the streets.

Committee members were not insensitive to the labor abuses that attended the street-corner markets. Nor were committee members insensitive to the poor labor conditions that plagued the occupation as a whole. As long-range goals, though not "immediately practical," the committee recommended inclusion of domestics in workers' compensation, minimum wage and maximum hours laws, and Social Security Insurance.[103] But the committee was concerned that housewives would not use centers that forced them to pay a minimum wage or limited domestics' hours, and so they did not require employment bureaus to enforce labor standards. Thus, although the bureaus provided workers with protection from bad weather and sexual harassment, they did not address the root problems of workers' exploitation. As Dora Jones, the African American president of the Domestic Workers Union, put it, the "main weakness" of the placement bureaus was that there was "no floor to the wages."[104]

By putting a roof over the Bronx "slave markets," the committee was able to allay several concerns: it guaranteed that domestic labor was the only thing being sold into employers' homes while also suppressing the public image of middle-class housewives offering paltry wages to desperate women. Committee members had been directed by the mayor to assess the street markets and come up with a solution. Frieda Miller, New York's commissioner of labor, expressed support for the project. The committee, therefore, wielded state power when it investigated the plight of street-market domestics. It did not, however, use that power to address the low wages, long hours, or labor exploitation that accompanied the public bartering for household service. Instead, it merely shielded the labor conditions in middle-class homes from public view.

Protecting the Middle-Class Home from Disease

This conflict between women's reform ideals and their gender ideology did not always produce political inertia. Domestic service lacked neither regulation nor reform in the 1930s. Activists may have been slow to address domestics' working conditions, but they quickly embraced measures requiring household workers to appear for physical examinations before going to work in middle-class homes. These laws were mostly local ordinances, enacted by city councils and local health departments in towns and cities in suburban New Jersey and New York. These ordinances, which many women activists vocally supported, reflected the expansion of women's organizing power from the city to the middle-class suburbs in the mid-twentieth century. Once again, the idea of the home as a place that was fundamentally different from other workplaces resurfaced in these reformers' arguments in favor of health examinations. In the eyes of the women reformers who lobbied for health regulations, housework's intimacy required that its workers be monitored in ways that industrial workers were not. The case of health regulations shows the ways in which progressive women activists viewed the middle-class home as an object of state protection but not as a target of labor reform. It therefore also reveals the tangled path along which organized women drew the line between the proper role of government in industry and in the middle-class home.

One of the earliest initiatives in the North to protect the middle-class home from diseases purportedly borne by domestic workers began in Newark, a New Jersey city ten miles west of New York City. In 1930, Thomas V. Craster, Newark's health officer, noted that domestics made up a large percentage of visitors to the city's venereal disease clinic. Craster was known for facing health issues head-on, no matter how unpopular, having waged "an unsuccessful campaign against kissing," along with a presumably equally futile attempt to convince dog owners that their pets were unsanitary.[105] After concluding that domestics posed a threat to his community's health, Craster passed an ordinance in 1931 requiring Newark's household workers to submit to twice-yearly Wasserman blood tests for syphilis. By 1939, the law had been amended, mandating that domestics file with the Health Department a physician's certification that they were free from "tuberculosis and any other contagious or communicable disease."[106] For domestics found to be in violation of the law, the fine for the first offense was twenty-five dollars. Thereafter, domestics who refused to be examined would have to pay a fine of fifty dollars.[107]

Thus, food handlers underwent physical exams only once a year but domestic workers in Newark would be examined twice as often. Food handlers, Craster explained, tested positive for syphilis only 2 percent of the time, while "approximately 20% of our domestics are under treatment for syphilis."[108] Furthermore, Craster argued, household workers posed a greater danger to Newark's middle-class citizens than did the city's restaurant cooks. In contrast to a short-order cook, a domestic, "by the nature of his or her employment," came "even more directly in contact with the family circle."[109] Newark domestics wishing to receive a health certificate allowing them to work in private homes appeared at the clinic twice yearly, where physicians conducted Wasserman blood tests for syphilis, chest x-rays to diagnose tuberculosis, vaginal smears to test for gonorrhea, and, if the physician thought it warranted, vincent angina smears to test for trench mouth.[110] To make sure that no domestics worked without being tested, the city maintained a "force of field investigators," who levied fines on employers and employees who flouted the law.[111] In 1932, just after the ordinance passed, a special team of female inspectors went door-to-door in Newark's middle-class neighborhoods, informing housewives of the new law and insisting that their workers receive physicals.[112] Privacy, it turned out, was a distinctly middle-class prerogative.[113]

Craster was not alone in worrying about the effect of unhealthy domestic workers on the families for whom they worked. His ordinance served as an example for health departments across the country, and particularly in the New York area.[114] In short order, the northern New Jersey towns of Summit, Englewood, and Tenafly passed their own ordinances. In New York, New Rochelle's city council considered a similar measure.[115] In 1939, Brooklyn assemblyman Charles H. Breitbart even introduced a bill to the New York State legislature requiring full-time domestic workers to prove that they were free of syphilis.[116] Perhaps most surprising was the role of progressive women's organizations, including New York–area branches of the League of Women Voters, the YWCA, and the Women's City Club, in proposing and lobbying for local health regulations.[117] What had seemingly begun with the public health obsession of one man had quickly developed into a movement for government regulation of the bodies of household workers.

Concerns about domestic workers bringing death and disease into the home were not new. Craster argued, for instance, that "the 'Typhoid Mary' story" showed "the danger to individual households of an undetected typhoid carrier employed as a domestic cook."[118] It was certainly not the first time that experts accused domestics of being carriers of disease, but the movement in a large northern city for routine examinations of domestics for venereal disease was new. Despite the publicity surrounding "Typhoid" Mary Mallon, a private household cook who was identified as the source of several typhoid infections between 1900 and 1907, there was little discussion of requiring domestics to be examined before they took work in private homes. In response to the threat posed by typhoid carriers like Mallon, many states enacted laws requiring restaurant cooks to be examined but made no effort to regulate household workers.[119] Why, then, did a public demand for health tests for domestics arise in the 1930s?

Part of the answer lies in the wave of "syphilophobia" that engulfed the country during the 1930s and 1940s.[120] Inspired by other public health successes, Surgeon General Thomas Parran, the former health commissioner of New York, began a nationwide campaign in the 1930s to wipe out syphilis. Parran believed that through a combination of public education and "Wasserman dragnets," syphilis might be "The Next Great Plague to Go."[121] An unintended consequence of Parran's focus on the eradication of syphilis, argues historian Allan Brandt, was "fear, stigma, and denial."[122] Although doctors and public health officials knew that syphilis could not be transmitted through household chores, public panic prompted municipalities to pass ordinances like Newark's requiring examinations for domestics.[123] Newark's ordinances targeting domestic workers were, rhetorically at least, in line with Parran's crusade to rid the world of syphilis. Newark's health department stated as its larger goal "the routine examination of the greatest possible number as a means of combating syphilis and tuberculosis through early detection, and the institution of proper treatment."[124] Health officials' focus on domestics as an occupational group, however, had deeper roots.

Race was central to domestic workers being singled out as a particular syphilitic threat. Since the early nineteenth century, doctors and medical experts had suspected African Americans of being especially susceptible to disease. After emancipation, public health programs similar to those enacted in northern New Jersey appeared throughout the South. For instance, white Atlantans declared tuberculosis a "Negro servant's disease" and, in 1905 and 1910, required all black domestics to pass a tuberculosis exam before entering service in private homes.[125] In southern cities like Atlanta, health ordinances served to reinforce the segregated white power structure by identifying African Americans as carriers of disease and portraying black women, among the few southerners to cross the color line, as a menace to white society.[126] Southern physicians depicted blacks as being particularly prone to syphilis, one calling African Americans in the early twentieth century a "syphilis-soaked race."[127] Episodes like the Tuskegee Experiment, in which U.S. Public Health Service doctors studied the effects of syphilis on 399 African American sharecroppers in Alabama between 1932 and 1972, all the while falsely assuring them that they were being treated, demonstrate that the idea that there was a connection between race and disease persisted well into the twentieth century.[128] Depictions of black women as particularly sexual fueled these ideas. Tellingly, few medical or cultural sources even hinted that white men might be the source of syphilis epidemics among domestic workers in white households. Instead, they focused on the disease they believed inherent in African American communities, which they imagined as being transmitted to white families in nonsexual ways. Of course, Newark's Health Department did not single out African Americans explicitly. Race, however, remained a persistent presence in their official publications. For example, Newark authorities listed Newark's African American domestics along with criminals and prostitutes as "reservoirs of infection . . . by reason of occupation, habits of life or lax moral codes."[129]

Public health policies targeting household workers in the 1930s can also be traced to the labor patterns that African American workers brought to the occupation. The change from live-in to live-out service presented a problem for many middle-class employers. When middle-class housewives employed live-in domestic workers, they were able to maintain a level of surveillance that they could not keep up in regard to African American women who came into their homes daily after World War I.[130] Employers and their advocates in newspapers and magazines had always depicted household workers as unhygienic and sexually promiscuous. But as long as the women lived in their employers' homes, middle-class women could monitor both their living conditions and their sexual partners. As African American women, long suspected of being promiscuous and prone to disease, took over the occupation, white housewives and reformers worried that they would bring sickness from African American communities into white middle-class neighborhoods. Black women's daily trips between their homes and their employers' homes seemed, in the minds of some, to increase the chances of disease transmission.[131] As early as 1915, domestic expert Christine Frederick suggested a way for *Ladies' Home Journal* readers to ease their fears about live-out domestics infecting their homes. Frederick suggested that "Delia," who was depicted in the accompanying image as a white maid, might live in her own neighborhood, and on "the street cars that morning she is 'going to work' just like any other girl."[132] Upon arriving at her employer's home, however, she "removes her wraps and changes her street dress for a uniform and apron, which are always left at the mistress's home (this helps to avoid danger from contagion, which is another minor objection raised by women to the sleeping-out plan)."[133] For further germ protection, Frederick counseled her readers, employers should insist on "scrupulous cleanliness" and perhaps even "that Delia take a bath every afternoon in her 'off-time' of one hour."[134]

In the 1930s, newspapers and magazines constantly assured employers that they were right to worry about the health of their domestic employees. The image of domestics who appeared to be healthy infecting the families, and especially the children, of their employers appeared repeatedly throughout the Depression. One pamphlet advertised that women "alive to the dangers" of employing "a household worker without a health test" could have their workers tested through one of several private New York employment agencies.[135] The pamphlet told the story of the tubercular maid in the home of a "prominent pediatrician," who infected his three children, killing one of them, before her disease was discovered.[136] A writer for the popular health magazine *Hygeia* told a similar story of a one-year-old girl who had contracted syphilis "from a maid who had kissed her," an infection that "might easily have been avoided by an examination before employment."[137] In the media, at least, there seemed to be agreement that, in the phrasing of a *Parents Magazine* article, "ailing servants are a threat to all the family."[138] Again and again, cultural depictions of the danger posed by infected domestic workers focused on the intimate relationship that these workers shared with middle-class families, a relationship that could not be found in other, more public, forms of work. Both experts and progressive women activists agreed that domestics should be treated differently than workers in public industry.

Reformers voiced their own concerns about domestics' insidious illnesses spreading to their family members. Organized women pointed to the intimacy of domestics with middle-class families as a reason that they, and not industrial workers, should be preemptively tested for disease. In 1934, Anna Silver, president of the Westchester League of Women Voters, wrote with horror about her neighbor's maid, infected with tuberculosis, who "slept in the same room with the youngest child" throughout a two-week vacation before the family learned of her infection.[139] She, for one, supported legislation requiring domestics to have health certificates before going to work in private homes. Silver was not alone. Women's clubs frequently discussed local ordinances regulating the health of domestics and debated whether or not they should be applied in and around New York. The Women's City Club wondered whether health ordinances might not be "of benefit," while Mrs. Loomis of the Westfield, New Jersey, YWCA felt that since "there have been one or two cases of typhoid carriers," her club would consider "health standards" alongside labor standards.[140] In the Westchester town of New Rochelle, twelve of the city's women's groups and several more Parent-Teacher Associations turned out to support a proposed city ordinance to test domestic workers for tuberculosis and venereal disease.[141] Other women's groups shared this concern, frequently injecting the subject into conversation at various New York conferences on domestic service. At the 1942 Forum on Household Employment, held by the NCHE, conference attendees concluded that tuberculosis posed "a much greater menace to children than social diseases because it is easily communicated to them."[142] Middle-class women attending a class led by the NCHE's Dr. Benjamin Andrews at a Brooklyn YWCA supported "a medical examination of the employee by a qualified physician within the past six months prior to engagement," including tests for venereal disease and tuberculosis.[143] Middle-class women shared the concerns of public health experts that the necessity of having domestic help put their children at risk of infection. To many, a government solution to this problem seemed only logical. The home, middle-class women argued, was a more intimate work environment than industrial work sites. The household's special status, progressive women's groups argued, therefore required that public health officials consider domestics' potential health problems more carefully than they would those of industrial workers.

Despite the best efforts of many middle-class employers, employment agencies, public health officials, and state legislators, the Breitbart bill requiring domestics to have physicals before going to work in private homes did not pass the New York State legislature.[144] That state legislators considered it worthy of debate reveals the distinction that many politicians and progressive women reformers drew between domestic service and other forms of women's paid labor. It also demonstrates widespread anxiety over changing conditions of domestic service in the mid-twentieth century. African American household workers' autonomy, combined with what many employers and public health experts believed was a racial tendency toward disease and promiscuity, fueled employers' fears that houseworkers might bring infection with them to work. Many reformers, employers, public health officials, and domestic experts eagerly turned to government authority to protect the middle-class home, even if it meant invading the personal privacy of workers. As this debate demonstrates, women's groups did not draw so strict a line between public and private that they were unwilling to pursue any legislation that touched the middle-class home. Instead, they prioritized their ideological and material stake in the middle-class home over their belief in a duty to advocate for the largest group of women workers.

Placing and Training Domestic Workers

The New York State legislature may have failed to protect the middle-class home from the ravages of worker-borne illness, but employment agencies and training programs did so enthusiastically. Private employment agencies continued to place domestic workers during this period, but as the Depression plunged the country into increasingly desperate economic straits, placing domestics also became a government project. Two government agencies, the NYSES and the WPA Household Training Program, opened their doors in the 1930s to household workers and potential employers. Both public and private agencies established policies in this period that reflected the priorities of decades of domestic service reform: providing middle-class homes with domestics who had been medically tested and trained in housework while allowing housewives to arrange hours and wages privately with their workers.

The WPA Household Training Program began in 1936, as part of an effort to "take nearly a half million unemployed young people — 'especially colored girls and women' — off the relief rolls."[145] The WPA Household Training Program employed home economists and other domestic experts to teach relief

Women taking part in a National Council on Household Employment
training program. (Courtesy of National Council on Household
Employment Records Collection, Kheel Center, Cornell University)

recipients the finer points of paid household labor. Like other New Deal
programs, the WPA Household Training Program's directors were state-level
appointees, although the program received funding from the federal government. New York City, like other large cities of its kind, hosted six training centers, two devoted to women of color. Many women's organizations,
including the YWCA, had members on the program's advisory board. The
WPA program brought to fruition domestic training ideas that organized
women had been suggesting and enacting privately for decades. Under WPA
tutelage, women between eighteen and thirty-five who had been referred
by the Home Relief Bureau learned housekeeping skills ranging from how
to clean a bedroom, including vacuuming the mattress, in forty-five minutes or less to, more vaguely, "personal hygiene."[146] The training could even
be individualized for each employer. For example, a WPA booster bragged,
"One employer returned a girl who could not make apple pie to suit her
husband. After our intensive post graduate training she was finally able to

A young woman scrubs an icebox as part of a wpa domestic training program in New York. (Courtesy National Archives and Records Administration, Washington, D.C.)

please him."[147] After placing a worker in a private household, wpa adminis-trators sent out a "follow-up report" asking employers to comment on their new employee's housekeeping abilities as well as her attitude, promptness, and dress.[148] Thus, women lucky enough to hire a wpa-trained domestic had wpa administrators working both before and after placement to get the best possible performance out of their new employee.

The wpa also assuaged the concerns of employers who worried about domestics' health. Before receiving any training, applicants underwent a "complete medical examination," which included a Wasserman blood test and gynecological smears to test for syphilis and gonorrhea and a urine test.[149] wpa administrators thought it important to pay "especial attention" to these communicable diseases, "since these workers live in close contact with the families who employ them."[150] In addition to the physical exam, wpa intake officers took detailed family histories, learning all they could about an applicant's family and personal history.[151] With this thorough investigation, the WPA tried to protect middle-class homes from the disease, incompetence, personal baggage, and lack of enthusiasm for housework that the WPA and employers associated with working-class domestic workers. Poor women who refused the medical examination or objected to such intimate questioning faced real consequences. As a WPA press release explained, "Refusal to take the course by a recipient of home relief is considered as a refusal to work, and relief is withheld in consequence."[152] Women struggling to support their families in the midst of the Depression could not afford to lose their relief check. As the WPA advertised in press releases, in the meetings of women's organizations, and in newspaper, magazine, and journal articles, women who took the course took the physical exam. Indeed, the only choice a woman on relief could make when referred to the program was the color of her uniform.[153] Private employment agencies quickly followed the government's example and required domestic workers to undergo a physical examination before being placed. In fact, a long list of New York's prominent private employment agencies signed on with the Murray Hill Health Service to offer health certificates for household workers upon the request of an employer.[154]

Discussions of working conditions were nearly absent from the WPA's program. WPA administrators argued that they could not mandate wages and hours. They were, they said, hamstrung by the prevailing low domestic wage and the occupation's exclusion from labor laws. Advisory board member Rose Schneiderman explained that administrators did "try not to place anybody unless the woman promises that there will be a 60-hour week."[155] The WPA could not, however, offer any guarantees. Wage standards were similarly lenient. In 1937, one WPA worker reported that its placement officers guaranteed domestics a minimum wage of thirty-five dollars per month for live-in work.[156] By 1938 that rate had gone up to forty or fifty dollars per month for live-in work and twelve dollars per week for day work.[157] Even at the highest of these wages, fifty dollars per month, a worker who put in a sixty-hour week earned only about twenty-one cents an hour, well under the minimum wage for workers covered by the FLSA.[158] The WPA had no way to ensure even this minimal standard after workers left its program. When administrators made follow-up visits to employers' homes, they respected employers' privacy, visiting "only upon invitation from the employer."[159] As YWCA leader and advisory board member Dorothy Wells admitted, "It seems to me that the [WPA] Intake Office might work a little more intensively with employers on standards."[160]

The NYSES, a state agency, had been placing domestics before the Depression, but the economic crisis sent many more women to its doors. Like the WPA, NYSES administrators did nothing to ensure that they sent applicants to jobs with basic wage and hour standards. City investigator Benson Ellis reported that, because the NYSES could not rely on labor laws to guarantee domestic workers a minimum wage or maximum hours, placement agents were forced to situate "women in jobs where pitiable oppression prevails."[161] NYSES administrators felt obliged to offer applicants whatever jobs came in. Workers, in turn, had to decide whether they were desperate enough to accept jobs with long hours and low pay. Many domestics apparently decided that such marginal income was not worth the effort since the NYSES reported that it would have been able to place far more domestics in private homes if workers were more willing to take "sub-standard jobs."[162] Workers, "aware of the long hours," regularly rejected sleep-in work and insisted on at least a fifteen-dollar weekly wage plus carfare.[163]

A Minimum Wage and Maximum Hours

The language of privacy that framed the language of the New York City Committee on Street Corner Markets and the progressive women's organizations' push for physical exams for domestics was also central to activists' arguments against legislation regulating the hours and wages of domestic workers in the New York State legislature. In 1938 and 1939, the WTUL attempted to pass three bills providing labor standards for domestic workers in New York State, one mandating a six-day, sixty-hour work week, one providing a minimum wage, and one including domestics in workers' compensation laws. In 1938, the New York WTUL sent the three bills to Bronx assemblyman Gerard Muccigrosso, who introduced them into the state Assembly. There they promptly "died a quiet death" in committee.[164] Not to be discouraged, the WTUL tried again in 1939, this time launching a public education campaign on the need for such legislation, working to recruit other women's organizations as allies, and sending a lobbyist to Albany to help the bills negotiate the state bureaucracy. WTUL leaders also watered down the bills' content, asking only for a sixty-hour week and dropping provisions for one day's rest in seven. Despite these efforts, the WTUL's bills once again met defeat. Casting about for someone to blame, the secretary of the New York WTUL lamented that "all three bills now lie under three little gravestones on which are carved the initials RIP — Republicans in Power."[165]

A closer look at the historical record, however, reveals that Republicans were not the only obstacle to extending wage and hour protections to domestic workers.[166] Had the New York WTUL's secretary been more honest with herself and her readers, she might have admitted that New York's progressive women's organizations, usually supportive of women's protective labor laws, shared blame for the failure of the legislation.[167] Even as they publicly decried "feudal" domestic labor relations, women's organizations disagreed when it came to reform. The WTUL saw legislation as the only way to ensure basic labor standards for domestics, but other women's organizations, such as the YWCA, the Women's City Club, the Consumers' League of New York, and the League of Women Voters, were leery of state intervention in household labor relations.[168]

Not everyone in these organizations, of course, agreed. Sometimes national leaders—particularly Mary Dublin and other leaders of the National Consumers' League—voiced support for protective labor legislation for domestic workers when local branches staunchly refused even to discuss the issue.[169] Sometimes the disagreement between local members and national leaders was reversed. In the YWCA, workers in the organization's Industrial Program supported including household workers in labor laws.[170] Some of the middle-class members of the YWCA's subcommittee on household employment agreed with them. But neither the subcommittee nor the YWCA National Board ever took a position on the legislation. Similarly, although some members of the Women's City Club exhibited support for household worker labor protections, they were unable to rally the organization as a whole around supporting the WTUL's bills in the state legislature. This disagreement highlights the important connections between local and national politics and complicates our picture of even the most progressive women's labor reform organizations.

After its initial legislative defeat in early 1938, the New York WTUL hoped to harness women's organizations' renewed interest in the plight of domestics coping with the Depression to persuade them to lobby the New York State legislature for an extension of wage and hour protections to household workers. Although the WTUL wanted to alleviate domestics' working conditions, it was also interested in bringing state labor protection to workers whose "whole legislative history" was defined by "exclusion, exemption, exception and negation."[171] The New York WTUL met repeatedly with New York's various women's organizations and distributed thousands of copies of a pamphlet explaining the legislation and asking for support.[172] The WTUL hoped its efforts would convince reluctant employers "that standards are necessary and that such standards will be beneficial not only to the worker but to the employer, or should I say to the family."[173]

Persuading household employers that government would exert a positive influence on the family, however, would not be easy. After sending out questionnaires to various organizations asking them to pledge their support for the legislation, the WTUL's legislative committee reported that "the responses on the whole, were poor."[174] WTUL leader Mary Dreier made numerous trips to meetings of the YWCA's subcommittee on household employment, where she sat through several lengthy debates and still could not get committee members to take a position on the legislation.[175] Again and again, Dreier attended YWCA subcommittee meetings and presented the WTUL legislation. Again and again, Dreier heard a laundry list of counterarguments, including "difficulty of enforcement, legislation has never been successful, people won't stand for it," and "conditions are not as bad as they are supposed to be."[176] The best the YWCA could do, after "much discussion," was inform its local branches of "the pros and cons for legislation."[177]

This discussion was repeated in the meetings of other progressive women's organizations. The League of Women Voters went on record in support of including domestics in workers' compensation protections but declared itself "not in a position to take up the question of hours and pay."[178] It then placed the wages and hours of domestics on the list of items "for study," where it remained until 1939, at which time it fell off the league's program entirely.[179] Even the Consumers' League of New York, usually supportive of wage and hour protections, approached the legislation gingerly. Given the "distaste" of its "membership for the subject," the Consumers' League split its stand, supporting the minimum wage and workers' compensation provisions but, after lengthy debate, refusing to approve limiting domestics' hours.[180] City investigator Benson Ellis could not even get two prominent consumers' groups to discuss the legislation with him because they worried it "would be embarrassing to their members, who also employ domestic help."[181]

Whatever their feelings about paying their domestics higher wages for shorter hours, middle-class activists' objections to the legislation overwhelmingly centered on their conviction that the government overstepped its bounds when it proposed to enter the private home. A 1939 Collier's magazine article spoke for many when its author warned that the "sociologists and legislators are after us," that they were "investigating our three-room flats and forty-room country houses," and that, most ominously, "their reports aren't flattering."[182] YWCA opponents of the legislation argued, in addition to their other complaints, that it represented "an effort to regiment the last stronghold—the home."[183] When the Women's City Club asked its members for their views on the legislation, they were barraged with telephone calls from members who complained that "they are good to their help, and they resent anyone outside of their home making suggestions about how to run it."[184] One Women's City Club member demonstrated the value clubwomen placed on privacy, stating on a club questionnaire, "I resent all these questions. There is too much talk about 'labor and industry' coming into the privacy of one's home."[185] Given these responses, the Women's City Club leadership decided not to support the WTUL legislation. All of these organizations supported industrial labor legislation, but the idea of applying those standards to the middle-class home proved controversial. WTUL leader Elisabeth Christman described a conference on domestic service labor legislation at which "opposition cropped out every jiffy" and expressed amazement "at one person who I thought was wholly committed to that kind of law being violently opposed to touching domestics because it touched her own household."[186]

It is tempting to view the resistance to labor regulation by organized white women like the one encountered by Christman as a case of simple racism. Race certainly shaped reformers' worldviews and influenced the way that white women reformers and employers approached household workers and domestic service. As white women, employers, even if they did not articulate it in just this way, assumed a racial and class privilege to control the workers in their homes while also directing their work. Reformers' motivations, however, were complex. Women's organizations had opposed state regulation of domestics' working hours since the turn of the century, when most domestics working in New York were white European immigrants.[187] Further, many women's organizations that opposed including domestics in labor laws supported regulation of other industries, including commercial laundries and hotels, which had large numbers of African American workers.[188] The place of the home in public policy also remained a key issue in this debate. In the reams of minutes that women's organizations produced throughout the 1930s on state-level labor protections for domestics, white women progressive activists focused repeatedly on the necessity of protecting the home from state intervention.[189] Most progressive women's organizations supported expanded government power to promote equity for women of all races working in industry but drew a fine line between public and private when they considered how to apply this power. The result, of course, was that white middle-class women reinforced the racial hierarchy in their homes, arguing for (and winning) control over their homes and the women, almost always black, who worked there.

This complexity was couched in the language of privacy. Even activists who voiced support for "decent labor standards in the home" insisted that the home could not be regulated like industrial workplaces.[190] The internal rhythms of the middle-class home and the intimate labor that took place there, they argued, could not be put on a standardized industrial schedule.[191] Unlike manufacturers, who objected most strenuously to minimum wage laws, women reformers worried most about hours laws. Although some were willing to pay their workers more, most organized women's groups saw government regulation of hours as an intolerable intervention into the household routine. As one YWCA member put it, "Housework cannot be regulated like factory work because of emergencies which arise in the household."[192] The Women's City Club legislative committee objected to the wording of the WTUL's hours bill limiting domestics to sixty hours because "under the present wording a maid sleeping in the same room as children who might need attention could be considered 'on duty.'"[193] Although middle-class women acknowledged domestics' poor working conditions, they rejected government regulation as an unreasonable restriction of the individualism of the home. Amey Watson, of the YWCA-affiliated NCHE argued that, although her group supported standards in household employment, standards were not the same as "standardization of the home, because that would be very unfortunate."[194]

Middle-class clubwomen nevertheless recognized that they had a labor problem brewing in their kitchens. As an alternative to legal restrictions on domestic workers' wages and hours, the Women's City Club, the NCHE, and the League of Women Voters circulated myriad versions of a voluntary agreement between 1938 and 1941. These agreements, their authors hoped, might serve as an informal contract between household workers and employers to set basic standards for domestic service. Progressive women's organizations' belief that voluntary agreements were enough to assure domestics fair wages and hours reflects their underlying faith in a gender ideology that posed the middle-class home as fundamentally different from cash-driven industries—and middle-class women as intrinsically interested in social justice for other women. Unlike greedy industrialists, who had to be compelled by law to treat their workers fairly, education seemed, to many organized women, enough to bring middle-class employers into line. Rather than government mandates, these clubs believed that education would persuade those housewives on the "die hard fringe," who sought to squeeze as much work out of their household employees for as little money as possible, to recognize that fair labor conditions benefited both workers and employers.[195] The League of Women Voters, for example, hoped that education might persuade employers "to comply with voluntary agreements affecting standards of working conditions and wages."[196] A Women's City Club member expressed a similar conviction that domestic service should be regulated not by law but rather by educational appeals to the essential "reasonableness" of middle-class employers.[197]

The form that voluntary agreements took, however, demonstrates that organized women's faith in even the most progressive middle-class employers was misplaced. Although the various versions of the agreements had slight differences, they all shared several common features. The agreements called for a sixty-hour week with one full day or two half days off per week. In addition, two hours of time "on call," during which the worker was in the home but otherwise "free to follow his or her own pursuits," would be measured as one working hour. This arithmetic would, as Domestic Workers Union leader Geraldine Connell observed, "legalize a seventy to eighty hour work week."[198] Women's City Club members who opposed the WTUL legislation countered that a voluntary agreement would allow for working conditions "adapted to each individual situation."[199] The League of Women Voters also supported the agreements because they produced a labor accord "gradually from discussion and education rather than through stringent imposition."[200] Voluntary agreements allowed employers to determine their own domestic schedule, arranged around household rhythms of meals, social engagements, and child care, while also keeping the home free of government mandates. Women's City Club board members seemed uncomfortable with even these minimal guidelines. Board members agreed to have the club's draft of a voluntary agreement released to the press, as long as the release was "worded so as not to convey that any particular members of the Club had signed this agreement."[201]

It is a testament to the power and persistence of organized women in winning passage of labor legislation that the WTUL was finally able to win inclusion of domestics under workers' compensation laws in 1946. Workers' compensation programs required employers to purchase insurance policies that would pay workers' medical expenses if they suffered an injury at work. Although it continued to introduce wage and hour provisions for domestic workers to the New York legislature, after 1939 the WTUL focused its lobbying efforts on the workers' compensation portion of its agenda. In 1940, the New York WTUL explained that from then on, rather "than press for passage of all three bills simultaneously," it would "concentrate on the workmen's compensation bill."[202]

Women's organizations were much less hostile to workers' compensation legislation, which would require employers to buy insurance policies to cover employees injured on the job. Workers' compensation, after all, protected employers from liability in the case of employee injury, placed a smaller financial burden on employers, and did not directly intervene in household labor relationships. Employers were willing to provide for an injured employee but balked at allowing the state to dictate their domestic schedule or private labor negotiations. Women's groups rallied to the cause. Citing statistics such as a finding that "home accidents killed 3,250 people" in New York State in one year, women's organizations began cataloging the grisly, if probably also one-of-a-kind, accidents that had befallen domestics while working in the home.[203] The League of Women Voters told of a woman who had "sustained a hemorrhage while helping to lift a barrel." The YWCA drew up a list of increasingly dire household accidents, including a domestic who had gotten hot oil in her eye while frying meat, one who lost her scalp to a wringer while washing clothes, another who had nearly had to have her leg amputated after crawling over broken glass while scrubbing the floor, and yet another who had died from an infected splinter she had gotten from an ironing board.[204] Poor Winifred, YWCA writers recounted, had fallen while taking care of her employer's baby, broken her spine, and wound up "wearing a cast from her hips up to the pit of her arms for a year."[205] In addition to protecting employees who had no health insurance, the bill's proponents argued, workers' compensation would protect guilt-ridden employers from being stuck with domestics' medical bills when freak accidents occurred in their homes. Women's organizations discussed workers' compensation legislation with much more sympathy than wage and hour regulations. In fact, the NCHE and the YWCA expressed tentative support for including workers' compensation as early as 1931.[206]

By 1940, this tentative support had solidified into a full-throated embrace. That year a coalition of women's organizations formed the Committee on Workmen's Compensation for Household Employees, which included delegates from the Consumers' League, WTUL, Women's City Club, League of Women Voters, and YWCA. The committee immediately began lobbying the state legislature to bring workers' compensation coverage to domestics. In 1941, the bill passed the New York State Senate, only to die in the Assembly.[207] In 1942 the committee sent a delegation to Albany to lobby state legislators directly. Although the bill did not make it out of the Assembly Rules Committee before the legislature adjourned for the session, WTUL leader Cara Cook bragged that the delegates had been impressed by "our persistence," since "everywhere they looked, there we were!"[208] In 1945, Governor Dewey, after enduring an intensive letter-writing campaign by New York's women's groups, asked the legislature in his annual message to pass the measure.[209] Finally, in 1946, the New York WTUL celebrated the workers' compensation bill's passage, reporting that, thanks to the "endorsement of the major women's organizations," the measure had passed and "like the walls of Jericho the opposition was crumbled into silence."[210] But even this success was only a paper victory for many New York domestic workers. The law covered only cities of 40,000 or more and only workers who were employed by the same employer for forty-eight hours or more per week. Women working outside major metropolitan areas and the African American day workers who dominated the domestic labor market in New York City and who worked for several different employers each week remained uncovered.[211]

Without the support of all of New York's women's organizations, or even most of them, the wage and hour legislation did not stand a chance against Republican opposition. Even the YWCA cited the "lack of interest among women's groups which have supported other kinds of labor legislation" as one obstacle to inclusion of domestic workers under state labor laws.[212] Despite the fact that New York's organized women agreed that domestics were an exploited class of workers and despite their years of work in support of labor legislation for women industrial workers, they were unable to come to a consensus on legislation that would bring state regulation to the middle-class home. Thus, also despite WTUL lobbyist Blanche Freedman's talk of the "uninterested, hard-boiled Republican lot" in the legislature, women's organizations' ambivalence about state regulation of the middle-class home contributed to the failure to bring basic labor standards to domestic workers in New Deal New York State.[213]

WOMEN'S HISTORIANS have traditionally attributed organized white women's maternalist approach to working-class women to a double standard based on ideas about class and gender. Even as they created welfare policies designed to keep single mothers out of the workforce, historians argue, reformers chose career over marriage and family for themselves and staunchly defended their right to government policy-making positions.[214] But while efforts to reform other industries and other women may have been based on reformers' view of the needs of working-class women, these women's efforts to reform domestic service were tied up with their own needs and those of the middle-class home. Women reformers claimed a right to a voice in public politics based on a gendered argument that, as women, they were especially qualified to speak about women's issues. That claim had its foundation in a view of the home as a gendered private space rather than as a workplace with the potential for labor exploitation. Inviting the government to regulate the middle-class home would acknowledge that many middle-class women could be just as self-interested as industrialists and that women reformers possessed no special authority when it came to social justice for the disadvantaged. Ironically, then, allowing the government to regulate domestic service would challenge progressive women's authority to advocate on behalf of women workers. White middle-class activists clearly believed that the privacy of the middle-class home was worth defending.

After a long campaign by women's groups and domestic service reform groups, some domestics won workers' compensation protection in 1946 in New York State, and in 1950, 1 million domestics became covered by Social Security. But despite their majority among working women, domestics would continue to be left out of wage and hour legislation until 1974. This history of, as the WTUL put it in 1937, "exclusion, exemption, exception and negation" is, in part, a legacy of an inability, even among those most passionately devoted to social justice for working women, to recognize the middle-class home as a site of labor and, sometimes, of exploitation.[215]

Five
Every Domestic Worker a Union Worker

MIDDLE-CLASS AFRICAN AMERICAN ORGANIZATIONS

AND DOMESTIC WORKERS CONFRONT LABOR

EXPLOITATION DURING THE DEPRESSION

When Corrine Washington was offered an opportunity to leave her job in a Richmond tobacco factory for domestic work in New York City in 1938, she jumped at the chance. An agent promised her a live-in position at twenty dollars a month, much less than the ten dollars a week she earned in the factory, but assured her that she would earn more if her employer liked her work.[1] Tobacco factory work was an onerous and dusty affair, requiring workers to spend hours on their feet doing repetitive tasks on the assembly line. African American women like Washington usually performed the dirtiest and most back-breaking chores in tobacco factories, and Washington could not have been sorry to leave the work behind.[2] An added benefit was escaping the racial restrictions of the Jim Crow South and joining New York City's famously vibrant black community. Washington's decision was made. She set off for New York in early January, and by January 3, 1938, she was working as a mother's helper for a Mrs. Spears in Queens.

After her arrival, things did not go as smoothly as she had probably hoped. One Thursday afternoon, after having worked for Mrs. Spears for nearly a month, Washington asked for a quarter to go to the movies. Spears gave her the money, but to Washington's shock, she "said that instead of going to the movies I should go to Flushing and look for another job." Spears insisted that Washington leave her house immediately. Washington, with no friends in New York and not even enough money to buy her own movie ticket, "begged her to let me stay until I had enough money so that I could return to Richmond." Her employer refused, Washington remembered, and "told me to pack my bags and hunt for another job."[3] When Washington asked for her wages, Spears again refused. Spears reminded Washington that she had only worked for twenty-five days and had not earned a full month's wage. Further, Spears claimed, she had paid the agent who had brought Washington to Queens $17.80, which she was deducting from Washington's pay. Washington was, as she put it, "alone in New York." But Washington had already learned about an organization that might help her. Alone and penniless, she did the only thing she could think of—she called the union.[4]

The machinery of the Domestic Workers Union (DWU), Local 149, of the American Federation of Labor (AFL)–affiliated Building Services Employees International Union, quickly began to turn. Dora Jones, the African American union president who also lived in Queens, took Washington into her home and supplied her with living expenses. Once Washington's immediate needs were taken care of, Jones went about addressing the larger problem. Washington was not the only young African American woman brought to New York to perform domestic work for a substandard wage. As Jones saw it, trafficked southern migrants who worked for less than the going rate depressed the wages of the domestics she represented. Jones secured the services of a lawyer, who drew up an affidavit based on Washington's description of her experience. Then Jones wrote to the National Association for the Advancement of Colored People (NAACP) asking for a representative to accompany her on a visit to Mayor Fiorello LaGuardia.[5]

In April, Jones and Charles Houston, the NAACP's special counsel, met with Mayor LaGuardia to discuss the problem of agents bringing young southern migrants to New York to perform cheap domestic labor.[6] Jones reiterated to LaGuardia her concern that new migrants working for low pay reduced "the wages and [threatened] the conditions of the workers in the industry," adding that it was unfair to migrants like Washington to be lured to New York with the promise of a job, only to be summarily dismissed. Finally, Jones argued, when young women like Washington were cast penniless onto the street, "they become the charge of the City of New York."[7]

This last argument held particular appeal to a mayor trying to guide his city through the twentieth century's worst fiscal emergency. Two months later, the commissioner of licenses warned the mayor that the crisis was growing. He reported nine cases of "very young" women with "no experience in house work" being brought to New York under similar circumstances to Washington's.[8] In 1939, Mayor LaGuardia responded, writing a series of strongly worded letters to various federal law enforcement and southern government officials, warning them of unlicensed agents working to entice young domestic workers to move to New York.[9]

The work of Dora Jones and the DWU on behalf of Corrine Washington is characteristic of the ways in which workers shaped the public debate over domestic service during the Depression. Throughout this period, African American domestics worked together to defend the few employment rights they had managed to acquire, as competition for jobs increased and wages and working conditions took a sharp dive. In the process, they challenged the power of employers to determine domestics' working conditions.

Middle-class African American reform organizations also tried to help. Many middle-class social justice organizations had been created with the mission of helping African Americans find a foothold in the New York job market. As the Depression worsened, however, middle-class African American organizations struggled to place domestic workers in a diminishing number of jobs. In the process, they became increasingly likely to bow to employer demands. In contrast, domestic workers, perhaps because they recognized how little they had to lose, refused to give ground to employers who wanted more labor in return for less pay. Workers also refused to submit to health examinations, rejecting the notion that they were somehow more likely to be infectious than their wealthy, white employers. As employers debated whether the private home should be subject to state authority, domestic workers consistently argued that the home was a workplace, whose workers deserved government protections. Far from the helpless figures portrayed in Depression-era reform literature, domestic workers challenged employers in increasingly public ways, even as the working conditions in private households worsened.

Domestic workers' unions like the DWU were among the first overtly political organizations that sought not only to change the conditions under which household workers labored but also to recast the terms of the debate over domestic service.[10] Middle-class employers and many middle-class women activists insisted that the home was, first and foremost, a private space; the DWU and other domestic worker activists argued that the home was a workplace, whose workers deserved fair treatment. The story of the DWU and other activist domestics is one of small victories and often overall defeat. Trade organizations represented only a small percentage of working domestics during this period, and the DWU did not function within the traditional union model. Its members were much more likely, for example, to recruit the help of more powerful political groups than they were to go out on strike. Nonetheless, the mere presence of working black women in New Deal policy debates belies the idea that domestics were inherently passive workers or that middle-class progressives, black or white, controlled the debate over domestic service.

The Work of Middle-Class African American Activists
In the years before the New Deal social safety net, poor people had few options in times of crisis. And African American poor people had even fewer options. White charitable agencies designed their programs to address the needs of poor and working-class whites and often either ignored or explicitly excluded African Americans. Middle-class black charity and social justice agencies stepped in to fill the gap, creating a network of social services that sustained the black community throughout the twentieth century.[11] The employment programs that these organizations ran all acknowledged women's need for employment, even if they did not applaud it. Because black women were more likely than white women to work outside the home, black social service organizations also supported families in which both men and women worked. All of these programs faced formidable obstacles, the most daunting of which was the discrimination that black women faced in nearly every avenue of employment, including domestic service. This racism and, in some cases, their own organizations' failure to put working-class women at the center of their programs stopped these organizations from offering domestic workers a viable solution to the Depression's declining working conditions.

Many of the programs African American social welfare agencies offered to black domestic workers during the Depression were continuations of the ones they had established when African Americans began to move to New York in large numbers in the 1910s and 1920s. These early programs focused first on finding employment for newly arrived black migrants. Employment bureaus and training programs offered educational and placement services, which organizers hoped would give young African American women a skill advantage, if not a racial one, over the untrained immigrant. For example, the Committee for the Protection of Colored Women, an organization that would later become the National Urban League, partnered with the White Rose Mission in 1913 to offer women migrants a place to stay, help finding employment, and training in various branches of housework, including general housekeeping, waiting, and laundry work.[12]

These middle-class black reformers also supported the families of black working mothers. As sociologist Elizabeth Ross Haynes argued in 1923, the most "perplexing" problem for African American domestic workers was "how to provide proper care and protection for their dependents while they are away from home at work."[13] In response, churches large and small opened day nurseries and kindergartens and hosted supervised play for domestics' children.[14] Grace Congregational Church ran a day nursery as well as a summer kindergarten. In the 1920s, Utopia Children's House and the Hope Day Nursery for Colored Children opened a mere three blocks apart in Harlem.[15] One researcher observed that the larger black churches offered so many services, clubs, and exercise and play spaces that they closely resembled secular social settlement houses that served poor immigrant neighborhoods.[16] Other churches encouraged black workers to join benevolent societies, which offered benefits to workers who became ill and supported their families when they died.[17] These social welfare programs were part of the effort of black churches and community organizations to support women's employment. By taking care of domestic workers' children, these organizations freed black women to leave their homes each day to work in someone else's.

These programs soldiered on after the stock market collapsed in 1929, but their efforts strained under the weight of the Depression's massive unemployment. Nannie Helen Burroughs, head of the National Training School for Women and Girls, a school for domestic workers in Washington, D.C., estimated that "one out of every four Negro household workers have no jobs," leaving a quarter of a million African American domestic workers dependent "on what relief they can get."[18] New York domestics who managed to keep their jobs worried about being displaced by new southern migrants willing to work for next to nothing. For example, in 1938, Mrs. F. R. Birch wrote to the NAACP to say she was "greatly concerned" about this situation. She was, she wrote, "very uneasy about my job as I need it very badly." Another domestic worker in her Brooklyn neighborhood undercut her wage by working for twenty-five dollars a month. The other worker had also, Birch complained, "sent to Ralford, NC for at least five girls to come here to Flatbush" to work for the same amount. As Birch explained, two of her friends had already "lost good jobs to girls working for $25.00 per mo.," and she now feared for her own. "I wonder," Birch asked, "if there can't be something done about this condition."[19] Birch's situation was hardly unique to Flatbush, Brooklyn.

Working conditions also deteriorated. The Urban League reported that wages in Brooklyn fell by half, and some days workers made only twenty or twenty-five cents an hour.[20] A Young Women's Christian Association (YWCA) study found African American domestics working in "so-called opportunity homes," where they worked for no wages other than room and board.[21] Many young women probably would have empathized with Norabell Harty, who begged the NAACP in 1934 to help her find a job "at anything but housework."[22] In order to keep her family afloat, Harty had dropped out of high school and had taken a job in which she did not even get time off for church. She needed a new job. Harty wrote, "I would love to work someplace that I'm considered human. So far, at the places I worked, I was either looked upon as something rare, or, the children treated me as dirt beneath their feet simply because I was 'nobody but the maid.'"[23] Echoing the desperation of many African American women in these circumstances, she wrote, "I'll do anything, but I'm getting so I can't stand houseworking any longer."[24] Unfortunately for Harty and other African American women like her, racial prejudice and the economic climate of the Depression prevented her from doing much else.

There were few services that African American middle-class activists could offer women like Norabell Harty. African American middle-class clubwomen in the National Council of Negro Women (NCNW) and the National Association of Colored Women (NACW) were increasingly politicized in the 1930s. They joined the chorus of voices calling for domestic workers' inclusion in the Fair Labor Standards Act and Social Security. They also supported the efforts of workers to unionize. The NCNW, for example, urged "all Negro groups to give their endorsement and support to those Domestic Workers Unions which are already in existence and foster the formation of more such unions."[25] Despite their support for the union and legal protections for domestic workers, neither the NCNW nor the NACW launched a comprehensive lobbying effort to address domestics' working conditions. Instead of directly lobbying government for labor reform, the NCNW called for black women's inclusion in government agencies like the Women's Bureau and the Children's Bureau. Once African American women were appointed to government offices, the NCNW reasoned, they would be better able to advocate for household workers.[26] The focus was on establishing a foothold for black women in the halls of political power, a foothold that white activists had already achieved.

Meanwhile, African American reform organizations like the YWCA's Harlem and Brooklyn branches and the Urban League focused on placing domestic workers in order to meet the unemployment crisis. Both the YWCA and the Urban League offered domestic employment services. The middle-class black clubwomen who ran the YWCA's segregated African American facilities, at 137th Street in Harlem and on Ashland Place in Brooklyn, ran training programs for houseworkers and offered new trainees help finding a job. The YWCA held its courses in a model apartment arranged to replicate "living conditions in a typical New York apartment and equipped with all modern appliances and conveniences."[27] Instructors taught courses with titles like "Maids for Business Women," "Social Health Problems," and "Employer and Employee Relationships," which stressed "work attitudes and habits."[28] These skills, YWCA administrators hoped, would "help the worker to secure her place" and, perhaps most significant, "meet the present demand for reliable efficient household employees."[29] Leaders of these organizations were aware that domestic workers often suffered labor exploitation. The YWCA's Anna Arnold Hedgeman decried the pitiable working conditions that domestic workers at her Brooklyn branch described in middle-class homes.[30] But given the Depression's crisis in employment, black middle-class organizations focused on finding jobs, any jobs, for unemployed black workers rather than on advocating for women who were already working.

As the Depression wore on, the Urban League and the YWCA only faced more difficulty finding positions for black women. Josephine Pinyon Holmes, an administrator for the YWCA in Brooklyn, reported in 1928 that "there is an increasing demand for light colored girls, so much so that it has become a serious problem with us."[31] Holmes spoke poignantly of the young black women "whose skin has reminded me of beautiful purple, almost black, pansy," who were hard to place but who needed "to work or become objects of charity and burdens on the community."[32] By 1931, the problem had gotten worse. That year, Henry Ashcroft of the Urban League recounted an increase in employers' calls for "attractive light colored girls to serve as maids and general house-workers."[33] YWCA and Urban League leaders continued to champion their training and placement programs, hoping to help black women find a competitive edge in employment.

In the Urban League, some leaders' discomfort with women's paid labor outside the home may also have been at work. The organization continued to offer employment services for African American women workers, and T. Arnold Hill, president of the Urban League, doggedly pushed state and federal agencies to do something about the exploitation going on in the Bronx street-corner markets.[34] Still, he attributed the exploitative conditions on those street corners to "the failure to pay the negro worker in general sufficient to keep these women off the corners."[35] For Hill, as for other Urban League leaders, "the negro worker" was male. When the Urban League discussed unemployment and labor exploitation of domestic workers, it argued that lack of jobs for black men meant that "Negro women have had to go to work in order to tide over families."[36] After all, Hill argued, "the woman has to go out and help on her rent," and even if domestic work paid only "10 or 25 or 5¢ an hour; she is going to feed her children."[37] Adding to black men's employment problems, worried Urban League leaders, was the threat that women might undercut the labor of their brothers, husbands, and fathers. Black women earned an even lower wage than black men, and there were reports that "women are fast replacing men in a number of lines." Urban League leaders despaired "that there is no telling how the situation will end."[38] The Urban League expressed outrage over domestic employment abuse and continued to offer domestic job placement. This strategy was doubly important because women's domestic work did not threaten black men's labor. The Urban League focused the bulk of its energies, however, on men's employment.

The YWCA and the Urban League made another concession to make their applicants more attractive to prospective employers. At the height of the Depression's stranglehold on the domestic labor market, both organizations began requiring their applicants to take physical examinations. Urban League placement secretary Eugene Roundtree believed offering employers a health certificate for their prospective household workers would "increase our percentage of calls at least 50%." The only flaw in this plan was that applicants were "very sensitive on the matter," and he hoped that an "educational campaign" among domestic workers would "get them to cooperate in an affair of this kind."[39] The working-class women in the YWCA training program might have been equally sensitive on the matter of health exams, but like patrons of the Urban League placement service, they were examined anyway. In the eighteen months leading up to March 1937, doctors examined 667 women as part of the YWCA's training program. YWCA administrators required not only a health examination but also a lengthy list of references, investigated by YWCA administrators, and a wage history.[40]

In an effort to retain some control over working conditions, YWCA administrators insisted on having access to employers' homes for follow-up visits. In the first month of service, administrators interviewed both workers and their employers and attempted to "correct weaknesses discovered on the part of employees" and the "rearrangement of work conditions."[41] That was the extent to which YWCA administrators felt they could push their power. After their training, YWCA graduates could expect to earn at least ten dollars per week, including meals. Even given an improbable forty-hour week, this wage amounted to just twenty-five cents an hour.[42] At sixty hours, the more likely work week for domestics, ten-dollar-a-week YWCA domestics made only sixteen cents an hour—hardly more than untrained workers earned as a result of standing on Bronx street corners. YWCA administrators did enforce some standards, including one afternoon and every other Sunday off and a private room for live-in workers. But with no labor laws to back their placement programs and a competitive labor market, YWCA employment office workers could not ensure domestics either a minimum wage or hours comparable to women working in industry.

While the YWCA and the Urban League strategized to make African American domestic workers more attractive to white housekeepers and the NCNW worked to expand opportunities for black women in general, black churches offered hope of a different kind. Larger churches opened their own employment bureaus and offered the chronically unemployed a food pantry, donations of clothing, and help navigating the complicated bureaucracy of the New Deal relief system.[43] Another important offering of black churches was spiritual. Store-front Holiness-Pentecostal churches and the Church of Father Divine, both of which attracted a mostly working-class following, taught congregants to look for a different version of success than the one embraced by larger American society. Rather than a definition of worthiness based on wealth and whiteness, working-class churchgoers found virtue in antimaterialism and obedience to God.[44] Father Divine, an African American religious leader with a large following, was also rumored to ply his congregants with occasional hearty meals and ice cream socials.[45] This spiritual and economic support did not, however, always pan out in favor of working women. Perhaps because Father Divine's followers turned their income over to the church, they were not picky about their hourly rate for domestic work. "Father Divine's people," one woman waiting on a Bronx street corner for day labor complained, "really spoil it for us when they come up here. I've known them to work for as little as ten cents an hour."[46] Another told Works Progress Administration (WPA) writer Vivian Morris that Father Divine followers were always "comin' 'roun' heah [shouting] 'peace sister' an wukkin' fo' nuthin'. Dere was a time w'en we got good prices on dis co'ner; but den dey come."[47] Some ministers interceded on behalf of church members to recover withheld wages or protested domestic workers' treatment to city government, but many churches could offer little more than spiritual forbearance to workers facing long hours and low pay.[48]

Dora Jones and the Domestic Workers Union

The DWU thus offered workers benefits they could not get elsewhere. Perhaps domestic labor activism was inevitable amid the heady unionism of the Depression and the increasing militancy of New York's black community. Regardless, in the 1930s, household workers stepped forward in increasingly organized ways to shape the debate over domestic service.[49] By far the most organized of these efforts was the DWU. As has often been the case for social change initiated by women, the DWU began after a group of women met to discuss their problems. As they pushed their employers' children through a park in Sunnyside, Queens, in 1934, an interracial group of nursemaids talked about the enormous amount of work they did each day, how little they were paid, and how weary they were by the end of the day. One complained, "My work is never done. . . . I'm so tired at night that all I can do is drop in bed. But what can I do?"[50] A former domestic worker among the group brought up the idea of organizing a union, and the DWU was born. In its early days, the union was actually made up of several unions of African American and Finnish women in Yorkville, Harlem, Portchester, and Sunnyside, Queens.[51] Dora Jones, an African American domestic worker, headed the Sunnyside contingent and went on to become the public face of the organization, guiding it through its initial organizing campaigns. As the union began to cohere, it established a headquarters in a Finnish neighborhood in Harlem, a location that was convenient to both its white immigrant and African American members. When those offices were destroyed in the 1935 Harlem riots, Jones and the other union members relocated their offices to the Upper East Side.[52]

The next year, in 1936, the DWU took out "a new lease on life" when the AFL issued the union a charter.[53] What had begun with a small group of nursemaids in Sunnyside, Queens, was now the DWU, Local 149, of the AFL-affiliated Building Services Employees International Union (BSEIU). The union trumpeted its slogan, "every domestic worker a union worker," and began organizing immediately.[54] The union called a mass meeting at the Harlem Labor Temple just four months after earning its AFL charter. In that

Dora Jones, the leader of the Domestic Workers Union in New York
City, ca. 1940. (Courtesy Daily Worker/Daily World Photographs
Collection, Tamiment Library, New York University)

meeting and in those that followed, speakers such as Rose Schneiderman, of the Women's Trade Union League (WTUL), A. Phillip Randolph, president of the powerful Pullman Porters Union, and Frank Crosswaith, president of the Negro Labor Committee, an organization dedicated to organizing black workers, gave rousing speeches to the crowd of working women.[55] Over the next years, the DWU worked hard to bring more domestics into the union. Focusing on apartment buildings with elevator operators who had already organized under the BSEIU, DWU organizers posted leaflets urging house-hold workers to turn out to fight for "time for recreation, church, family, and friends," as well as "an adequate wage, social security, and consideration on the job." DWU organizers promised potential recruits that with a union membership would come the chance to "speak for yourself, your rights, and your security."[56]

Estimates of DWU membership vary. In 1937, some sources claimed that the DWU had enrolled 1,000 members; others put the number closer to 350.[57] Either way, as the YWCA's Jean Collier Brown reported, by the late 1930s, New York's DWU was "one of the most active domestic workers' unions in the country" and served as a model for other working women.[58] After the DWU won its AFL charter in 1936, other locals surfaced in West-chester, Newark, and Brooklyn.[59] As late as 1950, the union, under the di-rection of a new president, Nina Evans, still had 250 participating mem-bers, women who had stayed in domestic work after many of their union sisters had taken industrial jobs during World War II.[60] The union was also successful in finding union jobs for some of its members. Women lucky enough to get jobs through the union hiring hall were guaranteed fifty cents an hour for day work, plus carfare and a signed contract from their employ-ers, pledging a sixty-hour week, one day off a week, and two weeks of paid vacation after one year of employment. Employers also agreed to pay their employees' union dues of fifty cents. With this contract, the DWU sought to create a closed union shop in New York's private homes by stipulating that employers hire "only members in good standing with the Union" and requiring nonunion employees to join the union by their second day on the job.[61] For their part, workers active in the DWU believed joining the union to be "the only decent thing that has happened to us."[62] One union domestic told a friend that joining the union was "one of the best things she ever did in her whole life."[63] Another worker, all too familiar with being asked to hang out of windows on the upper floors of apartment buildings with a rag and window-washing solution, quipped that after joining the DWU, "Never again will I horn in on the Window Cleaners' Union."[64] Yet another told an investigator, "Before I belonged, I quit two jobs, 'cause I just couldn't stand it, and then spent a month on the 'slave market' working by the day for 25¢ an hour. . . . I ain't never been sorry that I'm a Union member and I'll fight for the Union all I can."[65] As Dora Jones put it, "We have grown not spectacularly, but at a steady clip. The members we get—we hold."[66]

The success that the DWU had in organizing domestic workers was rooted in the historical context of Harlem during the Great Depression. Harlem's close quarters, a by-product of residential segregation and job discrimination, created deeply felt bonds of experience and interest among its African American residents.[67] A political fire, once ignited, spread rapidly. Rose Reed remembered, "One Sunday I was sitting next to a sister in church and I told her how hard I had been working. She showed me the way out." For Reed, the way out was the DWU. Reed then went on to try to recruit Vivian Morris, the WPA writer, after meeting her on the street. Reed told Morris, "Well I think the best thing that you could do would be to join up. . . . You can't fight your battles alone."[68] Another DWU member reported hearing about the union by word of mouth. She remembered, "A girl that lived next door to me told me about the Union."[69] Indeed, despite claims by DWU leadership that its members included "many races and nationalities" and pleas from Dora Jones for interracial unity, the DWU membership was made up almost entirely of African American women, many of them from Harlem.[70] Because black workers lived out, rather than living with their employers as immigrant workers had, they were able to create not just a sense of personal autonomy but also a community of shared experience and suffering, all of which fueled DWU organizing.

DWU leaders may have relied on Harlem's African American community to help recruit members, but in order to keep them they created a new and gendered sense of community at union headquarters. When WPA writer Vivian Morris visited DWU offices, she found a particularly homey tableau. A group of women sat around a long table sipping coffee, eating sandwiches, and discussing a recent newspaper story about the Depression's worsening domestic labor conditions. In the corner, another worker cooked a meal over a gas stove.[71] This scene, at once domestic and political, was no coincidence. The union provided the gas stove free of charge to day workers who had not found work in the union hiring hall. Meanwhile, DWU leaders had carefully stocked the room with books on trade unions and union pamphlets mixed in with popular fiction. A bulletin board full of newspaper clippings on the plight of domestic workers adorned the wall.[72] Union leaders created a domestic space that at once reinforced a gendered sense of community and worker solidarity. This strategy is evident in the DWU's other organizing techniques as well. The union regularly hosted teas, dances, and other social gatherings to raise funds for the organizing drive.[73] DWU leaders had unionized workers once thought impossible to organize by crafting an approach that brought a political sensibility to women's social gatherings.

There is some evidence that the DWU managed to spread its collective consciousness to the street-corner markets. For labor leaders as well as for white middle-class reformers, the markets often served as the prime example of the passivity of domestic workers as a class. DWU organizers spent time in the Bronx talking to the women waiting on sidewalks for day work, trying to persuade them to join the union. After weeks of talking in vain, organizers threw up their hands and sent letters to African American ministers, in order to, as Dora Jones put it, urge "them to impress upon these women the direct harm they do to themselves and others by going to these slave marts and accepting the low wages that these heartless employers offer them."[74] They also sent letters to white rabbis and clergymen in the area, asking them to "stress to their congregation that they should stop hiring the girls from the slave marts at starvation wages."[75] Although the markets did not seem to lose any business, something changed after union organizers visited the street corners. Wage rates began to climb.[76]

Higher wages were almost certainly the result of worker activism rather than a concession by penitent employers. At some markets, women who agreed to work for less than thirty cents an hour were "literally run off the corner" by other workers.[77] In the busy days before a holiday, a group of street-corner domestic workers collectively refused to work for a penny less than thirty-five cents an hour.[78] Bessie O'Banyon, an African American domestic originally from Massachusetts, confirmed these reports. She remembered that, while waiting at the street markets, she "almost had a fight . . . because one day these West Indian girls used to come in there and work for less." Other workers discovered that the newcomers had agreed to work for as little as fifteen cents an hour. "When the girls got on to that," O'Banyon exclaimed, "boy!"[79] Other workers were furious, and the atmosphere became so fraught that O'Banyon felt sure violence was imminent. O'Banyon was not the only worker to encounter such violence. Vivian Morris, the WPA writer, spoke to one worker who reported that when Father Divine's followers undercut wages on her corner, "me an anudder girl beat two of dem up so, one day, 'til dey uz nigh senseless. So now dey doan' come on dis [particular corner] no mo!"[80] Raising wages on the street corner to more than fifteen or twenty-five cents an hour was hardly a triumph for domestic workers or the DWU, but it demonstrated the viability of labor organizing as a strategy for improving the lives of household workers.

In addition to recruiting new members, the DWU also sought to make a difference for domestic workers across New York State. In partnership with the New York WTUL, the DWU launched an insistent campaign to pass legislation in the state legislature giving domestics workers a minimum wage, maximum hours, and inclusion in workers' compensation legislation. Representatives of the union, Dora Jones in particular, worked tirelessly between 1936 and 1940 to drum up support for the legislation with diverse organizations, including New York's women's organizations, the New York State Federation of Labor, the Negro Labor Committee, and the NAACP.[81] Although the WTUL authored the legislation, the DWU served as the link to black community organizations and to black workers. For their part, DWU organizers saw legislation as vital to the survival and success of the union. In Dora Jones's estimation, her union needed the recognition that state and federal government gave to industrial unions. Jones believed that legislation would provide the union, as she put it, "a new weapon to operate with." First, the union could act as a watchdog to expose violations of labor law. Jones asserted that "once workers learn that they are protected by law, they are eager for organization that can prevent the violations they see going on." Second, with legislation, household workers would have enough money and time off to attend union meetings and pay union dues. As Jones argued, "There is no doubt that should domestic workers be placed under minimum wage and maximum hour legislation, this union would see vigorous growth."[82]

The DWU brought the issues of legislation and organization to its constituents, allowing them to weigh in on the discussion. In a series of mass meetings, the DWU invited legislators, representatives from the WTUL and the New York State Federation of Labor to Harlem to discuss the legislation with domestic workers.[83] At one such meeting at the Abyssinian Baptist Church in Harlem, over 300 domestics appeared to hear talks from Dora Jones, Assemblyman William T. Andrews, and Wilford Gray of the NAACP.[84] An observer described the atmosphere in the room as one of "seething militancy," as domestic workers stood up to tell the audience about their worst job experiences. One worker reported that "most of us must do laundry work; we cook, we nurse the dog and nurse the baby. Many girls work so late they have to take a taxi home, and they make only $1.50 a day. . . . That means working for nothing, doesn't it?"[85] The meeting proved a powerful and politicizing experience for many women in the audience. After listening to the speakers, another worker stood to express a newfound conviction, announcing, "I'm here to fight."[86] By serving as a link between the WTUL and the black community, the DWU was able to provide the WTUL with organizational support, made up of both workers and black social justice organizations, which the WTUL had not been able to solicit from white middle-class women's groups.

The union also addressed the grievances of individual workers, especially when Dora Jones and other leaders felt the case might draw attention to larger issues facing household workers in New York. When Bessie Brown was beaten by her employers, the DWU used the case to put a spotlight on the frequent abuse that, as Jones put it, "domestic workers undergo at the hands of their employers."[87] After the beating, Brown pressed charges. As she took the stand in her employers' assault trial, Jones and other union members sat in the audience to lend their moral support. Brown testified that her employer, Mrs. Altshul, had called her "an impudent 'nigger' b——" and kicked her while Mr. Altshul beat her over the head with a telephone receiver.[88] Brown ultimately lost the case, but Dora Jones argued that, although "we wish we could have won," it was an "important step forward that we succeed in getting this case on the court calendar at all."[89] Jones and the DWU viewed Brown's suffering as intimately connected to the union's larger goals. Jones reminded readers of the *Amsterdam News*, New York's premier African American weekly, that ensuring labor protections for domestic workers like Brown could "only" be accomplished "through organization and legislation." Jones also commended Brown's courage in taking the case to court, commenting that "we need in our organization more Bessie Browns."[90] In this and other cases, the DWU inserted itself into individual grievances between household workers and their employers and used each case to further its larger organizational goals. Throughout the 1930s, the DWU assisted many workers like Brown. The leaders also sought help from sympathetic organizations like the National Negro Congress, a labor and civil rights group; the American Labor Party, a liberal, prolabor political party; International Labor Defense, a Communist-affiliated organization offering free legal services; the NAACP; the WTUL; and the YWCA. These alliances helped the union to support workers who had suffered racial discrimination or abuse on the job and to recruit new members in the process.[91]

In the end, the DWU was unable to create a mass labor movement, despite its successes in community organizing and the commitment of its members. Other factors severely limited the union's ability to achieve large-scale political change. Domestic workers lacked the legitimacy granted to other unions by New Deal labor legislation and faced major opposition from housewives and employment agents. Employers continued to insist that the home was a private space, which would be torn apart by labor conflict or protective legislation. As one employer wrote to the YWCA's Dorothy Wells, organizing domestic workers would be, in her mind and in the minds of her friends, at best "unfortunate." She argued, "If the privacy of the home is to be invaded by union organizers and 'sit down' strikes I think more and more people will manage to get along without domestic help."[92] Employment agents, worried about competition from union hiring halls, took a more methodical approach to thwarting DWU organizing. One group of agents, calling itself the New York Household-Placement Association and representing some of the largest and most prestigious employment agencies in the city, handed out flyers to domestic workers urging them to avoid the union. The pamphlet pointed to the allegedly high dues of unions like the Scenic Designers Union ("500.00!") or the Musician's Union ($50 plus $1.40 per month, "whether they work or not") and warned workers that by joining the union they would trade their "individual freedom" to become "part of a big machine." To make matters worse, the pamphlet claimed, expensive union dues would only go to "pay the big salaries of the Organizers and the Bosses."[93] Another employment agent sent pamphlets to employers asking, "Do you want your home disrupted by 'sitdown' or other strikes? And further—do you want your servant exploited by interests which have shamefully betrayed workers in other trades here in New York?"[94] With cries like "WORKERS! UNITE!!! PRESERVE YOUR FREEDOM FROM UNION TYRANNY!!!" employment agents, along with the employers they served, did what they could to block union organization and discourage employer support.[95]

By all accounts, these efforts had a significant effect on the DWU's efforts to place workers in union jobs. Although they had some success in reaching out to progressive housewives, employers by and large chose not to hire from the union hiring hall.[96] One worker, waiting at a Bronx union hiring hall situated near a thriving street-corner market, complained, "I sit and sit in the union and nobody comes. Them women won't hire nobody from the union; not when they can pick up a gal on the corner for fifteen cents."[97] Even those housewives who did hire from the union did so "more from pressure than persuasion."[98] As a result, the union had some trouble maintaining even the modest standards touted by the union hiring hall. The union's original goal to place domestic workers at fifty cents an hour for day work, a nine-hour day, and one day off a week deteriorated in the face of the Depression's poor job market and employer resistance.[99] DWU leaders admitted that given the "difficulties of organizing this particular industry," it was difficult to "fix standards of union work."[100] DWU leaders hoped that with legislation they might be better able to guarantee labor standards for their members, but given the Depression's circumstances, job standards had to be "interpreted leniently."[101]

A more serious concern for Dora Jones and her fledgling union was the organization's money problems. Outside of the legitimacy of a union charter, the BSEIU offered domestic workers very little other support, including financial assistance.[102] Financing a major organizing drive from the pool of union dues was also out of the question. Even the union's modest request for fifty cents from members was a stretch for workers struggling to feed their families, especially if they could not expect to see an immediate reward. One domestic worker explained that "50¢ a month dues is too high for most domestics to pay. Some of us have got to pay rent, buy food, and clothes for children. 50¢ a month is too much, that's all."[103] The union could not even muster the dues to join the Negro Labor Committee, although leaders professed their "willingness to cooperate" with its program.[104] By 1937, Dora Jones was worried, telling journalist Marvel Cooke, "We are really handicapped because of lack of money."[105]

Anxious for the future of a union with no funds, Dora Jones repeatedly made the rounds of larger organizations with both resources and sympathy for the domestic workers' cause. She met with the YWCA to "discuss ways and means of raising money" and informed the Negro Labor Committee that the DWU was happy to cooperate with the committee's program "but owing to financial difficulties were unable to meet their dues."[106] Jones finally pinned her hopes on the WTUL, which was by then already lobbying state government to pass labor legislation for household workers. In 1937, Jones asked the WTUL to find and pay for a full-time organizer. Citing "lack of money and personnel," the New York WTUL declined to help.[107] Jones tried again in June 1938, this time asking for a financial contribution "to aid the union in getting on its feet."[108] The WTUL did not respond, and six months later Jones returned with another plea for funds. The WTUL replied that, although they were "mindful of the urgent needs of this union and our special concern with their problem," the organization would not "depart from its usual policy of not making outright contributions to unions" and could help only through employer education and lobbying for labor legislation.[109] Although they had provided organizational help for other unions, like the laundry workers' union, the WTUL viewed investing funds and personnel in a domestic workers' union as an uncertain endeavor.[110] In addition, they were convinced that minimum wage, maximum hours, and workers' compensation legislation was the most effective way to solve domestic workers' labor problems.[111] Household workers, they argued, were difficult to organize and the WTUL had very limited funds. The WTUL viewed legislation as a much more efficient way of guaranteeing domestic workers' hours and wages. City investigator Benson Ellis, however, was highly critical of the WTUL decision not to fund the DWU. He argued that, although legislation was important, "the Domestic Workers' Union must have pecuniary assistance if it is to achieve this necessary legislation."[112] When state labor legislation failed to pass, the DWU was left with the impossible task of organizing poor workers in a competitive labor market with no ready source of funds.

Poverty notwithstanding, the DWU achieved several important goals. First, and perhaps most important, the union brought workers into public discussions about the future of domestic service. For the first time, domestic workers were participants in, rather than merely the subjects of, the debate about domestic work. In Harlem's mass meetings, legislators and reformers came to address domestic workers directly and hear their concerns. In the quiet club room of DWU headquarters, African American women working in the city's most depressed occupation engaged in political debate. Meanwhile, by intervening in cases like those of Corinne Washington and Bessie Brown, the DWU directly challenged the rhetoric of employers that cast domestic workers as fickle and immoral. These cases also amplified the DWU's political voice beyond the union's small membership. In the union's version of the story, domestic workers were the victims of cruel and abusive employers. As Dora Jones was always quick to point out, organization, along with wage and hour legislation, offered the solution. Progressives at the YWCA and the Women's City Club claimed that a voluntary agreement and employer education were enough to improve the conditions of domestic service, but the DWU argued that stories like Washington's and Brown's showed that bad employers were intractable and dangerous and had to be brought in line. Although the DWU had neither the finances nor the manpower to control the conversation over domestic service, Dora Jones and the rest of the DWU leadership brought a new and important voice to public debate.

Second, the DWU was able to shape the agenda of the middle-class organizations working on its behalf. For example, the DWU, working with the

BSEIU, had constructed a bill with stronger provisions than the WTUL's wage and hour bill. The DWU bill would have, among other things, limited domestics to a forty-eight-hour week rather than sixty hours. Only after WTUL leaders explained that there was no chance of passing a bill mandating less than a sixty-hour week did the DWU agree to work with the WTUL on its legislation.[113] Once the union was on board, the WTUL took seriously workers' views on its legislative agenda. When the Women's City Club suggested that it might be more willing to support the maximum hours bill if the sixty-hour work week counted two hours of time "on-call" as one hour of paid work, the New York WTUL legislative committee consulted the union. Geraldine Connell, a DWU leader, "pointed out" to the committee "that such a change would emasculate the Bill completely and negate the very purpose of the measure." Committee members could not deny this logic, and they agreed "that the measure be reintroduced in its present form."[114] The WTUL remained at the helm of the legislative campaign, pragmatically insisting, for instance, on introducing a bill in 1938 without a provision for one day's rest in seven, over workers' vocal objections. The DWU, however, was able, for the first time, to bring the voice of black women workers into the conversation of middle-class women and policy makers over how to reform domestic service.

"Why Humiliate One Class?": Domestic Workers and Physical Exams

A more effective, if less organized, example of domestics' political action was their effort to defeat health ordinances requiring them to take physical exams before entering service in private homes. As middle-class women in towns and cities around New York proposed these measures, domestic workers, whether in organized groups or in ad hoc alliances, turned out to express their indignation. With varying levels of success, workers in New Rochelle, New York, and Englewood, Newark, and Tenafly, New Jersey, expressed fury over allegations that they posed a particular health threat to middle-class families. In each of these towns, domestics insisted that they, not middle-class employers, risked infection through the intimacy of their labor. Time after time, domestics tied wage and hour legislation to protecting the health and safety of domestic workers.[115] Time after time, domestics demanded that government protect their labor rather than examining their bodies.

An example of just this kind of activism unfolded in New Rochelle, a northern suburb of New York City, in the spring of 1937. Councilman Wylie Troy, at the urging of local women's groups, introduced an ordinance to the city council requiring health examinations for domestics working in private homes. To him, these measures probably seemed entirely uncontroversial. After all, several townships in and around New York City had already passed such measures. Rose Richman Gurenson, chair of the Committee on Health for New Rochelle's Civic League, had submitted a dossier of data in support of the ordinance and claimed to have the approval of almost all of the town's white community organizations.[116] Soon after Councilman Troy proposed the measure, the City Council received endorsements of the measure from everyone from the American Legion to New Rochelle's League of Women Voters. Supporters included the Ladies' Aid Society of the First Methodist Episcopal Church, the Sisterhood of Beth El Synagogue, the Women's Democratic League, the Discussion-of-the-Month Club, the Garden Society, and the Parent-Teacher Association of nearly every school district in town.[117] In total, the *Amsterdam News* counted "twenty-eight organizations which had gone on record favoring the legislation, including all the prominent women's organizations and the Board of Education."[118] By June, letters began to stream into the office of the city clerk, most of them voicing support.[119]

Opponents of the ordinance, however, did not stay quiet. John Wallace, an African American politician who had run against Troy for his seat on the city council, was determined that the measure not pass without comment from workers. To publicize the issue, he wrote a full-page letter to the editors of the *New Rochelle Standard-Star*, which was then reprinted a week later in the *Amsterdam News*. In it, Wallace blasted the measure as discriminatory and unfair and urged New Rochelle's councilmen to vote it down.[120] Wallace's letter caused a stir in New Rochelle's African American community. As the date for the hearing on the ordinance approached, resistance grew among domestic workers and their advocates. Over the next few weeks, letters from houseworkers and their supporters began to appear in the city's newspaper, roundly condemning the regulation and asking the city council to reject it.[121] When the hearing was postponed to accommodate a WPA project to paint and redecorate the council chambers, the opposition used the time to gather its forces.[122] Five days before the hearing, New Rochelle's newspaper gleefully promised that the meeting would be "the best attended since that conducted two years ago on Councilman George I. Roberts' Charter amendment ending non-partisan elections for municipal offices."[123]

The meeting was indeed well attended. Domestics packed the council chambers, many having left work early to get to the meeting on time.[124] In fact, near the beginning of the proceedings, a worker in the audience chastised council members, explaining that "it wasn't fair to the domestics to hold the hearing on Monday night because Thursday was their night off."[125] Among the crowd was Theodore Archer, president of the Westchester City Household Workers, which represented over one hundred domestic workers. Walter Clemmens of the Household Employees of New York and representatives of the Communist Party also found seats in the audience.[126] Over the course of two hours, more than twelve speakers rose from the floor to denounce the ordinance, sometimes interrupting speeches by the measure's supporters. As each domestic stood to speak, the crowd voiced its support with shouts and nods.[127]

Supporters of the ordinance were taken aback. They had couched their support for the regulation in terms of protecting domestics from themselves and protecting the middle-class home from infection. How could anyone, they wondered, oppose that? Rose Gurenson, representing the New Rochelle Civic League, explained that the ordinance was not intended to be discriminatory but rather was designed to alert domestics who were infected with tuberculosis or a venereal disease that they were ill. After all, Gurenson posited, "If a domestic is not diseased, he or she need have no fear of the results of the medical examination, and should have no objection to taking it periodically. Isn't that so?" Furthermore, she argued, if a domestic were "diseased, he or she should be thankful of the opportunity to find it out in time to do something about it."[128] Regardless, Gurenson argued, housewives could not afford to take chances when the health and safety of their homes was at stake. "How," she wondered, "can we let the domestics 'alone' when their good health affects not only them but also our very households and is a matter of daily concern to us?"[129]

Domestic workers not only disagreed with this argument, they turned its logic on its head. Why, they asked, did everyone assume that they were any more likely to be sick than their employers? Further, they argued, household workers were much more likely to come in intimate contact with their employers' germs than the reverse. Representatives from domestic workers' organizations cataloged their most personal household chores, including handling dirty linens and cleaning employers' dirty bathrooms. Domestic workers did all this, they reminded listeners, while working long, unhealthy hours.[130] As one worker argued in a letter to the editor of the city newspaper, "The maid's life and health is just as important to her, as the lives of the family are to the employers."[131] Another wrote in to argue, somewhat more bluntly, "Those who must look for germs and disease should look first in their own back yard."[132] As another worker put it, "It was too bad that well-meaning organizations should spread through newspapers that domestics are disease-ridden."[133] If domestic workers should be required to produce health cards for the sake of their employers' well-being, the workers argued, then employers should also be required to produce health cards for the protection of their employees. "Why," workers argued, "humiliate one class?"[134] A law requiring household workers and not employers to be examined was discriminatory and unfair. As John Wallace put it, wealth did not make one immune from disease, and "what is good for the goose is always good for the gander."[135] Outraged workers shared this sentiment. A city council member had to ask one worker to remain seated after she became so irate that she jumped out of her seat to ask, "Who [is] going to protect the domestic?"[136] Middle-class employers, with the support of New Rochelle's middle-class women's organizations, had circulated the idea that domestic workers had an inherent tendency toward disease. Domestics, recognizing the racial and class biases in such an argument, turned middle-class women's logic inside out, painting employers as the party more likely to be sick.

Domestic workers also highlighted the hypocrisy of alleged progressives supporting measures to regulate the bodies of domestic workers under the guise of helping African American women. If progressives were so concerned with protecting domestics, household workers pointed out, they would enact protective labor legislation, not health measures. As one worker asked New Rochelle townspeople, why not instead "pass a law to give us an eight-hour day? That would give us a chance to see a little happiness and also to get some much needed rest. . . . After all, we are human beings although not treated as such."[137] Another worker chimed in, arguing that "the City Council should be occupied by more important matters than to meddle with the freedom and liberty of hard-working citizens." Instead they might actually "propose something that will give our so-called domestics a chance to live like other human beings."[138] John Wallace agreed, urging the council to "give the domestics a lift, or else let them alone."[139] Domestic workers tied whatever propensity they had to disease to their long hours and poor wages. As Theodore Archer reminded New Rochelle's city council members, domestics would love to spend time and money taking care of their health, but could not because of "long hours, improper food and small wages."[140] In domestics' view, the debate over labor legislation was directly tied to that over health ordinances. Labor legislation was the most humane and effective way to guard domestics' health, the ordinance's opponents argued.

Astonishingly, the domestic workers won. There is, unfortunately, no record of council members' private debate over the measure to explain this victory. There is, however, enough evidence to hazard a guess about how African American domestic workers beat back the town's white power structure to defeat the health measure. First, the *New Rochelle Standard-Star* reported that when the council finally cut off debate, domestic workers and their advocates had overwhelmed the "comparative handful" of representatives from women's clubs who had appeared in support of the ordinance.[141] Although New Rochelle's women's organizations had signed statements of support when the measure was first proposed, they were apparently unwilling to defend it under heavy opposition. Many of the women's organizations that had originally supported the ordinance prided themselves on their progressive pedigree and their work on behalf of working-class women. These groups, including New Rochelle's chapter of the League of Women Voters, were often local branches of national organizations that had lobbied hard for labor legislation and New Deal reforms. Publicly debating domestic workers would have freely exposed the labor conditions in middle-class homes. Further, white middle-class women's leaders like Rose Gurenson had been careful to frame their support for the measure in the clinical language of public health.[142] In their statements both before and during the meeting, domestic workers exposed the racial and class assumptions that were implicit in the health measure, a strategy that would surely have undermined middle-class women's self-image as advocates of working women.

While domestic workers' public opposition to the health ordinance worked to suppress progressive women's turnout at the city council meeting, a group of conservative doctors became the workers' unlikely allies. These doctors, among them Dr. Toothacher, the director of New Rochelle's venereal disease clinic, pointed out that, given domestics' low wages, the city would almost certainly have to pick up the tab for the testing. They doubted that the measure would uncover enough diseased domestics to make the expenditure worth it.[143] The members of New Rochelle's medical community who opposed the ordinance did not do so out of sympathy for domestic workers. Opponents felt that "the idea is good, but impracticable to enforce."[144] Nor did the measure's white opponents reject the connections the measure made among race, class, and disease. One suggested that a better plan than compulsory testing for household workers would be compulsory testing for people who accepted government relief checks.[145] Regardless, New Rochelle's city council members were convinced. An un-official poll at the end of the meeting revealed that most of the council members opposed the measure.[146]

This drama replayed across the New York region throughout the Depression. When a similar ordinance passed in Englewood, New Jersey, in 1934, over the objections of domestics who attended several city council hearings, workers immediately organized to oppose the legislation. In a series of mass meetings, the Englewood Domestic Employees Association quickly cohered, joined by a delegation from the neighboring community of Tenafly, which was facing down a similar ordinance. The organization argued that the measure discriminated against African American maids, casting them as sexually promiscuous and diseased. Black workers in Englewood reportedly called the measure "discriminatory" and argued that "they were being looked at as prostitutes."[147] In fact, the association argued, domestic workers put themselves at risk of disease each day they worked in middle-class and wealthy homes. If stemming the spread of venereal disease and tuberculosis was an important goal for the community, they argued, the town should also force employers to prove their own good health.[148] The association wanted the ordinance to be repealed or the measure's constitutionality to be tested in court.[149] A year and a half after domestics began their protest, Englewood's ordinance was repealed.[150]

Even where they did not formally organize, domestic workers consistently protested suggestions that they were more likely to be diseased than their white employers. As investigators went door to door in Newark, New Jersey, informing housewives of the city's new health ordinance for household workers in 1931, they met domestic worker after domestic worker who asked "how they were to know if the family they worked for was healthy." Workers added that they "did not think it fair for the domestic to have a card and the employer not."[151] Resistance from domestics to Newark's health ordinance was so entrenched that the city had to muster a "trained and sufficient force of field investigators" to ensure that domestics appeared for testing.[152] In New York City, domestic workers scrupulously avoided those employment offices that required a health exam before placement.[153]

Everywhere their argument was the same: if domestic workers should have to produce health cards then so should their employers. Workers invited to speak at the YWCA about the conditions of domestic labor weighed in on the matter of health standards for houseworkers. The workers described the danger they put themselves in while working in private homes.

One domestic, speaking to an audience of middle-class YWCA members, described working for a family during the flu epidemic of 1919 in which "the Mister was sick." She recounted that "nobody told me that he had the flu and I took care of him and I feel that the employers also then should have a health certificate of some kind."[154] Mary Turner agreed, remembering that she had once worked for a woman who was so ill that the doctor ordered her to burn the linens that she had been changing and laundering for weeks. She recalled, "I was not informed [that her employer was sick] until I had really been in danger."[155] Like the domestics who protested health ordinances in New Rochelle, Englewood, and Newark, these workers argued that their intimate care work put them at real risk for disease, and that it was they, not middle-class families, who needed protection.

As in New Rochelle, the vocal objections of domestic workers in various organizations did not go unnoticed in white women's organizations' discussions of domestic service. When a colleague wanted to include a paragraph supporting legislation requiring domestics to submit to physicals in a National Council on Household Employment Bulletin, Benjamin Andrews expressed concern. Pointing to the protests by the Englewood domestic workers, he confessed that he doubted "*vigorously* the advisability of this" and argued instead for "voluntary health certificates via placement agencies and via *employer education*."[156] Andrews shared the concerns of many middle-class housewives about the health of domestic workers, but as president of an organization committed to finding common ground between domestics and employers, he was wary of angering household workers by publicly supporting health laws. The WTUL's Mary Dreier agreed with members of the YWCA subcommittee on household employment that there should be public health laws for domestic service, so long as they included "a statement about health examinations for everybody," including employers.[157] Dreier's comments self-consciously echoed workers' objections to public health legislation: if employees had to submit to health exams, then so should employers. Members of the League of Women Voters showed a similar hesitancy, voting down a motion to support the bill pending in the New York State legislature requiring health examinations for domestic workers. Employers and members of white women's organizations continued to support public health laws aimed at household workers in meetings and in private conversation. But the forceful objections of domestics swayed some reform leaders to support workers, especially those in state and national organizations that had pledged to maintain cross-class bonds.

Winning battles like the one in New Rochelle over requiring physicals for houseworkers was no small victory for domestics. The city's domestic workers faced off against a power structure that included men in city government, white women who ran the city's community organizations and employed domestic workers in their homes, and local doctors who saw value in mass testing for venereal disease and had internalized racist stereotypes about black women as sexually promiscuous and more likely to be diseased. Improbably, these workers, who occupied the lowest rung on hierarchies of race, gender, and labor, won. They did so by carefully dissecting middle-class women's argument that intimate contact between workers and employers was likely to spread disease. Nobody, they argued, had more intimate daily contact with other people's germs than they did. It was not middle-class families that needed protection from diseased domestic workers, they argued, but domestics who needed protection from the germs they encountered in the course of their work. While white middle-class women framed their support for such measures in terms of protecting the private family, household workers consistently tied their health to the daily tasks of domestic work. Health, like hours and wages, they argued, was a labor problem, and the home was not just middle-class private space but a workplace. Domestic workers, they insisted, needed labor protections.

THESE DEMANDS DIFFERED significantly from middle-class black organizations' strategy to keep domestic workers employed and their families afloat through the Depression's employment crisis. African American social justice agencies and charity organizations cultivated a vision of race consciousness and uplift that sought to sustain black residents of Harlem. They believed that giving black women a competitive advantage, whether in training or placement, over the white women flooding the domestic employment market was vital to the survival of African American families. This single-minded concentration on employment for employment's sake, however, took middle-class black organizations' focus away from the conditions of women's paid labor. When employers demanded that placement agencies provide them with workers who had been personally and physically screened, social justice organizations by and large complied. Although all of these organizations vocally condemned the conditions under which African American women toiled during the Depression, they offered few programs to address the situation.

Domestic workers' brand of activism was necessarily more radical and sometimes more effective. The DWU created a gendered sense of solidarity among its workers, while also using more traditional organizing techniques like opening a union hiring hall and leafleting buildings and street corners to recruit members.[158] The DWU and other activist domestic workers were not able to create immediate and widespread change. But household workers shaped the agenda of white middle-class organizations like the WTUL, injecting African American women workers' voices into the debate over New Deal labor policy and, more tangibly, shaping the language of the wage and hour bills in the New York State legislature. The DWU also directly challenged employer rhetoric about domestic service and its workers, insisting that the occupation's poor working conditions could not be settled with a little employer education. There could be, they argued, no accord between household management and labor as long as reformers continued to view the middle-class home as a private space, governed by different rules than those of public industry.

Ironically, the Depression economy ultimately undermined the DWU's organizing efforts even as its political atmosphere energized its base. The DWU drowned in the economic crisis of the Depression while trying to support a membership of low-wage workers. Other organizations, many facing their own financial problems, did little to help. The DWU clearly demonstrated that domestic workers were not impossible to organize but that a union was impossible to maintain with no resources and little support. The 1930s, then, was a moment in which the history of domestic service might have changed direction—in which domestics might have begun negotiating with government and employers on the same terms as other workers. Many African American workers would escape domestic service for higher-paid industrial work during World War II and more permanently with the civil rights movement. Domestic service, however, would remain a low-paid, low-status occupation, plagued by long hours and poor working conditions. Despite the work of Dora Jones and the DWU, and despite the ad hoc organization of angry domestic workers in New Rochelle and elsewhere, the 1930s was a moment of promise that would remain unfulfilled.

Epilogue

THE WALLS OF JERICHO

On a balmy August day in 2004, a group of immigrant women workers, mostly Latina and Polish, stood on a street corner in Williamsburg, a rapidly gentrifying Brooklyn neighborhood. Like the African American domestics who had occupied Bronx sidewalks during the Depression, these workers waited for day work cleaning the houses of middle-class women who lived nearby. As the morning progressed, employers approached the group on foot or drove up to the curb and, after carefully considering their options, chose a worker to take home with them for the day. Although there was no formal organization among the workers, they pressured one another to uphold a basic wage, a strategy that did not always work. A consistent source of conflict were the workers, most of them poor, some undocumented, and many with families to support in their home countries, who sometimes broke ranks. A fifty-three-year-old Polish widow told a reporter, "We never talk to the Latinas—sometimes they agree to work for less."[1] Even when they upheld a wage standard, however, some of the women waiting in Wil-

174

liamsburg worked for less than New York State's minimum wage. Although unreported and untaxed labor for less than minimum wage is illegal under New York state and federal law, neither the workers nor their employers seemed particularly worried about being caught or punished. Williamsburg's street-corner market for domestic workers, as a *New York Times* reporter put it, was a rare, publicly visible indicator of the "vast underground economy of domestic service."[2]

It is hard to know the precise number of immigrant women working as domestics in New York today. The only thing that is certain is that Williamsburg's domestic workers are not the only women who are paid under the table for housework in middle-class homes. These workers operate without the legal protections, including minimum wage and mandatory overtime pay, that domestic workers won under an amendment to the Fair Labor Standards Act (FLSA) in 1974. Domestic Workers United, a New York domestic workers' union, estimates that there are anywhere from 200,000 to 600,000 household workers working in New York City today.[3] Scholars and research organizations agree that domestic work is on the rise, reporting that there was a 53 percent increase in hiring between 1995 and 1999. In 1999, 30 percent of employers who hired domestic workers did so for the first time.[4] According to a survey of 547 domestic workers that the organization conducted between 2003 and 2004, the work in today's middle-class homes is hard and the pay is low—26 percent of the workers surveyed earned wages that put them below the poverty line. A few earned less than minimum wage; 37 percent said they could not afford to pay rent or take out a mortgage; 40 percent said they could not afford a phone. The economic downturn in 2008 only made things worse. Domestic help was often the first expense that middle-class and wealthy families cut as they reassessed their finances. As Ai-jen Poo of Domestic Workers United pointed out, "Unlike other sectors getting hit, domestic workers have no safety net. . . . It's the invisible, untold story of this crisis."[5] Despite these poor wages, domestics worked hard. Half of the workers worked overtime, sometimes more than sixty hours a week, even though 67 percent said they did not receive overtime pay. Working conditions were also frequently unpleasant. A third of the workers surveyed said that their employers had at one time or another made them feel uncomfortable or had subjected them to verbal or physical abuse. Marilyn Marshall, a Brooklyn nanny, explained, "Because you work in a private house, almost anything goes. . . . They don't think of what you do as real work or of you as a real worker."[6]

HOW DID WE GET HERE? There has been quite a bit of legislation and debate over domestic service in the seventy-odd years since African American workers waited in Depression-era street-corner markets. Most notably, in 1974 the federal government passed legislation guaranteeing live-out domestic workers a minimum wage and overtime pay. Many middle-class and elite women also think differently about domestic service than organized women's groups did in the 1930s. With the dawning of the women's movement, feminists began to see housework as an issue that united women across class lines. Echoing the sentiment the Women's Trade Union League expressed in its 1919 resolution, feminists argued that household workers' poor wages reflected the lack of status accorded to women's labor in general. Despite this legislative and cultural transformation, many household workers still face labor exploitation in middle-class homes. Domestic labor continues to structure political, social, and now global hierarchies and is still the subject of public debate. And yet domestic service continues to be a labor relationship that is largely worked out between employers and workers with very little state regulation. In fact, somewhere between 80 and 95 percent of domestic employers pay their workers under the table.[7] Although much has changed for domestic workers in the twenty-first century, the categories of public and private still shape domestic service in important and instructive ways.

The inclusion of domestic workers under FLSA laws was supposed to make a real difference for workers in middle-class homes. In 1974, in an unprecedented move, the U.S. Congress amended federal labor law to include live-out domestic workers. It was the first time that domestics had been included in any protective labor legislation. In a dramatic departure from the squabbles over the Women's Trade Union League's New York State wage and hour legislation in 1938, women's organizations almost unanimously supported the amendments. Representatives from the National Organization for Women (NOW), a reorganized National Council on Household Employment, and the National Consumers' League traveled to Washington, D.C., to testify in favor of the legislation. A host of other women's organizations wrote letters to federal lawmakers and signed petitions urging Congress to amend the FLSA to apply to domestics. Among this latter group were the American Association of University Women, Church Women United, the National Association of Colored Women, the National Council of Jewish Women, the National Council of Negro Women, the National Women's Political Caucus, the Women's Equity Action League, and the National Board of the Young Women's Christian Association.

In the explosion of gender analysis ignited by the women's movement in the 1960s and 1970s, organized middle-class women began to see housewives and domestics as suffering from a shared gendered oppression.[8] Feminist organizations and other middle-class women's groups viewed the poor wages of domestics as a product of the cultural, political, and economic devaluation of women's labor. These organizations also cast poverty as a women's issue that their members had a responsibility to address. Women's groups therefore lined up to lend their support to an FLSA that recognized housework as labor that deserved government protection.

None of the representatives from women's groups admitted in congressional testimony that middle-class women were part of the problem. Perhaps they were trying to head off criticism that any law governing labor relations in private homes would be unenforceable. Whatever her reasons, Kee Hall, a student and a young member of NOW, argued, "Having been exploited themselves in the workforce, women are becoming more and more sensitive to the exploitation of other women."[9] Even Dorothy Haener, NOW's official spokesperson at the hearings and a veteran of the United Auto Workers Women's Department, rejected any suggestion that the legislation was unenforceable in the millions of private homes across the country. The members of NOW, Haener argued, took "exception" to the idea that "women who employ household help would object very strongly to paying an adequate wage."[10] Edith B. Sloan, chair of the National Council on Household Employment and a young African American feminist, testified that the council believed "that those who claim the law cannot be enforced are misunderstanding the determination and desire of the average American citizen to voluntarily obey the law."[11] Although the women's movement had inspired organized women to reach across class lines to advocate for domestic workers for the first time, many activists could still not imagine that middle-class women would purposely exploit the domestics working in their homes. As Kee Hall put it, "Women know what housework is. It is dirty, tedious work and they are willing to pay to have it done because they, more than anyone else, know what it is worth." Hall insisted that "women will be willing to pay the minimum wage, whatever it may be in order to employ household help."[12] Although white middle-class activists admitted that most domestics worked for very low wages, they did not explicitly acknowledge the exploitation that domestics still faced in many middle-class homes. Feminists agreed, for the first time, that the middle-class home was a workplace for many working-class women, but they seemed hesitant to focus on middle-class women's participation in labor exploitation.

Domestic workers, however, were not as quick to sign on to middle-class activists' version of sisterhood. Domestics had plenty of evidence that some women abused the paid workers in their homes without regard to the law. Pointing to the fact that household workers often were not enrolled in Social Security even though many were eligible, Geneva Reid, chair of the Household Technicians of America, argued that "some employers are too lazy and too cheap to readily comply with the law."[13] In the view of domestic workers, employers were no more likely to treat their workers fairly than was management in public industry. Sisterhood, in Reid's view, was no guarantee of workplace equity. Instead, Reid argued that in order for domestics to be able to fight effectively for a decent wage and fair treatment in middle-class homes, they needed "a legal base, a law that says that we too are entitled to the minimum wage offered to other workers of the land."[14] Legislators had long excused domestics' exclusion from FLSA laws by arguing that their inclusion would be unenforceable and that amending the law was therefore not worth the government ink. Reid and her supporters countered that domestic workers, many of them newly politicized by the civil rights movement and the women's movement, would provide enforcement for the FLSA's provisions through collective organizing and by bringing to justice employers who failed to pay their workers a minimum wage or overtime pay.[15]

Given domestic workers' historical exclusion from all protective labor legislation, the passage of the 1974 FLSA amendments was a tremendous achievement. It was a legislative victory that could not have been won without the participation of a coalition of middle-class and working-class women's organizations and labor leaders. These groups faced vigorous opposition to the legislation from manufacturing and antiunion groups. But their persuasive gendered argument, along with the pressure they put on legislators, ultimately won the day. Although racial and class tension clearly still existed, the women's movement created ideological bonds and a sense of common purpose between domestic workers and middle-class women that had not existed before. Both groups argued that it was a grave injustice that domestics had been excluded from protective labor legislation. This cross-class coalition of women activists demanded that government leaders finally acknowledge, as Geneva Reid put it, "that our services, too, are of value to our society."[16]

Geneva Reid was right, however, when she suggested that legislation alone was not enough to guarantee basic labor standards in middle-class homes. Reid hoped that inclusion of domestic workers in the FLSA would allow unions like hers to recruit more members, help workers to insist on fair hours and pay, and give workers legal standing with which to bring recalcitrant employers into line. All of these goals, though, depended on a politically empowered workforce. The civil rights movement served as a political model to organize African American domestic workers, and it also helped to open a host of occupations to black women, who had previously been confined to domestic work.[17] Middle-class women, both black and white, who hoped to take advantage of the professional opportunities provided by the women's movement still needed workers to keep their houses clean and to care for their children and the elderly. As African American working-class women began to leave domestic employment for higher-paid and higher-status occupations, immigrant women, many of them undocumented and desperate to support families left behind in developing nations, quickly took their place in middle-class kitchens.[18]

These new immigrant workers, many without legal working papers and all in the country conditionally, are less likely than American citizens to participate in a union or publicly challenge employers who break the law. Undocumented workers who charge their employers in court with sexual or physical abuse usually receive a work visa, but workers who press wage and hour claims get no such consideration from immigration authorities.[19] Undocumented immigrant workers are therefore forced to think very carefully before taking their employers to court for FLSA violations. Furthermore, U.S. immigration law is structured in a way that ensures a docile immigrant domestic labor force. If workers who were brought into the country on employer-sponsored visas leave their employers, no matter how abusive, they also lose their legal immigration status.[20] Although these requirements affect all immigrant workers, not just domestics, labor abuses are easier to hide in private homes, not least because government regulators are not really looking for them. Neither NOW's imagined cross-class sisterhood nor Reid's vision of a politicized and organized domestic labor force have materialized to enforce FLSA laws. Many domestic workers, therefore, still experience working conditions in private homes that have long since been abolished in industry.

Paid housework is thus perhaps even less visible to the public and to researchers than it was at the turn of the century or during the Great Depression. Undocumented workers are often missed by Department of Labor statisticians and government census takers. Although domestic service is still imagined to be an entirely private occupation, scholars are beginning to demonstrate the occupation's important role in global politics. For instance, in order to meet the requirements, often called "Structural Adjustment Programs," for World Bank or International Monetary Fund loans, poor countries devalue their currency and cut social programs. Impoverished families in developing nations are therefore left with fewer government programs to rely on and are forced to send family members abroad to seek jobs paid in more valuable currency.[21] This strategy, it turns out, is a pragmatic one for struggling families in poor countries. The remittances workers send home top 300 billion dollars per year, almost three times the total amount that developing nations receive in foreign aid.[22] Women are increasingly likely to go abroad to support their families, creating what some scholars have called a "feminization of migration."[23] Most of these women end up performing some sort of poorly paid care work, whether taking care of young children, cleaning and cooking for middle- and upper-class families, or caring for the elderly.

Hiring a household worker therefore often means participating in a system of global labor exploitation. Barbara Ehrenreich suggests that domestic service continues to pose a serious dilemma for feminists today. Contributing to some form of global labor exploitation, she says, is unavoidable for most people who live in western consumer society. Everyone at one time or another buys clothing made in a sweatshop or eats produce picked by migrant laborers. But there is something different, Ehrenreich argues, when Americans bring that exploitation home. Even scrupulously fair employers, she asserts, must face the fact that "someone is working in your home at a job she would almost certainly never have chosen for herself—if she'd had a college education, for example, or was a native-born American with good English skills—[and] that the place where she works . . . is the same place where you sleep."[24] Feminists, she argues, should avoid hiring domestic workers at all and should instead divide household labor equitably among male and female family members. Scholar Bridget Anderson agrees, arguing that although "a working couple might need someone to look after their children or elderly relatives, no one *has* to employ a cleaner in the same way."[25] Cleaning and housekeeping, Anderson claims, too often "simply expresses the employer's status, leisure, and power."[26] The household is too intimate a space, scholars like Ehrenreich and Anderson believe, to accommodate comfortably both private family life and what they view as an inherently degrading form of labor.

Workers, as usual, have other ideas. Far from viewing domestic work as inherently degrading, domestics argue that their labor helps to create the public face of the city in which adults with families and household responsibilities get up every day and go to work in the public sector. These workers recognize the connections between their labor and city politics. As one New York short-term baby nurse explained, "We could close down the city. . . . If there's a garbage strike, the trash just lies there. If there's a postal strike, the mail doesn't get delivered. But if the nannies were to strike it would be different. You can't just leave a baby around until there's someone ready to take care of it."[27] Indeed, Domestic Workers United asserts that "domestic work forms the invisible backbone of New York City's economy."[28] It is political exclusion, they contend, not the work itself, that makes domestic labor prone to exploitation. The New York union points out that domestics are still excluded from most federal and state protective labor legislation. The National Labor Relations Act does not recognize the right of domestic workers to unionize; the FLSA still does not require overtime pay for live-in workers or home health aides; the Occupational Safety and Health Act explicitly excludes domestic workers; and Title VII, which prohibits employment discrimination on the basis of race, religion, gender, and national origin, does not apply to employers with fewer than fifteen employees.[29] If domestic work were more comprehensively written into public law, union leaders argue, paid household workers would be less likely to suffer exploitation in private homes.

Domestic labor is thus once again the subject of politics and labor legislation. In 2003, Domestic Workers United helped to pass a "Nanny Bill" in New York City that requires employment agencies to post a "code of conduct" in several languages that explains to potential workers their rights under state and federal labor law.[30] More recently, the union lobbied for and won the Domestic Worker Bill of Rights, which the governor signed into law during the summer of 2010. The measure requires employers to pay domestic workers a living wage and either provide health insurance or add two dollars an hour to their wages.[31] The Bill of Rights establishes a forty-hour work week and requires one day's rest in seven and three paid vacation days. Finally, the Bill of Rights specifically outlaws trafficking in domestic workers and removes language in New York State labor laws that excludes domestic workers.[32] The final bill does not, however, allow workers to sue employers who violate the law.

Domestic Workers United's support for this legislation demonstrates the feelings of many workers that a publicly regulated workplace would solve what some feminists see as a hopeless Gordian knot of private exploitation.

Progress toward publicly regulating the home, however, is slow. Workers in private homes continue to labor under conditions that are far different from those experienced by workers in the public sphere. As we debate domestic labor, whether and how much it differs from the paid labor that takes place in public will continue to be a central issue.

Notes

Introduction

1. Salmon, *Domestic Service*, 1–2.

2. Historian David Katzman describes the "servant problem" as "the bread and butter" of women's magazines, other mainstream publications, and social science journals. Katzman, *Seven Days a Week*, 223. See also Matthews, *Just a Housewife*, 97; and Vapnek, *Breadwinners*, 104.

3. Salmon, *Domestic Service*, 146n1.

4. Caroline Booker to Lucy Maynard Salmon, n.d., box 49, folder 5, Lucy Maynard Salmon Papers.

5. Salmon, *Domestic Service*, 168.

6. Caroline Curtiss Johnson to Lucy Maynard Salmon, December 20, 1889, box 49, folder 4, Lucy Maynard Salmon Papers.

7. A. H. Jones to Lucy Maynard Salmon, December 12, 1889, ibid.

8. In a recent book, Alana Erickson Coble argues that organized women's reform efforts, along with other cultural and economic trends, made domestics more autonomous and respected by their employers after 1920. Coble focuses on the changing, and, she would argue, constantly improving, personal relationship between employers and domestics. Overall, hers is an extremely positive narrative of domestic service and addresses neither women's organizations' opposition to labor legislation nor the reforms

they did pass, including the employment agency law or health regulations. See Coble, *Cleaning Up*.

9. See, for example, Storrs, *Civilizing Capitalism*, esp. 198–221; Quadagno, *Transformation of Old Age Security*, 115–16; Kessler-Harris, *In Pursuit of Equity*, esp. 101–16; and Mettler, *Dividing Citizens*, 20.

10. Salmon, *Domestic Service*; Katzman, *Seven Days a Week*; Dudden, *Serving Women*. See also Hunter, *To 'Joy My Freedom*; Van Raaphorst, *Union Maids Not Wanted*; Clark-Lewis, *Living-In, Living-Out*, 97; Romero, *Maid in the U.S.A.*; and Coble, *Cleaning Up*. Phyllis Palmer and Faye Dudden, however, do investigate the national battle over labor legislation and domestic workers. See Palmer, *Domesticity and Dirt*; and Dudden, "Experts and Servants."

11. Katzman, *Seven Days a Week*, 287. Some historians argue that domestic service declined after 1910, citing a decrease in domestics as a percentage of working women and in the number of families per 1,000 employing domestics. These figures do not, however, measure the percentage of middle-class families employing at least one servant. As the working-class population grew, the total number of families employing household workers declined. That does not, however, change the centrality of employing a domestic to the middle-class experience. In addition, African American women performing paid domestic labor after World War I worked sometimes sporadically and often informally, especially during the Depression, when women took whatever work they could get. African American women did not often live with their employers, as immigrant domestics had before World War I. It seems likely, then, that domestic workers were not accurately counted by census takers after the 1910 census.

12. Approximately 43 percent of New York City women wage earners worked in domestic service in 1880; 33 percent did so in 1900; and approximately 14 percent did so in 1920. This latter number held steady, according to census takers and social investigators, through 1940, when between 13 and 19 percent of working women in New York City worked as domestics. Nationally, domestics represented approximately 42 percent of working women in 1880, 37 percent in 1900, 25 percent in 1920, and 30 percent in 1930. As previously noted, it seems likely that census takers underestimated the number of women working in domestic service after 1910, both in New York City and across the country. Nevertheless, as late as 1930, domestic service represented the second most likely occupation for working women in New York City and the most likely occupation for working women in the nation as a whole. See Katzman, *Seven Days a Week*, 284, 287; Coble, *Cleaning Up*, 18, 19; and Ellis, *A Socio-economic Study of the Female Domestic Worker in Private Homes*, 2.

13. On New York Progressive women's importance in national welfare movements, see Fitzgerald, *Habits of Compassion*, 11; Orleck, *Common Sense and a Little Fire*; Kessler-Harris, *In Pursuit of Equity*; Boris, *Home to Work*; and Gordon, *Pitied but Not Entitled*.

14. This history is ably charted in Dudden, *Serving Women*.

15. See Scobey, *Empire City*, 183; and Dudden, *Serving Women*, 119. In her investigation of the working conditions of domestic workers at the turn of the twentieth century, Frances Kellor found domestics in crowded apartments sleeping on top of the dining room table or in the family bathtub. Kellor, *Out of Work*, 110.

16. See Meyerowitz, *Women Adrift*, 28, 70, 78; and Diner, *Erin's Daughters in America*, 83. Reformers constantly lamented native-born women's refusal to take housework jobs and embarked on numerous (almost always ill-fated) programs to try to convert

native-born factory workers to domestic work. See Vapnek, *Breadwinners*, chap. 4; and Deutsch, *Women and the City*, chap. 2.

17. Diner, *Erin's Daughters in America*, 77; Walter, *Outsiders Inside*.

18. Diner, *Erin's Daughters in America*, esp. chaps. 1 and 4.

19. Daniels, *Coming to America*, 129.

20. See Jacobson, *Whiteness of a Different Color*; Ignatiev, *How the Irish Became White*; Gordon, *Great Arizona Orphan Abduction*; and Roediger, *Wages of Whiteness*.

21. The change from white live-in service to black live-out service is chronicled in Katzman, *Seven Days a Week*; Palmer, *Domesticity and Dirt*; and Clark-Lewis, *Living-In, Living-Out*. See also Hunter, *To 'Joy My Freedom*.

22. Maureen Fitzgerald argues that historians must begin to tell the story of working-class women alongside that of middle-class reformers. Fitzgerald, *Habits of Compassion*, 7.

23. The classic work on cultural expectations for nineteenth-century middle-class women is Barbara Welter, "Cult of True Womanhood." Excellent historiographical discussions of the development of separate spheres as an organizing concept for women's historians include Kerber, "Separate Spheres"; Richter, *Home on the Rails*, 6; and Turbin, "Refashioning the Concept of Public/Private," 43–44.

24. As with each of these historiographies, there is an enormous literature on women's female networks. See, for example, Rosenberg, "Female World of Love and Ritual"; Sklar, *Florence Kelley and the Nation's Work*; Sklar, "Hull House in the 1890s"; and Lebsock, *Free Women of Petersburg*.

25. Among many fine examples of this scholarship, see Pascoe, *Relations of Rescue*; Ryan, *Cradle of the Middle Class*; Hewitt, *Women's Activism and Social Change*; and Flanagan, *Seeing with Their Hearts*.

26. See Deutsch, *Women and the City*; Gordon, *Pitied but Not Entitled*; Storrs, *Civilizing Capitalism*; Dye, *As Equals and as Sisters*; Muncy, *Creating a Female Dominion*; Skocpol, *Protecting Soldiers and Mothers*; and Sklar, *Florence Kelly and the Nation's Work*.

27. Most scholars depict Progressive white women's reform groups as middle class. See Muncy, *Creating a Female Dominion*, xii; Flanagan, *Seeing with Their Hearts*, 29; Gordon, *Pitied but Not Entitled*, 44; and Sklar, *Florence Kelley and the Nation's Work*, xii.

28. Landon R. Y. Storrs makes this point for the National Consumers' League. Storrs, *Civilizing Capitalism*, 28–30.

29. Ibid., 33, 282n71; Records of the National Council of Negro Women; Records of the National Association of Colored Women's Clubs, 1895–1992.

30. See also Hedgeman, *The Trumpet Sounds*, 37; and White, *Too Heavy a Load*, 132–33.

31. Hart, *Bound by Our Constitution*, 170.

32. On the regulation of working-class homes by the state, see Gordon, *Pitied but Not Entitled*.

33. See, for example, Davidson and Hatcher, *No More Separate Spheres*. Michael Schudson argues that the public sphere was never a place of rational political discourse, as posited by Habermas. Schudson, "Was There Ever a Public Sphere."

34. See Habermas, *Structural Transformation of the Public Sphere*.

35. Ritter, *Constitution as Social Design*, 262–87; Forbath, *Law and the Shaping of the American Labor Movement*; Zelizer, *Purchase of Intimacy*; Boydston, *Home and Work*, 142–63; Kleinberg, "Gendered Space"; Stiehm, "Government and the Family."

36. Boydston, *Home and Work*, 142–63.

37. See Orleck, *Common Sense and a Little Fire*; and Storrs, *Civilizing Capitalism*.

38. Addams, "A Belated Industry."

39. "Domestic Service," 7; Salmon, *Domestic Service*, 129.

40. Sutherland, *Americans and Their Servants*, 5; Van Raaphorst, *Union Maids Not Wanted*, 13; Strasser, "Mistress and Maid," 64; Clark-Lewis, *Living-In, Living-Out*, 97; Katzman, *Seven Days a Week*, ix.

41. In her study of Chicana maids in the American Southwest, Mary Romero points out that these formulations inaccurately remove domestic service from a "sphere of capitalist production in which race and gender domination are played out." Romero, *Maid in the U.S.A.*, 93.

42. As Faye Dudden has persuasively argued about an earlier period, domestic service developed "parallel to industrialization," not outside of it. Ruth Cowan also points out that the home was constantly shaped by new technologies, as various tasks were mechanized or removed from home production entirely. See Dudden, *Serving Women*, 8; and Cowan, *More Work for Mother*.

43. See Kessler-Harris, *In Pursuit of Equity*; Boris, *Home to Work*; Storrs, *Civilizing Capitalism*; and Gordon, *Pitied but Not Entitled*.

Chapter One

1. "Bold Man Defends the Servant Girl."

2. Ibid.

3. Pascoe, *Relations of Rescue*; Ryan, *Cradle of the Middle Class*; Hewitt, *Women's Activism and Social Change*; Gordon, *Pitied but Not Entitled*; Storrs, *Civilizing Capitalism*; Muncy, *Creating a Female Dominion*.

4. See, for example, Richardson, *Long Day*, 56–57; Pettengill, *Toilers of the Home*, vi; Bensley, "Experiences of a Nursery Governess," 26; and Salmon, *Domestic Service*, 130. On native-born women's unwillingness to take domestic work, see also Meyerowitz, *Women Adrift*, 70; Vapnek, *Breadwinners*, chap. 4; and Diner, *Erin's Daughters in America*, 83.

5. Klink, "Put Yourself in Her Place," 169.

6. "The Reason Why."

7. "Martyrdom of the Housewife."

8. Urban historian David Scobey points out that even "merely 'comfortable'" New Yorkers "needed at least a cook and a maid to maintain themselves." Sarah Deutsch concurs: "Middle-class/elite matrons seemed to have no conception of a legitimate household without servants." See Scobey, *Empire City*, 183; and Deutsch, *Women and the City*, 66.

9. Phyllis Palmer makes this argument for the interwar years, but her analysis holds true for the late nineteenth century as well. See Palmer, *Domesticity and Dirt*, 5; Mintz and Kellogg, *Domestic Revolutions*, 58, 117; and Cowan, *More Work for Mother*.

10. As Tera Hunter points out for the South, employer complaints of "shortages" of domestic workers probably reflected a lack of workers who were "compliant and submissive" rather than a shrinking domestic labor force. Hunter, *To 'Joy My Freedom*, 237.

11. "An Unsettled Question," 59.

12. "Is the Home Disappearing?"

13. Robb, "Our House in Order," 354.

14. See also "Is the Home Disappearing?"; "Irish Servants Are Scarce"; Kellor, "The Problem of the Young Negro Girl from the South"; Sheldon, "Servant and Mistress," 3018;

and Goldwin Smith, "Passing of the Household," 422. The issue of New Yorkers leaving apartments and single-family homes for boardinghouses and hotels for want of "help" was still being written about with concern into the late 1920s. See "To Save the Great American Home"; and Fraser, "Servant Problem."

15. See Scacchi, "American Interiors"; and Scobey, *Empire City*, 174–85.

16. One of reformers' chief objections to tenement life was the indiscriminate mixing of families and neighbors and their boarders. See Riis, *How the Other Half Lives*, 1–2; and Brace, *Dangerous Classes of New York*, 55.

17. See Gilman, *Women and Economics*; and Cowan, *More Work for Mother*.

18. "Laundry Reforms Needed."

19. Mary Mortimer Maxwell, "The Family Washing."

20. Davis, "Recovery of Family Life," 673.

21. See Strasser, *Never Done*, chap. 6; and Cowan, *More Work for Mother*.

22. L. Seely, *Mrs. Seely's Cook Book*, 32.

23. Ibid., 8–24.

24. Scobey also notes that between 1850 and 1875 seven of ten New York property owners lived in the upper wards of Manhattan and that 96 percent of single-family dwellings and apartment houses (as opposed to boardinghouses and tenements) were built uptown. Scobey, *Empire City*, 115–18.

25. Riis, *How the Other Half Lives*, 14; Campbell, *Prisoners of Poverty*, 113.

26. *Report of the Tenement House Committee*, 4–8.

27. S. Josephine Baker, *Fighting for Life*, 58.

28. Scobey argues that Victorian New Yorkers recognized an "interconnection between spatial and social disorder" and that "'uptown' was a place of genteel domesticity, marked by the absence of both commercial densities and tenement crowds." See Scobey, *Empire City*, 181, 115.

29. Kellor, *Out of Work*, 20; Kellor, "Intelligence Office," 458.

30. Kellor also reported that more than two-thirds of New York intelligence offices were "owned or managed by women." Kellor, *Out of Work*, 19, 35.

31. McArdell, "Help! Help! Help!," 479, 482.

32. F. E. V. Odell & Co., *Servant's Exchange Pamphlet*, New-York Historical Society.

33. "Kitchen Drama."

34. Ibid.

35. Flagg, "I Should Say So," 111.

36. Taft, "How Is the Refined New York Family."

37. Commissioner George Bell to Mayor John P. Mitchel, May 16, 1916, box 38, folder 326, Files of Office of the Mayor, Mitchel Administration.

38. Kellor, *Out of Work*, 49.

39. "Plague of the Household."

40. Dudden, *Serving Women*, 217–18.

41. Kellor, "Criminal Sociology: II," 519–20.

42. Kellor, *Out of Work*, 98–99.

43. Campbell, *Prisoners of Poverty*, 236.

44. Ibid.

45. "Another View of the Matter," 3.

46. Sarah Deutsch argues that reformers hoped that domestic service would bind "different classes into a single family, albeit unequal." Deutsch, *Women and the City*, 65.

47. Goodwin, "An Appeal to Housekeepers," 753.

48. Ibid., 759.

49. Kellor, "Immigrant Woman," 402.

50. "Why Is It That So Many Servant Girls Go Insane?"

51. Whipple, "Domestic Service," 25.

52. "Phases of Domestic Service."

53. "Domestic Servants Needed"; "A 'Downtrodden' Mistress."

54. Spofford, *Servant Girl Question*, 31.

55. For example, Annie McLaughlin wrote to Mayor Mitchel in 1916 complaining that her employer had warned, "If you ever leave, I will never let you get another position." An unemployed McLaughlin wrote that it did "seem as if she carried out her threat." Annie McLaughlin to Mayor John P. Mitchel, September 21, 1916, box 48, folder 493, Files of Office of the Mayor, Mitchel Administration. See also Kellor, *Out of Work*, 115.

56. "About Servants in Liveries—and in General."

57. Coffey, *Irish in America*, 143; Diner, *Erin's Daughters in America*, 85.

58. "The People to Whom We Confide Our Children."

59. Cusack, *Advice to Irish Girls in America*, 174.

60. Spofford, *Servant Girl Question*, 32–33.

61. See Jacobson, *Whiteness of a Different Color*, chap. 2.

62. Deutsch, *Women and the City*, 74.

63. Goodwin, "An Appeal to Housekeepers," 758.

64. "One Who Tried Domestic Service."

65. MacLean, "Diary of a Domestic Drudge," 603.

66. "Statement by Mrs. Joseph Allen of Seal Harbor, ME about Helen Tangney and Bridie Kennedy," July 15, 1927, box 4, folder 42, Annie Ware Winsor Allen Papers. The incident occurred late in Allen's life at her family home in Maine, but Allen had begun her housekeeping in New York City, during which time she published a pamphlet, "Both Sides of the Servant Question," advising employers on the management of domestic workers. It is also worth noting that the Social Reform Club stated as its mission a special dedication to "the improvement of the condition of wage-earners." 1898 Social Reform Club Annual Report, Constitution, List of Members (New York: Allied Printing Trades Union Label Council, 1898), 2, box 4, folder 38.

67. Henrietta MacLauren Richards Diary, vol. 5, January 22, 1887.

68. Kneeland, *Commercialized Prostitution*, 101–6. Sarah Deutsch notes that similar studies, with similar findings, had taken place in Boston. Deutsch, *Women and the City*, 57.

69. Forrester, "The 'Girl' Problem," 378.

70. Kellor, *Out of Work*, 99.

71. Ibid., 100.

72. "Servant Girls."

73. Bailey, "Livin'-Out Girls," 309.

74. Kellor, *Out of Work*, 15.

75. See Dudden, *Serving Women*, 215–19; and Deutsch, *Women and the City*, 62–64.

76. See Rorer, "How to Treat and Keep a Servant"; Godman, "A Nine-Hour Day for Domestic Servants," 399; Taft, "How Is the Refined New York Family"; and "A Servant on the Servant Problem," 503.

77. Salmon, *Domestic Service*, 152n1.

78. Taft, "How Is the Refined New York Family."

79. Doughty, "Evolution in the Kitchen," 389.

80. Hotchkiss, "Advice to Employers."

81. "Mr. Coster's Servant Girl."

82. Godman, "A Nine-Hour Day for Domestic Servants," 399.

83. "The Maidservant."

84. Wagner, "Into Such Hands Do We Commit Our Children."

85. Gilman, *Concerning Children*, 219.

86. Bensley, "Experiences of a Nursery Governess—VIII," 180.

87. Rorer, "How to Treat and Keep a Servant."

88. Rose, "White Woman's Burden."

89. Wagner, "Into Such Hands Do We Commit Our Children."

90. Gilman, "The Irresponsible Nursemaid."

91. Although Kathy Piess argues that domestics did not have the leisure time to participate in these "cheap amusements," public concerns about domestics' recreation suggest otherwise. See Piess, *Cheap Amusements*.

92. "Kitchen versus Slop Shop."

93. Bacon, "We and Our Servants," 354.

94. Agnes M., "True Life Story of a Nurse Girl," 2266.

95. MacLean, "Diary of a Domestic Drudge," 602.

96. "Why 100,000 Domestics Are Needed Here."

97. Lillian Pettengill complained of an employer who left small change lying around the house in order to test her honesty. Kellor recounted the story of a worker who was driven to ruin after having been falsely accused of stealing and fired with no reference. See Pettengill, *Toilers of the Home*, 215; and Kellor, *Out of Work*, 115.

98. "Servant Girls."

99. A cursory search of the *New York Times* and the *New York Tribune* revealed at least sixty-seven separate reports of families robbed by their domestics between 1870 and 1930, many of these crimes warranting several articles. Sixty of these reports fell between 1877 and 1907.

100. Rose, "White Woman's Burden."

101. Kellor, *Out of Work*, esp. 45–46.

102. "Invitations to Theft."

103. "A Servant Girl's Fiendish Revenge."

104. "An Insane Woman as a Servant."

105. McArdell, "Help! Help! Help!," 479.

106. Grace Eulalie Matthews Ashmore Diary, August 14, 1907, vol. 16, box 2, Grace Eulalie Matthews Ashmore Papers.

107. As these stories demonstrate, the gulf that historian Christine Stansell demonstrated between working-class and middle-class mores for public behavior in the early nineteenth century remained alive and well into the early twentieth century. Stansell, *City of Women*, 58–61.

108. Thompson, "The Servant Question," 521.

109. Abel, "Training School for Servants," 502; Godman, "A Nine-Hour Day for Domestic Servants," 398.

110. Salmon, *Domestic Service*, 129.

111. Scobey, *Empire City*, 176.

112. "Privileges of Servants," 614.

113. "A Servant's View of the Situation."

114. Klink, "The Housekeeper's Responsibility."

115. Kellor, "Immigrant Woman," 406.

116. See Deutsch, *Women and the City*, 56–67.

117. Dorr, "Prodigal Daughter," 684.

118. Untitled speech, ca. 1904–5, reel 8, frame 202, Margaret Dreier Robins Papers, in James, *Papers of the Women's Trade Union League*.

119. Frederick, "Suppose Our Servants Didn't Live with Us."

120. Although scholars argue that it was not a part of the rhetoric of female reformers, the vulnerable position of domestics vis-à-vis their male employers was part of public discussions of domestic service. See Dudden, *Serving Women*, 215–19; Deutsch, *Women and the City*, 62–64; and Kellor, *Out of Work*.

121. "Servant Girls."

122. Wilson, "How We Treat Servants and How They Treat Us," 64.

123. Pettengill, *Toilers of the Home*, vii.

124. Kellor, *Out of Work*, 96–97.

125. Rorer, "How to Train a Green Cook."

126. Klink, "The Housekeeper's Responsibility," 376.

127. Godman, "Ten Weeks in a Kitchen," 2463–64.

128. McMahan, "Something More about Domestic Service," 401.

129. "Why There Is a Servant Question."

130. Campbell, *Prisoners of Poverty*, 224.

131. "Why There Is a Servant Question," 5.

132. McArdell, "Help! Help! Help!," 483.

133. Comstock, "Mistress Problem," 15.

134. *Ladies' Protective Union and Directory*.

135. "The Servant Girl Question: Miss M. C. Jones in the Pittsburgh Dispatch."

136. "Experiences of a 'Hired Girl,'" 779.

137. "Domestic Service," 7.

138. "What the Servant Sells."

139. Ibid.

140. Rubinow and Durant, "Depth and Breadth of the Servant Problem," 580.

141. "The Reason Why."

142. Thompson, "The Servant Question," 523; Coman, "Problem of Domestic Service," 652.

143. "One Who Tried Domestic Service."

144. Historian Amy Dru Stanley notes that the image of the enslaved and abused female body was a particularly effective weapon in the arsenal of free labor advocates for the "family wage." See Stanley, *From Bondage to Contract*.

Chapter Two

1. "Finns of New York."

2. Naisyhdistys Pyrkijä celebrated its golden jubilee in 1943. See Ross, *Finn Factor*, 22–23; and Ekman, Olli, and Olli, *History of Finnish American Organizations in Greater New York*, 161.

3. Ekman, Olli, and Olli, *History of Finnish American Organizations in Greater New York*, 161.

4. See Diner, *Erin's Daughters in America*; and Mageean, "Making Sense and Providing Structure," esp. 238.

5. See Richardson, *Long Day*, 56–57; Pettengill, *Toilers of the Home*, vi; Bensley, "Experiences of a Nursery Governess," 130; Meyerowitz, *Women Adrift*, 70; Diner, *Erin's Daughters in America*, chap. 4; Klapper, "Jewish Women and Vocational Education," 113; and Sinkoff, "Educating for 'Proper' Jewish Womanhood," 582.

6. See Matovic, "Embracing a Middle-Class Life," esp. 290; Lintelman, "America Is the Woman's Promised Land"; and Nadel, *Little Germany*, 63.

7. Van Raaphorst, *Union Maids Not Wanted*, 13. See also Katzman, *Seven Days a Week*, 234; and Dudden, *Serving Women*, 230, 232.

8. Lintelman, "America Is the Woman's Promised Land"; Lintelman, "More Freedom, Better Pay"; Lynch-Brennan, *Irish Bridget*; Sinke, *Dutch Immigrant Women*; Wehner, "German Domestic Servants in America," 271–73; Matovic, "Embracing a Middle-Class Life," 293.

9. See Wehner, "German Domestic Servants in America," 290; Lynch-Brennan, *Irish Bridget*; Hotten-Somers, "Relinquishing and Reclaiming Independence," 238; and Diner, *Erin's Daughters in America*, 94.

10. See, for example, Astrid Henning Oral History Interview, Della McGovern Oral History Interview, and Catherine Leddie Oral History Interview, in New York City Immigrant Labor Project; and Lillian Amundsen Oral History Interview, Lisa Nelson Oral History Interview, Elizabeth Dalbey Oral History Interview, Ellen Brady Oral History Interview, Margaret Convery Horan Oral History Interview, and Mary Margaret Mullins Gordon Oral History Interview, in Ellis Island Oral History Collection.

11. A. E. Johnson Employment Registry Book.

12. Historians of working women have emphasized the importance of looking past masculine definitions of class consciousness, including focusing solely on unions and strikes, when examining women's paid labor. Sharon Harley defines working-class consciousness as simply "the expression of shared interests and the articulation of work-related concerns." Historian Nan Enstad argues that scholarly focus on unionism as evidence of worker identity "reifies historically constructed notions of who and what can be recognized as political," based on "nineteenth century divisions between public and private." Carole Turbin also warns against assuming that women's "temporary" status in the workforce denoted a lack of commitment to their occupation or to their class. Harley, "When Your Work Is Not Who You Are," 43; Enstad, *Ladies of Labor, Girls of Adventure*, 121, 88; Turbin, *Working Women of Collar City*, 73.

13. Katzman places the average hours of domestic service at twelve to fifteen per day. Katzman, *Seven Days a Week*, 112–16.

14. Arnold Schrier figures remittances from Irish workers in the United States, many of whom worked in domestic service, to their families in Ireland at $5 million per year by the 1890s. See Schrier, *Ireland and the American Emigration*; and Diner, *Erin's Daughters in America*.

15. Katzman, *Seven Days a Week*, 312.

16. See Kessler-Harris, *Out to Work*, 78–79.

17. Rembiénska, "A Polish Peasant Girl in America," 118.

18. "A Servant Girl's Letter," 36.

19. Rembiénska, "A Polish Peasant Girl in America," 118, 120.

20. "Defense of Servant Girls."

21. Lillian Amundsen Oral History Interview, Ellis Island Oral History Collection.

22. Aili Howard Oral History Interview, ibid. See also Salmon, *Domestic Service*, 146n1.

23. "Trials of a Governess."

24. See Kellor, *Out of Work*. See also "Why There Is a Servant Question," 5; McArdell, "Help! Help! Help!," 483; and Comstock, "Mistress Problem," 15.

25. Kellor, "Intelligence Office," 459.

26. Salmon, *Domestic Service*, 147n2.

27. Ibid.

28. Ibid.

29. "The Servant Girl Question: Miss M. C. Jones in the Pittsburgh Dispatch."

30. Salmon, *Domestic Service*, 147n2.

31. Kellor, *Out of Work*, 147.

32. Ibid.

33. "Trials of a Governess."

34. Agnes M., "True Life Story of a Nurse Girl," 2263.

35. Astrid Henning Oral History Interview, New York City Immigrant Labor Project.

36. Ibid.

37. Ibid.

38. Ibid.

39. Ibid.

40. "Card from Servant Girls."

41. Ibid.

42. Ibid.

43. Rose, "White Woman's Burden."

44. See "Kitchen Autocrats Stirred Up"; and "No Union for Servant Girls."

45. For a chart depicting various attempts at unionization of household workers in the United States, see Christiansen, "Making of a Civil Rights Union," 77–82. Tera Hunter discusses African American washerwomen's attempts, in the face of white opposition, to organize a union in 1880s Atlanta. Hunter, *To 'Joy My Freedom*, esp. chap. 4. See also Foner, *Women and the American Labor Movement*, 241–43; Van Raaphorst, *Union Maids Not Wanted*, chap. 7; and Katzman, *Seven Days a Week*, 234–35. The Women's International Label League in Chicago was able to organize about 300 household workers in 1901. Their demands included a ban on work before 5:30 A.M., union procedures for settling grievances with employers, union wages, the right to receive male callers, and time off on Mondays for shopping at sale counters. By the end of the year, however, attendance at union meetings had dwindled to between eight and twelve members and the union attempt had fizzled. See "Plans a Union of Housemaids"; "Working Women Organize"; "Servant Girls Make Rules," 1; "Union Maid the Kitchen Queen," 1; "The Servant Girl's Union"; "The Union Servant Girl," 3; and "Maids' Union Is Dying." See also Sutherland, *Americans and Their Servants*, 133–37.

46. "No Union for Servant Girls."

47. Murolo, *Common Ground of Womanhood*, 12.

48. See Hood, "Subways, Transit Politics, and Metropolitan Spatial Expansion," 191–212; and Kenneth T. Jackson, *Crabgrass Frontier*, 20–44.

49. "Domestic Service," 7.

50. "Kitchen versus Slop Shop," 12.

51. See Hood, "Subways, Transit Politics, and Metropolitan Spatial Expansion," 191–212; and Kenneth T. Jackson, *Crabgrass Frontier*, 20–44.

52. Lillian Amundsen Oral History Interview, Ellis Island Oral History Collection.

53. Mary Heany Oral History Interview, ibid.

54. Astrid Henning Oral History Interview, New York City Immigrant Labor Project.

55. Mary Condon Oral History Interview, New Yorkers at Work Oral History Collection.

56. See Piess, *Cheap Amusements*, 88–114.

57. Historian Kathy Piess contends that "the relatively isolated nature of [domestics'] labor, its long hours, and task-oriented rhythms did not reinforce a concept of leisure as a separate sphere of social life." Domestics themselves, however, named dancing as their favorite activity on days off. Piess, *Cheap Amusements*, 39.

58. Kamphoefner, Helbich, and Sommer, *News from the Land of Freedom*, 599.

59. Agnes M., "True Life Story of a Nurse Girl," 2263.

60. Ibid., 2265.

61. Grace Eulalie Matthews Ashmore Diary, January 23, 1911, vol. 19, box 3, Grace Eulalie Matthews Ashmore Papers.

62. Mary Heany Oral History Interview, Ellis Island Oral History Collection.

63. Ann Kelly Craven Oral History Interview, ibid.

64. Lillian Amundsen Oral History Interview, ibid.

65. Kamphoefner, Helbich, and Sommer, *News from the Land of Freedom*, 595.

66. Ibid., 599.

67. Patricia Kelleher makes this argument for Chicago. Kelleher, "Young Irish Workers," 198. Sarah Deutsch has also noted that live-in domestics created a community that "overlay spatially" that of their employers. Deutsch, *Women and the City*, 19.

68. Our Lady of the Rosary Home for Immigrant Girls Registry Book, 1906–7; U.S. Bureau of the Census, *Thirteenth Census*.

69. U.S. Bureau of the Census, *Thirteenth Census*. Kelleher presents a similar analysis for domestic workers in Chicago. Kelleher, "Young Irish Workers," 198.

70. *The People v. Bertha Schade*, trial transcript, October 3, 1889, box 370, folder 3471, 2.

71. Lillian Amundsen Oral History Interview, Ellis Island Oral History Collection.

72. Astrid Henning Oral History Interview, New York City Immigrant Labor Project.

73. Kellor, *Out of Work*, 5.

74. Dudden, *Serving Women*, 119; Scobey, *Empire City*, 183; Sutherland, *Americans and Their Servants*, 115.

75. "Card from Servant Girls."

76. Helen D. Brown to Lucy Maynard Salmon, February 10, 1889, box 49, folder 5, Lucy Maynard Salmon Papers.

77. "Days Out," 427.

78. "Servant Girls Extravagant," 5.

79. "The Servant Question."

80. "The Maidservant."

81. "Servant Quest Now."

82. Ibid.

83. Deshon, *Guide for Catholic Young Women*, 69–70.

84. "A Servant Girl for Her Class."

85. "A Sunday Night Stroll."

86. Rembiénska, "A Polish Peasant Girl in America," 118.

87. Ibid., 119.

88. Enstad, *Ladies of Labor, Girls of Adventure*, 10.

89. "A Servant Girl for Her Class."

90. Historian Carl Ross argues that Finnish immigrant women were particularly influenced by the Finnish women's movement and brought its precepts and organizational goals with them to the United States. See Ross, *Finn Factor*; and Ross and Brown, *Women Who Dared*.

91. Seller, *Immigrant Women*, 174.

92. Ibid., 175.

93. Ibid.

94. Ekman, Olli, and Olli, *History of Finnish American Organizations in Greater New York*, 1.

95. "Swedes in Brooklyn."

96. See McDannell, "Going to the Ladies' Fair." Hasia Diner argues that Irish women were less likely than Irish men or women of other ethnicities to form autonomous women's mutual aid organizations. See Diner, *Erin's Daughters in America*, 125.

97. Ann Kelley Craven Oral History Interview, Ellis Island Oral History Collection.

98. Harris, "Come You All Courageously," 177.

99. *Annual Report of the Mission of Our Lady of the Rosary*, 1899, 47.

100. Ibid.

101. McDannell, "Going to the Ladies' Fair," 237.

102. *Annual Report of the Mission of Our Lady of the Rosary*, 1887, 5. See also "Helping Irish Girls."

103. Cusack, *Advice to Irish Girls in America*, 41.

104. Deshon, *Guide for Catholic Young Women*, 203.

105. *The People v. Annie Kane*, statement of Max Schmittberger, September 8, 1880, box 19, folder 248.

106. *The People v. Bertha Schade*, trial transcript, October 3, 1889, 5, box 370, folder 3471.

107. Tera Hunter makes a similar argument about the practice of "pan toting" among African American domestics in Atlanta. Hunter, *To 'Joy My Freedom*, 67.

108. Weatherford, *Foreign and Female*, 253. Daniel Sutherland also discusses domestics buying marked-up goods from grocers and splitting the profits. Sutherland, *Americans and Their Servants*, 64.

109. Weatherford, *Foreign and Female*, 253.

110. Cusack, *Advice to Irish Girls in America*, 98.

111. "Dishonest Servant Arrested."

112. Kamphoefner, Helbich, and Sommer, *News from the Land of Freedom*, 596.

113. "Card from Servant Girls."

114. Astrid Henning Oral History Interview, New York City Immigrant Labor Project.

115. Ibid.

116. Kellor, *Out of Work*, 30.

117. Ibid.

118. Ibid.

119. "Swedes in Brooklyn."

120. *Report of the Commissioner of Licenses*, 1908, 7.

121. Kellor, *Out of Work*, 36.

122. *Report of the Commissioner of Licenses*, 1910, 8.

123. Kellor, *Out of Work*, 35.

124. Ibid.

125. *Report of the Commissioner of Licenses*, 1910, 7.

126. *People v. Mike Horin, Pauline Horin, and Katie Hordi*, trial transcript, June 4, 1912, indictment no. 1831, John Jay case no. 1565, reel 201, frame 1402, John Jay Trial Transcript Collection. This meeting was an unlucky one for Paness, who was then defrauded by Hordi's cousin.

127. Astrid Henning Oral History Interview, New York City Immigrant Labor Project.

128. "Domestic Chaos."

129. Kellor, *Out of Work*, 64.

130. Ibid.

131. "Problem Hard to Solve."

132. Ibid.

133. Kellor, *Out of Work*, 121.

134. Della McGovern Oral History Interview, New York City Immigrant Labor Project.

135. "Irish Servants Are Scarce." Like Irish women, Swedish domestics used networks of friends and family to find new employment when they were out of work or wished to change jobs. See Matovic, "Embracing a Middle-Class Life," 293; and Lintelman, "America Is the Woman's Promised Land."

136. "Problem Hard to Solve."

137. "Why 100,000 Domestics Are Needed Here."

138. Catherine Leddie Oral History Interview, New York City Immigrant Labor Project.

139. Sarah Gillespie Oral History Interview, Ann Walsh Oral History Interview, and Elizabeth Horan Schmid Oral History Interview, in Ellis Island Oral History Collection. Elizabeth Clark-Lewis argues that African American workers also used such word-of-mouth networks to find jobs in early twentieth-century Washington, D.C. Clark-Lewis, *Living-In, Living-Out*.

140. "About Servants in Liveries — and in General."

141. "The Servant Girl Question: Miss M. C. Jones in the Pittsburgh Dispatch."

142. "Servant Girl Question," *Brooklyn Daily Eagle*, March 10, 1897.

143. "More Servant Girl Letters," *Brooklyn Daily Eagle*, March 19, 1897.

144. Lisa Nelson Oral History Interview, Ellis Island Oral History Collection.

145. Arthur von Briesen to Rachel Ellison, June 4, 1914, box 6, folder 7, Arthur von Briesen Papers.

146. "War Prices for Servant Girls." See also Lintelman, "America Is the Woman's Promised Land," 389–90.

147. Grace Eulalie Matthews Ashmore Diary, January 25, 1911, vol. 19, box 3, Grace Eulalie Matthews Ashmore Papers.

148. *People v. Mike Horin, Pauline Horin, and Kate Hordi*, trial transcript, reel 201, frames 1432–33, John Jay Trial Transcript Collection.

149. Henrietta MacLauren Richards Diary, October 6, 1886, vol. 3. See also October 5, 1885, October 7, 1885, January 6, 1886, January 8, 1886, January 15, 1886, May 5, 1886, May 12, 1886, May 18, 1886, October 27, 1886, vol. 4, ibid.

150. Grace Eulalie Matthews Ashmore Diary, October 10, 1907, vol. 16, box 2, Grace Eulalie Matthews Ashmore Papers.

151. October 17, 1907, October 26, 1907, ibid.

152. See, for example, Dudden, *Serving Women*, 232–33; Van Raaphorst, *Union Maids Not Wanted*, chap. 7; and Katzman, *Seven Days a Week*, 234–35.

153. Hasia Diner notes that the demand for domestics allowed them to "set some of the terms of their employment and in essence to 'shop around' for an ideal situation." See Diner, *Erin's Daughters in America*, 85.

154. Rembiénska, "A Polish Peasant Girl in America," 119–20.

155. Aili Howard Oral History Interview, Ellis Island Oral History Collection.

156. Ibid.

157. Astrid Henning Oral History Interview, New York City Immigrant Labor Project.

158. George Bell to Mayor John Mitchel, May 16, 1916, box 48, folder 491, Files of Office of the Mayor, Mitchel Administration.

159. Kamphoefner, Helbich, and Sommer, *News from the Land of Freedom*, 602.

160. Schmitt, *History of the Legal Aid Society*, 1–28.

161. See Regan, Paterson, Goriely, and Fleming, *Transformation of Legal Aid*.

162. Rosalie Leow Whitney, "The Legal Aid Society and Its Work for Households," *Bulletin of the Inter-Municipal Committee on Household Research* (December 1904): 9.

163. Von Briesen, "Servant Problem Involves a Recognition of Rights."

164. McCook, "Judicial Aspect of the Work of the Legal Aid Society," 19.

165. Edward McGuire to Arthur von Briesen, March 19, 1909, box 7, folder 7, Arthur von Briesen Papers.

166. Sarah Mehler to Arthur von Briesen, September 14, 1905, box 7, folder 1, ibid.

167. *Legal Aid Review* 4, no. 1 (January 1906): 5.

168. G. Dexter Richardson to Arthur von Briesen, September 7, 1910, box 6, folder 2, Arthur von Briesen Papers.

169. Edward McGuire to Arthur von Briesen, March 19, 1909, box 7, folder 1, ibid.

170. Arthur von Briesen to Leonard McGee, March 6, 1913, box 6, folder 5, ibid.

171. Leonard McGee to Arthur von Briesen, October 7, 1914, box 6, folder 7, ibid.

172. Claghorn, *Immigrant's Day in Court*, 482.

Chapter Three

1. Godman, "A Nine-Hour Day for Domestic Servants," 397.

2. Klink, "The Housekeeper's Responsibility," 379.

3. See, for example, Mary Roberts Smith, "Domestic Service," 689; Abel, "Training School for Servants," 501; Davis, "Recovery of Family Life," 675; Forsyth, "Seven Times a Servant," 157; and Barker, *Wanted, a Young Woman to Do Housework*, 1.

4. Robb, "Our House in Order," 353; "Is the Home Disappearing?"

5. Tarbell, "Woman and Democracy," 220.

6. "Is the Home Disappearing?"

7. Salmon, *Domestic Service*, 274.

8. Margaret Dreier Robinson, Untitled Speech on the Work of the Municipal League, ca. 1904, Margaret Dreier Robins Papers, reel 8, frame 184, in James, *Papers of the Women's Trade Union League*.

9. Faye Dudden dealt with women's turn-of-the-century reforms only briefly in her conclusion, in which she observes that middle-class reformers' "analyses of the servant problem were not always incisive" and that they "did not always understand that the

stigma" working women attached to domestic service "reflected poor wages, hours, and working conditions." Deutsch argues that although organized women critiqued domestic service's hours and wages, they continued to hail the occupation as "the normative, idealized, and unregulated standard." Other historians have examined individual immigrant women's homes, demonstrating ethnicity's effect on middle-class women's reform efforts. None have connected these diverse reforms to reveal a comprehensive picture of women's domestic labor reform agenda. See Dudden, *Serving Women*, 239; Deutsch, *Women and the City*, 63, 75; Klapper, "Jewish Women and Vocational Education," 113; Sinkoff, "Educating for 'Proper' Jewish Womanhood," 582; and Moloney, "A Transatlantic Reform."

10. See Scott, *Natural Allies*; Kessler-Harris, *Out to Work*, 187; Orleck, *Common Sense and a Little Fire*; Flanagan, *Seeing with Their Hearts*; and Sklar, *Florence Kelley and the Nation's Work*.

11. Scott, *Natural Allies*, 104.

12. Ibid.

13. See Murolo, *Common Ground of Womanhood*.

14. Kessler-Harris, *Out to Work*, 184.

15. Ibid., 187.

16. Woloch, *Muller v. Oregon*, 112.

17. On the consequences of protective labor laws for women workers, see Lehrer, *Origins of Protective Labor Legislation for Women*; Rhode, *Justice and Gender*; Willoughby, "Mothering Labor"; Aldrich and Buchele, *Economics of Comparable Worth*; Aldrich, "Gender Gap in Earnings during World War II"; Baer, *Chains of Protection*; Lipschultz, "Hours and Wages"; and Wikander, Kessler-Harris, and Lewis, *Protecting Women*.

18. Deutsch, *Women and the City*, 56; Kessler-Harris, *Out to Work*; Vapnek, *Breadwinners*, chap. 4; Secretary's Report to the Executive Board, April 16, 1908, reel 1, frame 322, Records of the New York Women's Trade Union League, in James, *Papers of the Women's Trade Union League and Its Principle Leaders*.

19. *Bulletin of the Inter-Municipal Committee on Household Research* (November 1904): 5.

20. Mary White Ovington, "The Colored Woman in Domestic Service in New York City," *Bulletin of the Inter-Municipal Committee on Household Research* (May 1905): 10.

21. "Women and Business." See also "Plague of the Household"; Mary Roberts Smith, "Domestic Service," 686; Bacon, "We and Our Servants," 358; Taylor, "Housework as a Business," 1005; and "Experiences of a 'Hired Girl,'" 780.

22. See Mary Bancroft Smith, *Practical Helps for Housewives*; and Barker, *Wanted, a Young Woman to Do Housework*.

23. See Katzman, *Seven Days a Week*, 135–37, 179–81, 250–53; and Strasser, "Mistress and Maid."

24. "A 'Downtrodden' Mistress."

25. "The Club and the Domestic Problem."

26. Ibid.

27. Stone, *Problem of Domestic Service*, 15. See also "Household Work"; "An Unsettled Question," 60; "Kitchen Autocrats Stirred Up"; "The Club and the Domestic Problem"; Kingsley, "The Maid and the Mistress," 296; "Why Domestic Service Is a Problem," 301; and "The Spectator," 241.

28. Godman, "A Nine-Hour Day for Domestic Servants," 398.

29. *Fifth Annual Report of the Young Women's Christian Association of the City of New York*, 17.

30. "By Women, for Women."

31. Working Women's Protective Union, *Report of Its Condition.*

32. *Annual Report of the Alliance Employment Bureau of the New York Association of Working Girls' Societies.*

33. Murolo, *Common Ground of Womanhood,* 12.

34. See, for example, Vrooman, "Manual Training for Women."

35. Christian Aid to Employment Society, *Annual Report,* 11.

36. West, "Domestic Service," 413.

37. Mary Bancroft Smith, *Practical Helps for Housewives,* 192.

38. "Training Girls for Servants." The *New York Times* report quotes from the *Tenth Annual Report for the Shelter for Respectable Girls and Servants' Training-House for Young Girls* and notes that it was run by the Episcopal Church of the Holy Communion.

39. "A Home for Working Girls."

40. "Tiring of Factory Life."

41. "Its Care of Servants."

42. Secretary's Report to the Executive Board, April 16, 1908, Records of the New York Women's Trade Union League, reel 1, frame 322, in James, *Papers of the Women's Trade Union League.*

43. *Twenty-fourth Annual Report of the Wilson Industrial School for Girls (and Mission) for the Year Ending December 31, 1876* (New York, 1877), box 1, folder 2, Records of the Goddard-Riverside Community Center; *Thirty-third Annual Report of the Wilson Industrial School for Girls (and Mission) for the Year Ending December 31, 1885* (New York, 1886), 10, box 1, folder 4, ibid.

44. Huntington, *Little Lessons for Little Housekeepers; Twenty-third Annual Report of the Wilson Industrial School and Mission for the Year Ending December 31, 1875* (New York, 1876), 5, box 1, folder 2, Records of the Goddard-Riverside Community Center.

45. *Twenty-sixth Annual Report of the Wilson Industrial School for Girls (and Mission) for the Year Ending December 31, 1878* (New York, 1879), 7, box 1, folder 3, Records of the Goddard-Riverside Community Center.

46. *Thirty-second Annual Report of the Wilson Industrial School for Girls (and Mission) for the Year Ending December 31, 1884* (New York, 1885), 11, box 1, folder 4, ibid.

47. *Nineteenth Annual Report of the Wilson Industrial School and Mission for the Year Ending December 31, 1871* (New York, 1872), 18, box 1, folder 1, ibid.

48. Ibid.

49. Ibid.; *Twenty-seventh Annual Report of the Wilson Industrial School for Girls (and Mission) for the Year Ending December 31, 1879* (New York: Sears & Cole, Stationers and Printers, 1880), 6, box 1, folder 3, ibid.

50. "Kitchen-Garden."

51. Ibid.

52. "The Servants' Side."

53. *Report of the Commissioner of Licenses,* 1913, 10.

54. "Girls for Domestic Service," *New York Times,* January 9, 1879, 8.

55. *Twenty-fourth Annual Report of the Wilson Industrial School for Girls (and Mission) for the Year Ending December 31, 1876* (New York, 1877), 5, box 1, folder 2, Records of the Goddard-Riverside Community Center.

56. *Forty-third Annual Report of the Wilson Industrial School for Girls (and Mission) for the Year Ending December 31, 1895* (New York, 1896), 8, box 1, folder 6, ibid.

57. *Fifty-eighth Annual Report of the Wilson Industrial School for Girls for the Year Ending December 31, 1910* (New York, 1911), 6, box 1, folder 7, ibid.

58. *Sixty-second Annual Report of the Wilson Industrial School for Girls for the Year Ending December 31, 1914* (New York, 1915), box 1, folder 8, ibid.

59. National Council of Catholic Women, *Directory of Boarding Homes*. Various other ethnic and religious groups established their own homes. Historian Deirdre Moloney reports that in Boston fifteen different organizations had agents on the wharf to meet incoming immigrants. Moloney, "A Transatlantic Reform," 55.

60. "City Missionary Work."

61. "Not Enough 'Green Girls.'" "Green girls" were in particular demand because they provided middle-class women with cheap labor. Employers regularly paid new immigrant workers less than the going rate, based on their lack of experience. See, for example, McCulloch-Williams, "Logic of the Servant Problem"; and Ramsey, "How a Bride Can Train a Cook."

62. "To Found a Training School"; *Bulletin of the Inter-Municipal Committee on Household Research* (December 1904): 11.

63. "Not Enough 'Green Girls.'"

64. Ibid.

65. "To Found a Training School."

66. Untitled Proposal for a Domestic Training School, Margaret Dreier Robins Papers, reel 8, frame 160, in James, *Papers of the Women's Trade Union League*.

67. *Bulletin of the Inter-Municipal Committee on Household Research* (February 1905): 6.

68. *Annual Report of the Mission of Our Lady of the Rosary*, 1887, 13.

69. *Annual Report of Our Lady of the Rosary of the City of New York*, 1891, 14.

70. *Annual Report of the Mission of Our Lady of the Rosary*, 1885, 6.

71. Ibid., 1887.

72. *Annual Report of Our Lady of the Rosary of the City of New York*, 1905, 4.

73. Ibid., 1891, 8.

74. Rose Sommerfeld, "Twenty-five Years in the Clara De Hirsch Home for Working Girls," 1924, box 3, folder 22, Records of the Clara de Hirsch Home for Working Girls. See also *Yearbook New York Section Council of Jewish Women*, 1906–7, box 139, Records of the National Council of Jewish Women.

75. Report to the President and Members of the Board of the Clara De Hirsch Home for Working Girls, January 24, 1900, 16, box 1, folder 3, Records of the Clara de Hirsch Home for Working Girls.

76. *Bulletin of the Inter-Municipal Committee on Household Research* (February 1905): 11.

77. Report of the Clara de Hirsch Home for Immigrant Girls, 1904–10, 8, box 4, folder 14, Records of the Clara de Hirsch Home for Working Girls.

78. President's Report to the Officers and Directors of the Clara de Hirsch Home for Working Girls, in Minutes of Member Meetings, dated January 24, 1900, 9, box 1, folder 3, ibid.

79. Report of the Clara de Hirsch Home for Immigrant Girls, 1904–10, 6, box 4, folder 14, ibid.

80. Ibid.

81. Ibid.

82. Ibid.

83. Report of the Clara de Hirsch Home for Immigrant Girls, 1914, 5, box 4, folder 13, ibid.

84. Report of the Clara de Hirsch Home for Immigrant Girls, 1904–10, 4, ibid.

85. Ibid., 5.

86. Sinkoff, "Educating for 'Proper' Jewish Womanhood," 576.

87. White Rose Industrial Association Working Girls Home Pamphlet, ca. 1918, Records of the White Rose Mission and Industrial Society; Report of the White Rose Home, Summer 1906, 1, ibid. The White Rose Mission lived up to its advertising—its constitution allowed no more than three white people on the Board of Directors. See Constitution of the White Rose Mission and Industrial Association, ibid.

88. Report of the White Rose Home, Summer 1906, 1, ibid.

89. White Rose Industrial Association Working Girls Home Pamphlet, ca. 1918, ibid.

90. White Rose Mission Settlement description of work, n.d., ibid.; White Rose Industrial Association Working Girls Home Pamphlet, ca. 1918, ibid.

91. Report of the White Rose Home, Summer 1906, 1, ibid. In its first three months, the mission sheltered over 100 women. In 1918, the administrators reported an average of seven lodgers per day, with 237 total for the year. In 1920, administrators still averaged seven lodgers per day and helped 130 find work. Report of the White Rose Home, Summer 1906, ibid., 2; White Rose Industrial Association Working Girls Home Pamphlet, ca. 1918, ibid.; "White Rose Industrial Association, An Appeal to Our Friends," 1920, ibid.

92. Report of the White Rose Home, Summer 1906, 2, ibid.

93. Ibid.

94. Ibid.

95. White Rose Mission Settlement description of work, n.d., 2, ibid.; White Rose Industrial Association Working Girls Home Pamphlet, ca. 1918, ibid.

96. This reform agenda placed the White Rose Mission squarely within the context of other middle-class black women's reforms in the late nineteenth and early twentieth centuries. See White, *Too Heavy a Load*; and Gilmore, *Gender and Jim Crow*.

97. White Rose Industrial Association Working Girls Home pamphlet, ca. 1918, Records of the White Rose Mission and Industrial Society.

98. See Higginbotham, *Righteous Discontent*, esp. 185–229; White, *Too Heavy a Load*, esp. 68–78; and Guy-Sheftall, *Daughters of Sorrow*.

99. Constitution of the White Rose Mission and Industrial Association, 1, Records of the White Rose Mission and Industrial Society.

100. White Rose Mission Settlement description of work, 2, ibid.

101. Report of the White Rose Home, Summer 1906, 3, ibid.

102. White Rose Industrial Association Working Girls Home Pamphlet, ca. 1918, ibid.; Report of the White Rose Home, Summer 1906, 1, ibid.

103. Partial History of White Rose Mission and Industrial Association, n.d., ibid.; White Rose Mission Settlement description of work, n.d., 1, ibid.

104. See "A Rebuttal by Margaret Dreier to Commissioner Keating," ca. 1904, Margaret Dreier Robins Papers, reel 8, frame 167, in James, *Papers of the Women's Trade Union League*; Draft Annual Report of the Inter-Municipal Committee on Household Research, n.d., 10, box 49, folder 10, Lucy Maynard Salmon Papers; *Bulletin of the Inter-Municipal Committee on Household Research* (May 1905): 2.

105. "Irish Servants Are Scarce." See also Diner, *Erin's Daughters in America*, 80–94.

106. Sinkoff, "Educating for 'Proper' Jewish Womanhood," 585.

107. Report of the Clara de Hirsch Home for Immigrant Girls, 1904–10, 6, box 4, folder 14, Records of the Clara de Hirsch Home for Working Girls.

108. Ibid., 5.

109. "White Rose Industrial Association, An Appeal to Our Friends," 1920, Records of the White Rose Mission and Industrial Society.

110. Scholars of immigrant homes have given various explanations for the insistence on domestic work as the best occupational path for new immigrants. Melissa Klapper argues that the Clara de Hirsch Home represented an effort by Jewish middle-class women to "reconcile the American middle-class ideology of feminine domesticity with the need among poor immigrant women to earn a living." Nancy Sinkoff argues for a "complex interplay of self-interest, social control, and sisterhood." Deirdre Moloney argues that immigrant homes for Irish women in Boston constituted an effort to control immigrants' sexual behavior and to protect them from the threat of "white slavery." These works offer engaging analyses of various ethnic reform efforts, but they do not look at immigrant homes as a group nor as a part of a larger effort to reform domestic service. See Klapper, "Jewish Women and Vocational Education in New York City, 1885–1925," 113; Sinkoff, "Educating for 'Proper' Jewish Womanhood," 582; and Moloney, "A Transatlantic Reform," 50–66.

111. *Ladies' Protective Union and Directory*, 3.

112. Christian Aid Association, *Annual Report*.

113. Untitled Proposal for a Domestic Training School, n.d., Margaret Dreier Robins Papers, reel 8, frame 154, in James, *Papers of the Women's Trade Union League*.

114. *Ladies' Protective Union and Directory*, 3–4.

115. Christian Aid to Employment Society, *Annual Report*, 5.

116. *Bulletin of the Inter-Municipal Committee on Household Research* (December 1904): 11.

117. Ibid.

118. *Bulletin of the Inter-Municipal Committee on Household Research* (February 1905): 11.

119. "Golden Rule Club."

120. Fitzpatrick, *Endless Crusade*, 17.

121. "Bills Passed in Albany"; Cumming, Potter, and Gilbert, *Constitution of the State of New York*; Hoxie, *Civics for New York State New York*; U.S. Bureau of the Census, *Twelfth Census*, 430–33.

122. Kellor, *Out of Work*, 150.

123. "Employment Office Evils."

124. Fitzpatrick, *Endless Crusade*, 138.

125. Minutes of the Regular Monthly Meeting of the Board of Directors, April 24, 1898, 41, box 1, folder 1, Records of the Clara de Hirsch Home for Working Girls; Minutes of the Regular Monthly Meeting of the Board of Directors, December 16, 1904, 168, ibid.; Minutes of the Regular Monthly Meeting of the Board of Directors, January 20, 1905, 170, ibid.; Minutes of the Regular Monthly Meeting of the Board of Directors, February 17, 1905, 173, ibid.; Minute Book of the Prospect Heights Division of the Woman's Municipal League, April 13, 1905, box T-2, Records of the Citizens Union.

126. John N. Bogart to Mayor George B. McClellan, March 19, 1906, box 45, folder 455, Files of Office of the Mayor, McClellan Administration; Frances Kellor, Untitled Statement, n.d., Margaret Dreier Robins Papers, reel 8, frames 101–26, in James, *Papers of the Women's Trade Union League*.

127. *Bulletin of the Inter-Municipal Committee on Household Research* (November 1904): 1. On the Women's Educational and Industrial Union in Boston, see Vapnek, *Breadwinners*, chap. 4; and Deutsch, *Women and the City*.

128. *Bulletin of the Inter-Municipal Committee on Household Research* (November 1904): 1.

129. Draft Inter-Municipal Committee on Household Research First Annual Report, n.d., 3, box 49, folder 10, Lucy Maynard Salmon Papers.

130. Ibid., 2.

131. *Bulletin of the Inter-Municipal Committee on Household Research* (March 1905): 3

132. Kellor, *Out of Work*, 45, 88.

133. *Report of the Commissioner of Licenses*, 1907, 7.

134. Draft Inter-Municipal Committee on Household Research First Annual Report, n.d., 18, box 49, folder 10, Lucy Maynard Salmon Papers. Some scholars have taken Kellor to task, arguing that she viewed African American women as a scourge on the city. Hazel Carby has written that Kellor defined "black female urban behavior . . . as pathological." More recently, Marcy Sacks has argued that Kellor viewed African American women as particularly responsible for bringing prostitution and other urban problems to New York City, writing that Kellor's employment agency reform was informed by her "opposition to the growth of New York's black population." Kellor shared the prejudices of many of her contemporaries, but she was also a racial liberal and one of the founders of the Urban League. Kellor may have seen African American women as particularly naive but not necessarily as inherently promiscuous. Furthermore, Kellor, like other reformers, viewed the "servant problem" as one that mostly affected European immigrants and their white middle-class employers. See Carby, "Policing the Black Woman's Body in an Urban Context," 740; and Sacks, *Before Harlem*, 24.

135. See Odem, *Delinquent Daughters*.

136. *Report of the Commissioner of Licenses*, 1909, 4.

137. Herman Robinson to Hon. William J. Gaynor, October 3, 1911, box 38, folder 324, Files of Office of the Mayor, Gaynor Administration.

138. George H. Bell to Sophie J. Laux, July 7, 1915, box 47, folder 485, Files of Office of the Mayor, Mitchel Administration; E. Kaufmann to B de N Creuger, October 14, 1915, box 38, folder 324, ibid.; E. Kaufmann to Samuel Martin, November 25, 1916, box 48, folder 493, ibid.

139. *Report of the Commissioner of Licenses*, 1906, 1. In other years, the commissioner reported similar figures. In 1909, the commissioner reported having refunded $3,243.56 to employees of a total $4,029.45 recovered from employment agents. In 1910, he reported refunding $3,204.50 to employees out of a total $3,763.35 in fees. See ibid., 1909, 16; and ibid., 1910, 19.

140. Ibid., 1912, 11.

141. Complaint against Pauline A. Neinchil, March 3, 1911, box 38, folder 324, Files of Office of the Mayor, Gaynor Administration. Unfortunately, the records of the Office of Commissioner of Licenses have been lost, and it is impossible to tell how often employers, as compared to employees, used this office to air grievances. Employers, however, were more likely to complain to the mayor if they did not like the result.

142. Hearing transcript, March 8, 1907, box 45, folder 456, Files of Office of the Mayor, McClellan Administration.

143. "Employment Office Evils."

144. Ernest L. Williams to Margaret Chanler, March 25, 1904, Margaret Dreier Robins Papers, reel 8, frames 637–58, in James, *Papers of the Women's Trade Union League*.

145. "Keating, Solomon, of New York Employment Agencies."

146. Kellor asserted that more than two-thirds of New York intelligence offices were "owned or managed by women." Kellor, *Out of Work*, 35.

147. "Commissioner Keating Names His Inspectors."

148. Kellor, *Out of Work*.

149. Ibid.

150. Kellor, Untitled Document, n.d., Margaret Dreier Robins Papers, reel 8, frame 45, in James, *Papers of the Women's Trade Union League*.

151. Frances Kellor, Untitled Statement, n.d., Margaret Dreier Robins Papers, reel 8, frame 107, ibid.

152. Kellor, *Out of Work*, 24. See also Frances Kellor, Untitled Statement, n.d., Margaret Dreier Robins Papers, reel 8, frames 110–12, 125, in James, *Papers of the Women's Trade Union League*.

153. Margaret Dreier, Untitled Statement, n.d., Margaret Dreier Robins Papers, reel 8, frame 168, in James, *Papers of the Women's Trade Union League*.

154. *Report of the Commissioner of Licenses*, 1910, 7; Kellor, *Out of Work*, 30.

155. Kellor, *Out of Work*, 23.

156. Fitzpatrick, *Endless Crusade*, 135, 207–9.

Chapter Four

1. Evelyn Seely, "Our Feudal Housewives," 614.

2. "Housewives Want No Servants' Union."

3. Ibid.; Evelyn Seely, "Our Feudal Housewives," 614.

4. See Gordon, *Pitied but Not Entitled*.

5. See Storrs, *Civilizing Capitalism*; Gordon, *Pitied but Not Entitled*; and Boris, *Home to Work*.

6. See Cott, *Grounding of Modern Feminism*, 83–114; and Schuyler, *Weight of Their Votes*.

7. Deutsch, *Women and the City*, 219–83.

8. See ibid., 138–63; Ingalls, "New York and the Minimum-Wage Movement"; Storrs, *Civilizing Capitalism*, 46–59, 178–84; and Cott, *Grounding of Modern Feminism*, 117–42.

9. "Miss Swartz Takes a Stand," *1926–1927 Quarterly Report*, reel 24, frames 8–9, in Scott and Perry, *Grassroots Women's Organizations*.

10. The Progressive women's groups I examine in this chapter—the YWCA, the Consumers' League of New York, the New York Women's City Club, the WTUL, and the League of Women Voters—all opposed the ERA because they worried it would nullify protective labor legislation. See, for example, Browder, "Christian Solution of the Labor Situation"; Heath, "Negotiating White Womanhood," 90; Sharer, *Vote and Voice*, 158; Cott, *Grounding of Modern Feminism*, 123–24, 126–29; Young, *In the Public Interest*, 110; Perry, "Women's Political Choices after Suffrage," 421–22; and Reginald Wilson, "Women Clash at Hearing on 48-Hour Bill," February 25, 1925, reel 20, frame 467; "Women Urge Passage of the 48-Hour Week Bill in State," *New York Commercial*, March 11, 1925, reel 20, frames 467–68; "Miss Swartz Takes a Stand," *1926–1927 Quarterly Report*, reel 24, frames 8–9; Report of the Executive Secretary, February 1933, 5, reel 4, frame 167; Civic Secretary Report, January 1937, 6, reel 4, frame 590; Board of Directors Meeting, June 3, 1936,

4, reel 4, frame 535; Report of Executive Director, January 1936, 6, reel 4, frame 487; and Board of Directors Meeting, December 1, 1937, 1, reel 4, frame 652, all in Scott and Perry, *Grassroots Women's Organizations*, 11. See also Cott, *Grounding of Modern Feminism*, 117–42; and Butler, *Two Paths to Equality*.

11. See Cott, *The Grounding of Modern Feminism*, 117–42; and Butler, *Two Paths to Equality*.

12. See Gordon, *Pitied but Not Entitled*, 87–108; Orleck, *Common Sense and a Little Fire*, 138; Storrs, *Civilizing Capitalism*, 39; and Muncy, *Creating a Female Dominion*.

13. Orleck, *Common Sense and a Little Fire*, 162–63.

14. Deutsch, *Women and the City*, 220–56.

15. Report of the President, May 1938, 1, reel 1, frame 518, in Scott and Perry, *Grassroots Women's Organizations*.

16. Quoted in Storrs, *Civilizing Capitalism*, 34.

17. See Kessler-Harris, *In Pursuit of Equity*, 105–16; Storrs, *Civilizing Capitalism*, 196–205; and Mettler, *Dividing Citizens*, 203–6.

18. See Daniels, *Guarding the Golden Door*.

19. Kessler-Harris, *Out to Work*, 116, 227.

20. Marsh, *Suburban Lives*, 135–47. See also Kenneth T. Jackson, *Crabgrass Frontier*, 172–90.

21. Haynes, *Negro at Work*, 63. See also Sacks, *Before Harlem*, 112.

22. U.S. Bureau of the Census, *Twelfth Census*, Census Reports, vol. 1, Population, pt. 1, 594.

23. Du Bois, *The Philadelphia Negro*, 467. Tera Hunter confirms that blacks "were relegated to the bottom of the labor market in the 'plainer establishments.'" Hunter, "'Brotherly Love' for Which This City Is Proverbial Should Extend to All," 80. See also Vapnek, *Breadwinners*, 108.

24. Lemann, *Promised Land*, 6.

25. Clark-Lewis, *Living-In, Living-Out*, chap. 2.

26. Katzman, *Seven Days a Week*, 293.

27. Ovington, *Half a Man*, 147.

28. Greenberg, *Or Does It Explode*, 44.

29. *Report of the Department of Licenses*, 1922, 18.

30. U.S. Bureau of the Census, *Fifteenth Census*, vol. 3, pt. 2, 265–79.

31. On the move from live-in to live-out work, see Clark-Lewis, *Living-In, Living-Out*.

32. Marsh, *Suburban Lives*, 105.

33. Ruth Cowan makes this argument for housewives, although I would argue she underestimates the number of servants in middle-class homes. Cowan, *More Work for Mother*. See also Palmer, *Domesticity and Dirt*, 47–52.

34. See Palmer, *Domesticity and Dirt*, chaps. 2 and 3.

35. Blanche Bell to Frances Perkins, August 7, 1933, box 289, Division of Research, Unpublished Materials, 1919–72, Domestic Workers Household Employment, Records of the Women's Bureau.

36. Evelyn Stretch to Franklin Delano Roosevelt, July 25, 1933, ibid.

37. May Donath to Frances Perkins, February 17, 1934, box 290, ibid.

38. Margaret Hudson, Helen Bosak, Hattie McMillan, Irene Bosak, Agatha Miklas, Kathleen Moody, and Kady Micska to Eleanor Roosevelt, July 24, 1937, box 291, ibid.

39. Browder, "Christian Solution of the Labor Situation"; Heath, "Negotiating White Womanhood," 90.

40. Young Women's Christian Associations, U.S. National Board, *Commission on Household Employment*, 4.

41. Ibid., 33.

42. Ibid.

43. Ibid., 19.

44. Ibid.

45. Minutes of Meeting of the National Committee [*sic*] on Household Employment, February 16, 1939, 1, part I, series IV, box 5, Records of the National Urban League; Dudden, "Experts and Servants."

46. See, for example, Erna Magnus, "The Coverage of Domestic Servants (Household Employees) by Social Insurance," September 30, 1939, box 1, folder 3, National Council on Household Employment Records.

47. Code of Ethics, n.d., box 3, folder 18, ibid.

48. Sergel, *Women in the House*, 59, 83.

49. Benjamin R. Andrews to Martha Ines Baum, 1–2, box 1, folder 28, National Council on Household Employment Records.

50. "Resolutions No. 51 and 52 adopted by Seventh Biennial Convention, National Women's Trade Union League of America," 1919, National Women's Trade Union League Papers, reel 2, frames 440–41, in James, *Papers of the Women's Trade Union League*.

51. Ibid.

52. For the scholarly debate over the WTUL and elitism, see Dye, *As Equals and as Sisters*, 4; and Orleck, *Common Sense and a Little Fire*, 129.

53. See Palmer, "Outside the Law."

54. See Orleck, *Common Sense and a Little Fire*, 129.

55. Hedgeman, *The Trumpet Sounds*, 37.

56. On working-class activism within the YWCA, see Browder, " From Uplift to Agitation" and "Christian Solution of the Labor Situation."

57. Scholars disagree about how much organizing the WTUL pursued in the 1930s; see Dye, *As Equals and as Sisters*, 4; and Orleck, *Common Sense and a Little Fire*, 161.

58. Minutes of the Special Committee on Organizers in Training, March 1, 1938, Records of the New York Women's Trade Union League, reel 4, frame 278, in James, *Papers of the Women's Trade Union League*.

59. Minutes of the Executive Board Meeting, January 3, 1939, Records of the New York Women's Trade Union League, reel 4, frame 414, ibid. Benson Ellis, a researcher for the city's Department of Investigation, harshly criticized the league for not offering financial support to the Domestic Workers Union. See Ellis, *A Socio-economic Study of the Female Domestic Worker in Private Homes*, 69–70.

60. For instances in which WTUL members solicited the opinion of the Domestic Workers Union, see Minutes of the Legislative Committee, December 13, 1939, reel 4, frame 529, Records of the New York Women's Trade Union League, in James, *Papers of the Women's Trade Union League*; and Minutes of the Legislative Committee, February 14, 1938, reel 4, frame 263, ibid.

61. Lula Jane Cotter to Franklin Delano Roosevelt, April 30, 1936, frames 535–37, National Women's Trade Union League Papers, ibid.

62. Elisabeth Christman to Lula Jane Cotter, June 1, 1936, reel 2, frame 540, National Women's Trade Union League Papers, ibid.

63. See Orleck, *Common Sense and a Little Fire*; and Dye, *As Equals and as Sisters*.

64. See Dawley, *Struggles for Justice*; and Rodgers, *Atlantic Crossings*.

65. Mintz and Kellogg, *Domestic Revolutions*; May, *Homeward Bound*, 41–42.

66. Gertrude Ebert to Franklin Delano Roosevelt, May 29, 1933, box 289, Division of Research, Unpublished Materials, 1919–72, Domestic Workers Household Employment, Records of the Women's Bureau.

67. Mrs. Lillye Mehlinger Coleman to Frances Perkins, December 14, 1933, ibid.

68. Anna Cose to Frances Perkins, August 21, 1933, ibid.

69. Leadership Division, National Board of the YWCA, "Brief on Household Employment in Relation to Trade Union Organization," 1938, National Women's Trade Union League Papers, reel 2, frame 590, in James, *Papers of the Women's Trade Union League*.

70. "Placement Problems of Household Employees," n.d., 1, Young Women's Christian Association of the USA, National Board, Records, 1876–1970.

71. "Do Servants Need a Code?," 36.

72. Anonymous to Frances Perkins, September 7, 1933, box 289, Division of Research, Unpublished Materials, 1919–72, Domestic Workers Household Employment, Records of the Women's Bureau.

73. DJ to Eleanor Roosevelt, December 27, 1933, ibid.

74. Julia Mauer to Eleanor Roosevelt, June 10, 1938, box 292, ibid.

75. Cora Coker Interview, New York City Immigrant Labor Project.

76. Cora Coker Interview index, ibid.

77. Bessie O'Banyon Interview, tape 191, side B, ibid.

78. Gray, *Black Female Domestics*, 156.

79. See Evelyn Seely, "Our Feudal Housewives," 613.

80. Offord, "Slave Markets in the Bronx," June 29, 1940, 780.

81. Jacqueline Jones, *Labor of Love, Labor of Sorrow*, 205.

82. Confidential Report of the Committee on Street Corner Markets to Frieda S. Miller, Industrial Commissioner, State of New York, May 15, 1940, reel 228, frame 2378, Papers of Mayor Fiorello LaGuardia.

83. Minutes of Committee on Extending Labor Law Protection to All Workers, 80, October 31, 1938, box 12, folder 178, Clara Mortenson Beyer Papers.

84. Baker and Cooke, "Bronx Slave Market," 330.

85. See, for example, Marvell Cooke, "Bronx Slave Market: 'Paper Bag Brigade' Learns How to Deal with Gypping Employers," *Daily Compass*, January 10, 1930, Schomburg Center for Research in Black Culture, Clipping File, 1925–74, Subject: Domestic Workers; Garfield, "An Afternoon on the Auction Block"; Cooke, "Modern Slaves"; "Discovered: A Modern Slave Block," 5; "Slave Markets"; Cooke, "Bronx Slave Market Flourishes"; Jeffries, "New York Slave Markets"; Cooke, "Bronx Slave Market as Active as Ever"; Mitchell, "Slave Markets Typify Exploitation of Domestics"; Offord, "Slave Markets in the Bronx," June 29, 1940, 780; Tom O'Connor, "Maid Wanted: Eight Cents an Hour Offered," *PM*, January 15, 1941, 14, box 4, folder 14, National Council on Household Employment Records; Tom O'Connor, "Negro Domestics Earn Pittance in 'Slave Markets,'" *PM*, January 16, 1941, 14–15, ibid.; Marvell Cooke, "I Was a Part of the Bronx Slave Market," *Daily Compass*, January 8, 1950, Schomburg Center for Research in Black Culture, Clipping File, 1925–74, Subject: Domestic Workers; Marvell Cooke, "Bronx Slave Market, Where Men Prowl and Women Prey on Needy Job-Seekers," *Daily Compass*, January 9, 1950, ibid.; Marvell Cooke, "Some Ways to Kill the Slave Market," *Daily Compass*, January 12, 1950, ibid.

86. Mayor Fiorello LaGuardia to Charlotte E. Carr, May 7, 1937, reel 114, frame 2807, Papers of Mayor Fiorello LaGuardia. Interestingly, the subject line of this letter reads "Re: *Alleged* Slave Market for Negro Domestic Workers" (emphasis added).

87. Ibid.

88. Minutes of Conference on Street-Corner Markets for Domestic Workers Held in Commissioner Miller's Office, December 18, 1939, reel 228, frame 2378, Papers of Mayor Fiorello LaGuardia; Offord, "Slave Markets in the Bronx," June 29, 1940.

89. An early Conference on Street-Corner Markets also hosted members of the Urban League, the Domestic Workers Union, the National Association for the Advancement of Colored People, the New York State Employment Service, the city's welfare office, and the Works Program Administration household training program. See Minutes of Conference on Street-Corner Markets for Domestic Workers Held in Commissioner Miller's Office, December 18, 1939, reel 228, frames 2208–10, Papers of Mayor Fiorello LaGuardia.

90. Charlotte Carr to Mayor LaGuardia, April 5, 1937, reel 114, frame 2808, ibid.

91. Confidential Report of the Committee on Street Corner Markets to Frieda S. Miller, Industrial Commissioner, State of New York, May 15, 1940, reel 228, frame 2377, ibid.

92. Minutes of the Committee on Extending Labor Law Protection to All Workers, 80, October 31, 1938, box 12, folder 178, Clara Mortenson Beyer Papers.

93. Confidential Report of the Committee on Street Corner Markets to Frieda S. Miller, Industrial Commissioner, State of New York, May 15, 1940, reel 228, frame 2377, Papers of Mayor Fiorello LaGuardia.

94. Minutes of the Sub-committee Meeting of the Committee on Street Corner Markets, August 20, 1941, 1, box 3, folder 20, National Council on Household Employment Records.

95. O'Connor, "Negro Domestics Earn Pittance in 'Slave Markets.'"

96. Cooke, "Slavery . . . 1939 Style."

97. Offord, "Slave Markets in the Bronx," June 29, 1940.

98. Confidential Report of the Committee on Street Corner Markets to Frieda S. Miller, Industrial Commissioner, State of New York, May 15, 1940, reel 228, frame 2388, Papers of Mayor Fiorello LaGuardia.

99. Minutes of the Sub-committee Meeting of the Committee on Street Corner Markets, August 20, 1941, 1, box 3, folder 20, National Council on Household Employment Records. See also Mettler, *Dividing Citizens*, 203–4.

100. "Free Neighborhood Job Centers" flyer, n.d., reel 228, frame 2663, Papers of Mayor Fiorello LaGuardia.

101. Ibid.

102. Minutes of the Sub-committee Meeting of the Committee on Street Corner Markets, 1, August 20, 1941, 1, box 3, folder 20, National Council on Household Employment Records.

103. Confidential Report of the Committee on Street Corner Markets to Frieda S. Miller, Industrial Commissioner, State of New York, May 15, 1940, reel 228, frame 2374, Papers of Mayor Fiorello LaGuardia.

104. Dora Jones, "A Self-Help Program of Household Employees," 26.

105. "Craster Now Turns to Push for Purification of Washing," *Newark Evening News*, March 5, 1939, Newark Public Library, Clippings File, Subject: Newark-Health, 1927–30.

106. Examination of Domestic Employees (ordinance adopted September 1, 1930—

amended August 1, 1939) by the Department of Health, Newark, reel 97, Young Women's Christian Association of the USA, National Board, Records, 1876–1970.

107. Ibid.

108. Department of Health, *Health Report for the City of Newark*, 1939, 55.

109. "Tells of Newark's Health Test Work," *Newark Evening News*, October 27, 1932, Newark Public Library, Clippings File, Subject: Newark—Health, 1927–30.

110. See Department of Health, *Health Report for the City of Newark*, 1944, 22; ibid., 1937, 41.

111. Ibid., 1936, 26.

112. Department of Health, *Health Report for the City of Newark, Covering the "Depression Years,"* 1930–1935, 1935, 9.

113. Historians have noted the disregard of government officials and social reformers for the privacy of the poor. See Gordon, *Pitied but Not Entitled*.

114. Similar laws appeared in North Carolina and Florida. See Mrs. Alvin Bossak, Debate, "Should Household Employment Be Regulated?," January 30, 1940, Records of the Women's City Club of New York, 1916–80, in Scott and Perry, *Grassroots Women's Organizations*.

115. See Katherine Gardner to Emma Gunther, box 1, folder 24, National Council on Household Employment Records; Ellis, *A Socio-economic Study of the Female Domestic Worker in Private Homes*, 53; and Public Hearing on the Medical Examination of Domestics, *New Rochelle City Council Minutes for 1937*.

116. Warren, "Venereal Tests for Servants Proposed."

117. Agenda for Meeting on Household Employment, February 29, 1942, reel 91, frame 299, *Records of the National Consumers' League*; Debate, "Should Household Employment Be Regulated?," January 30, 1940, reel 20, frame 267, Records of the Women's City Club of New York, 1916–80, in Scott and Perry, *Grassroots Women's Organizations*.

118. Charles V. Craster, "The Medical Examination of Domestic Servants," n.d., reel 97, Young Women's Christian Association of the USA, National Board, Records, 1876–1970.

119. On the Mary Mallon case, see Leavitt, *Typhoid Mary*.

120. Brandt, *No Magic Bullet*, 155.

121. Ibid., 138, 140.

122. Ibid., 155.

123. Ibid., 156. Pippa Holloway argues that in Virginia such measures were connected with other state efforts to enforce public order and reinforce Jim Crow racial and class hierarchies. Holloway, *Sexuality, Politics, and Social Control in Virginia*.

124. Department of Health, *Health Report for the City of Newark*, March 1944, 4.

125. See Hunter, *To 'Joy My Freedom*, 187–218.

126. Ibid., 197; Holloway, *Sexuality, Politics, and Social Control in Virginia*.

127. Brandt, *No Magic Bullet*, 157.

128. See, for example, Brandt, "Racism and Research." The classic work on the Tuskegee Experiment emphasizing the role of race is James Jones, *Bad Blood*.

129. Department of Health, *Health Report for the City of Newark*, 1936, 15–16.

130. Elizabeth Clark-Lewis argues that African American domestic workers chose to live out in order to gain just this kind of autonomy from employer surveillance. Clark-Lewis, *Living-In, Living-Out*; see also Katzman, *Seven Days a Week*.

131. See Hunter, *To 'Joy My Freedom*, 187–218.

132. Frederick, "Suppose Our Servants Didn't Live with Us."

133. Ibid.

134. Ibid.

135. Committee on Health Tests for Household Workers, "Health Tests of Household Workers," n.d., box 4, folder 50, National Council on Household Employment Records.

136. Ibid.

137. Kruglick, "Real Servant Problem," 400.

138. Batchelder, "Healthy Help," 26.

139. Anna Silver to Mrs. Reynolds, August 8, 1934, box 1, folder 26, National Council on Household Employment Records.

140. "Should Household Employment Be Regulated?," frame 270, Minutes of the Meeting of the Sub-committee on Household Employment, January 26, 1939, reel 97, Young Women's Christian Association of the USA, National Board, Records, 1876–1970.

141. "Domestics' Medical Test Hearing Sought June 14."

142. Forum on Household Employment Report of the Findings Committee, April 30, 1942, 4, box 1, folder 10, National Council on Household Employment Records.

143. Personnel Problems Involved in Household Employment Management, Summary of Course Taught by Benjamin Andrews at the Brooklyn YWCA, July 1941, box 3, folder 50, National Council on Household Employment Records.

144. Unfortunately, the New York legislature's discussions of the Breitbart bill have been lost and no further information is available.

145. Mackenzie, "Domestic Help: National Issue."

146. Public Information Bulletin of the WPA, 3–5, March 1, 1937, box 11, folder e49, reel 4, Universal Negro Improvement Association, Central Division, New York Records, 1918–59.

147. Talk by Mrs. Harriet Dennis at the Herald-Tribune Conference, April 27, 1937, box 2, folder 55, National Council on Household Employment Records.

148. Standards for Trainees of WPA Household Training Program Recommended by Advisory Board, 1, February 15, 1939, reel 98, Young Women's Christian Association of the USA, National Board, Records, 1876–1970.

149. Ibid.

150. Public Information Bulletin of the WPA, 2, March 1, 1937, box 11, folder e49, reel 4, Universal Negro Improvement Association, Central Division, New York Records, 1918–59.

151. Dorothy P. Wells, "Report on Visit to WPA Household Employment Centers," 2, July 21, 1936, box 4, folder 6, National Council on Household Employment Records.

152. Public Information Bulletin of the WPA, 2, March 1, 1937, box 11, folder e49, reel 4, Universal Negro Improvement Association, Central Division, New York Records, 1918–59.

153. National Committee on Household Employment Bulletin V, December 1936, part 10, reel 12, frame 372, in Bracey and Harley, *Papers of the NAACP*.

154. See Committee on Health Tests for Household Workers, "Health Tests of Household Workers," n.d., box 4, folder 50, National Council on Household Employment Records.

155. Minutes of Committee on Extending Labor Law Protection to All Workers, 18, October 31, 1938, box 12, folder 178, Clara Mortenson Beyer Papers.

156. Talk by Mrs. Harriet Dennis at the Herald-Tribune Conference, April 27, 1937, box 2, folder 55, National Council on Household Employment Records.

157. Standards for Trainees of WPA Household Training Program Recommended by Advisory Board, 2, February 15, 1939, reel 98, Young Women's Christian Association of the USA, National Board, Records, 1876–1970.

158. See Mettler, *Dividing Citizens*, 203.

159. Standards for Trainees of WPA Household Training Program Recommended by Advisory Board, February 15, 1939, 4, reel 98, Young Women's Christian Association of the USA, National Board, Records, 1876–1970.

160. Dorothy P. Wells, "Report on Visit to WPA Household Employment Centers," July 21, 1936, 2, box 4, folder 6, National Council on Household Employment Records.

161. Ellis, *A Socio-economic Study of the Female Domestic Worker in Private Homes*, 23.

162. 1936 Annual Report of the Service Division of the NYS Employment Service Harlem Office, 1936, part 10, reel 11, frame 461, in Bracey and Harley, *Papers of the NAACP*.

163. Ibid.

164. Report of the Committee on Labor and Industry, May 1938, reel 1, frame 536, in Scott and Perry, *Grassroots Women's Organizations*.

165. New York Women's Trade Union League, *Annual Report, 1938–1939*, 3.

166. The resistance that labor reformers faced in state legislatures after 1938 made a united front on the part of reformers in demanding labor legislation for domestic workers all the more important. See Ingalls, "New York and the Minimum-Wage Movement," esp. 197; McGuire, "Catalyst for Reform"; Storrs, *Civilizing Capitalism*, 198, 220–21; Mettler, *Dividing Citizens*, 205–10; and Patterson, *The New Deal and the States*.

167. The cleavage among organized women over the issue of labor legislation has gone largely unnoticed. See Coble, *Cleaning Up*, 94; and Storrs, *Civilizing Capitalism*, 220–21.

168. Historians who have examined efforts to expand wage and hour protections under state law have tended to agree with the WTUL secretary that the conservative bent of state legislatures after 1938 made expansion of labor protections on a state level impossible. Most of these historians, however, have looked at state legislation from a national perspective. See Storrs, *Civilizing Capitalism*, 198, 220–21; Mettler, *Dividing Citizens*, 205–10; and Patterson, *The New Deal and the States*, esp. 143–45.

169. Storrs, *Civilizing Capitalism*.

170. Browder, " From Uplift to Agitation"; Browder, "Christian Solution of the Labor Situation."

171. WTUL Resolution, December 19, 1937, reel 2, frame 551, National Women's Trade Union League Papers, in James, *Papers of the Women's Trade Union League*. See also Report of Work, December 1937, reel 4, frame 203, Records of the New York Women's Trade Union League, ibid.; Mettler, *Dividing Citizens*, 203–4; and Kessler-Harris, *In Pursuit of Equity*, esp. 64–116.

172. Cara Cook, "Help Wanted!," 1939, reel 2, frames 707–23, National Women's Trade Union League Papers, in James, *Papers of the Women's Trade Union League*.

173. Elisabeth Christman to Miss White, May 31, 1932, reel 2, frame 513, National Women's Trade Union League Papers, ibid.

174. Minutes of the Legislative Committee Meeting, January 24, 1938, reel 4, frame 217, Records of the New York Women's Trade Union League, ibid.

175. See Minutes of the Meeting of the Sub-committee on Household Employment, December 2, 1937, January 7, 1938, February 4, 1938, January 26, 1939, reel 97, Young Women's Christian Association of the USA, National Board, Records, 1876–1970.

176. Minutes of the Meeting of the Sub-committee on Household Employment, January 26, 1939, reel 97, Young Women's Christian Association of the USA, National Board, Records, 1876–1970.

177. Ibid.

178. New York City League of Women Voters Board of Management Report, January 17, 1938, 2, box 13, Records of the League of Women Voters of the City of New York.

179. See Minutes of the Annual Convention—New York City League of Women Voters, May 24, 1938, 4, box 13, ibid.; Program of 1939 Annual Convention of the New York City League of Women Voters, 30–31, box 26, ibid.

180. Hours restrictions were always more controversial than a minimum wage in debates over household worker labor laws. Minutes of Board of Directors, January 10, 1939, 4, box 6B, folder 1, Consumers' League of New York City Records; Minutes of Board of Directors, February 17, 1939, 3, box 6B, folder 1, ibid. See also Storrs, *Civilizing Capitalism*; and Ingalls, "New York and the Minimum-Wage Movement."

181. Ellis, *A Socio-economic Study of the Female Domestic Worker in Private Homes*, 61.

182. Lane, "Listen Mrs. Legree," 27.

183. Minutes of the Meeting of the Sub-committee on Household Employment, January 26, 1939, 2, reel 97, Young Women's Christian Association of the USA, National Board, Records, 1876–1970.

184. Emma Bugbee, "Mrs. Marconnier Tells of Test of Pay-Hour Rules for Servants," *New York Herald-Tribune*, June 12, 1939, clippings file, reel 21, frame 554, in Scott and Perry, *Grassroots Women's Organizations*.

185. Ibid.

186. Minutes of Committee on Extending Labor Law Protection to All Workers, October 31, 1938, 18, box 12, folder 178, Clara Mortenson Beyer Papers.

187. See "A 'Downtrodden' Mistress"; and "The Club and the Domestic Problem."

188. Ellis, *A Socio-economic Study of the Female Domestic Worker in Private Homes*, 61. See also Orleck, *Common Sense and a Little Fire*; and Storrs, *Civilizing Capitalism*.

189. Of course, such talk had the effect of disadvantaging New York's African American women as a group since nearly 60 percent worked as domestics. U.S. Bureau of the Census, *Fifteenth Census*, 4:1134.

190. 1939 Annual Convention Program of the New York City League of Women Voters, 53, box 26, Records of the League of Women Voters of the City of New York.

191. Eileen Boris and Rhacel Salazar Parreñas argue for intimate labor as a lens through which to view classed, gendered, and racialized power relations. Boris and Parreñas, *Intimate Labors*.

192. Minutes of the Meeting of the Sub-committee on Household Employment, January 7, 1938, reel 97, Young Women's Christian Association of the USA, National Board, Records, 1876–1970.

193. Report of the Civic Secretary, March 2, 1938, reel 4, frame 688, in Scott and Perry, *Grassroots Women's Organizations*.

194. "Do Servants Need a Code?," 36.

195. Cara Cook, "Help Wanted!," 1939, reel 2, frames 714–15, National Women's Trade Union League Papers, in James, *Papers of the Women's Trade Union League*.

196. Notes on the Labor Program, September 1938, 2, box 4, Records of the League of Women Voters of the City of New York.

197. Debate, "Should Household Employment Be Regulated?," January 30, 1940,

reel 20, frame 279, Records of the Women's City Club of New York, 1916–80, in Scott and Perry, *Grassroots Women's Organizations*.

198. Summary of Findings on Conferences on Household Employment, 1928–31, box 2, folder 6, National Council on Household Employment Records; Suggested Voluntary Agreement, ca. 1938–39, reel 4, frames 756–57, in Scott and Perry, *Grassroots Women's Organizations*; Proposal for a Voluntary Agreement in Household Employment, 1941, reel 97, Young Women's Christian Association of the USA, National Board, Records; 1939 Annual Convention of the New York City League of Women Voters Program, 1939, box 26, Records of the League of Women Voters of the City of New York; Minutes of the Legislative Committee, December 13, 1939, National Women's Trade Union League Papers, reel 4, frame 529, in James, *Papers of the Women's Trade Union League*.

199. Debate, "Should Household Employment Be Regulated?," Records of the Women's City Club of New York, 1916–80, reel 20, frame 267, in Scott and Perry, *Grassroots Women's Organizations*.

200. Program of 1939 Annual Convention, 53, box 26, Records of the League of Women Voters of the City of New York.

201. Board of Directors Minutes, December 7, 1938, reel 4, frame 748, in Scott and Perry, *Grassroots Women's Organizations*.

202. New York Women's Trade Union League, *Annual Report, 1939–1940*, 20; Wilma Duntze to Dr. Hazel Kyrk, April 14, 1931, box 2, folder 49, National Council on Household Employment Records.

203. "It Can Happen in Your Home: 32,000 Deaths Each Year from Home Accidents," n.d., box 3, folder 36, National Council on Household Employment Records.

204. Statement re: Workmen's Compensation Bill for Domestic Workers, March 12, 1940, box 41, League of Women Voters of the City of New York Records; Sergel, *Women in the House*, 123.

205. Sergel, *Women in the House*, 125.

206. Wilma Duntze to Dr. Hazel Kyrk, April 14, 1931, box 2, folder 49, National Council on Household Employment Records.

207. New York Women's Trade Union League, *Annual Report, 1941–1942*.

208. Cara Cook to Sponsors and Contributors, May 8, 1942, 2, box 1, folder 43, National Council on Household Employment Records.

209. New York Women's Trade Union League, *Annual Report, 1945*; Fannie Hurst to Governor Thomas E. Dewey, November 1945, box 9C, folder 15, Consumers' League of New York City Records. For the text of the governor's message, see State of New York, *Public Papers of Thomas E. Dewey*, 4.

210. New York Women's Trade Union League, *Annual Report, 1946*, 4.

211. See Leonard S. Clark, New York County Lawyers' Association, Report on State Legislation, Report no. 124 on S. Int 371, Pr 1182, same as A. Int 370 Int 871 Pr 904, New York Bill Jacket Collection.

212. Proceedings of the Symposium on Household Employment, November 1939, 15, reel 98, Young Women's Christian Association of the USA, National Board, Records, 1876–1970.

213. Minutes of the Women's Trade Union Leagues' Regular Membership, March 6, 1939, reel 4, frame 455, Records of the New York Women's Trade Union League, in James, *Papers of the Women's Trade Union League*.

214. Gordon, *Pitied but Not Entitled*; Orleck, *Common Sense and a Little Fire*.

215. WTUL Resolution, December 19, 1937, reel 2, frame 551, National Women's Trade Union League Papers, in James, *Papers of the Women's Trade Union League*.

Chapter Five

1. "Affidavit of Corrine Washington," April 14, 1938, part 10, reel 12, frame 879, in Bracey and Harley, *Papers of the NAACP*; Lawrence, "Uncover Job Racket in Case of Virginia Girl."

2. See Beverly W. Jones, "Race, Sex, and Class."

3. "Affidavit of Corrine Washington," April 14, 1938, part 10, reel 12, frame 879, in Bracey and Harley, *Papers of the NAACP*.

4. Ibid., frames 878–80; Lawrence, "Uncover Job Racket in Case of Virginia Girl."

5. Dora Jones to NAACP, April 19, 1938, part 10, reel 12, frame 877, in Bracey and Harley, *Papers of the NAACP*.

6. Ibid.

7. Ibid.

8. Paul Moss to Mayor Fiorello LaGuardia, June 22, 1939, reel 123, frames 467–68, Papers of Mayor Fiorello LaGuardia.

9. Mayor Fiorello LaGuardia to Olin Dewitt Talmadge Johnston, Mayor Fiorello LaGuardia to Mayor of Cheraw, South Carolina, Mayor Fiorello LaGuardia to Mayor of Bennettsville, South Carolina, Mayor Fiorello LaGuardia to Mayor of McCall, South Carolina, June 1939, reels 468–74, frames 468–74, Papers of Mayor Fiorello LaGuardia.

10. Domestic workers' unions have rarely appeared in histories of the New Deal. See Orleck, *Common Sense and a Little Fire*, 165–66; Palmer, *Domesticity and Dirt*, 127; and Van Raaphorst, *Union Maids Not Wanted*, esp. chaps. 5 and 7.

11. The literature on middle-class black reform organizations is both long and rich. Some examples include Cash, *African American Women and Social Action*; White, *Too Heavy a Load*; Salem, *To Better Our World*; Giddings, *In Search of Sisterhood*; Weiss, *National Urban League*; Weisenfeld, *African American Women and Christian Activism*; and Higginbotham, *Righteous Discontent*.

12. Minutes of the Committee for Protection of [Colored] Women, April 7, 1913, part I, series XI, box 1, Records of the National Urban League; White Rose Industrial Association Working Girls Home pamphlet, ca. 1918, Records of the White Rose Mission and Industrial Society.

13. Elizabeth Ross Haynes, "Negroes in Domestic Service in the United States," reprinted from *Journal of Negro History* 8, no. 4 (October 1923), reel 98, Young Women's Christian Association of the USA, National Board, Records, 1876–1970.

14. "The Negro Church Today," reel 2, no. 7, Writer's Program Collection.

15. Greater New York Federation of Churches, *Negro Churches of Manhattan*, 24; Greenberg, *Or Does It Explode*, 58–59.

16. "The Negro Church Today," 3, reel 2, no. 7, Writer's Program Collection.

17. Greater New York Federation of Churches, *Negro Churches of Manhattan*, 23.

18. "America's Number One Problem in Education: An Interview with Nannie Helen Burroughs, Outstanding Negro Woman Educator, on the 'Servant Problem,'" part I, reel 12, frame 290, National Negro Congress Records.

19. Mrs. F. R. Birch to NAACP, March 8, 1938, Records of the NAACP, part 10, reel 12, frames 815–16, in Bracey and Harley, *Papers of the NAACP*. Thurgood Marshall replied

to Birch, explaining that the NAACP could not help and suggested that she contact the Urban League. Thurgood Marshall to Mrs. F. R. Birch, March 7, 1938, part 10, reel 12, frame 814, in Bracey and Harley, *Papers of the NAACP*.

20. "Conditions of Negro Domestics in Various Parts of the United States," September 27, 1933, part I, reel 1, frame 471, National Negro Congress Records.

21. "Summary of Second Conference," April 13 and 14, 1931, 8, box 2, folder 51, National Council on Household Employment Records; "Placement Problems of Household Employees," reel 97, Young Women's Christian Association of the USA, National Board, Records, 1876–1970.

22. Norabell C. Harty to NAACP, June 20, 1934, part 10, reel 11, frame 987, in Bracey and Harley, *Papers of the NAACP*.

23. Ibid., frames 987–88.

24. Ibid., frame 987.

25. "Report of the Commission on Findings of the National Council of Negro Women," October 1941, box 1, folder 10, DcWaMMB, Records of the National Council of Negro Women. I was also unable to find much evidence of National Association of Colored Women programs specifically related to domestic workers. Boehm and Williams, *Records of the National Association of Colored Women's Clubs, 1895–1992*. See also White, *Too Heavy a Load*, 132–33; and Storrs, *Civilizing Capitalism*, 33, 282n71.

26. For an example of this kind of thinking, see Conference on the Participation of Negro Women and Children in Federal Programs, Morning Session, April 4, 1938, series 4, box 1, folder 5, Records of the National Council of Negro Women.

27. The Young Women's Christian Association of the City of New York Annual Report (1935), 6, and Description of Placement Program at the 137th St. YWCA, n.d., reel 98, Young Women's Christian Association of the USA, National Board, Records, 1876–1970.

28. The Young Women's Christian Association of the City of New York Annual Report (1935), 6, ibid.

29. YWCA Trade School General Announcement (1933–34), 19, Schomburg Center for Research in Black Culture, Clipping File, 1925–74, Subject: Domestic Workers.

30. Hedgeman, *The Trumpet Sounds*, 37–39.

31. Transcript of Conference on Employer-Employee Relationships in the Home, October 17, 1928, 45, box 2, folder 28, National Council on Household Employment Records.

32. Ibid., 46.

33. Henry E. Ashcroft to T. Arnold Hill, April 10, 1931, series IV, box 5, Records of the National Urban League.

34. Minutes of Committee on Extending Labor Law Protection to All Workers, October 31, 1938, 81, box 12, folder 178, Clara Mortenson Beyer Papers.

35. Ibid.

36. "Trends in Household Employment 1931," n.d., 3, part I, series IV, box 5, Records of the National Urban League.

37. Minutes of Committee on Extending Labor Law Protection to All Workers, October 31, 1938, 81–82, box 12, folder 178, Clara Mortenson Beyer Papers.

38. Eugene V. Roundtree to T. Arnold Hill, April 8, 1931, 2, part I, series IV, box 5, Records of the National Urban League.

39. Ibid.

40. Description of Placement Program at the 137th St. YWCA, Schomburg Center for Research in Black Culture, Clipping File, 1925–74, Subject: Domestic Workers.

41. Ibid.

42. Ibid.

43. Waring Chuny, "Activity of the Churches during the Depression," 1–3, reel 2, no. 7, Writer's Program Collection.

44. Taylor, *The Black Churches of Brooklyn*, xvii, 57.

45. "The Negro Church Today," 10.

46. Cooke, "Slavery . . . 1939 Style."

47. Vivian Morris, "Price War in the Bronx Slave Market," December 14, 1938, Records of the Works Progress Administration, Federal Writers' Project Collection, Folklore Project.

48. Gray, *Black Female Domestics*, 63.

49. Cheryl Lynn Greenberg argues that "blacks in Harlem and other northern urban communities protested more often and more overtly than did rural southern blacks." Greenberg, *Or Does It Explode*, 217.

50. Cooke, "Modern Slaves."

51. Mary Ford to Julia Brown, June 18, 1936, reel 98, Young Women's Christian Association of the USA, National Board, Records, 1876–1970; Vivian Morris, "Domestic Workers' Union," February 7, 1939, Records of the Works Progress Administration, Federal Writers' Project Collection, Folklore Project.

52. Ibid.

53. Domestic Workers Union Local 149, All-Day Symposium on Household Employment, n.d., box 3, folder 33, National Council on Household Employment Records.

54. Esther Cooper Jackson, "Negro Domestic Worker in Relation to Trade Unionism," 43.

55. Ibid.; Mary Ford to "Dear Friend," April 15, 1937, part 10, reel 12, frame 532, in Bracey and Harley, *Papers of the NAACP*.

56. "Household Workers: Why This Difference in Working Conditions?," n.d., box 3, folder 33, National Council on Household Employment Records; Cooke, "Modern Slaves"; Offord, "Slave Markets in the Bronx," June 29, 1940, 781.

57. *The Nation* and the Negro Workers' Council reported that the DWU had recruited 1,000 members; Marvel Cooke, the *Amsterdam News*, and Benson Ellis, a special New York City investigator, put DWU membership at 350. See Evelyn Seely, "Our Feudal Housewives," 614; Workers Council Bulletin, no. 16 prepared by the Negro Workers' Councils, May 28, 1937, 7, reel 98, Young Women's Christian Association of the USA, National Board, Records, 1876–1970; and Cooke, "Modern Slaves." See also Ellis, *A Socio-economic Study of the Female Domestic Worker in Private Homes*, 67.

58. Brown, *Concerns of Household Workers*, 641.

59. Resolution introduced to New York State Federation of Labor Convention, by Local 130 of the DWU BSEIU, of Westchester County, box 3, folder 33, National Council on Household Employment Records; "Domestics Plan to Form Union"; Wesley Courtwright, "Brief History of the Domestic Workers' Association Brooklyn Local," reel 3, no. 27, Writer's Program Collection; "Domestic Workers," February 18, 1938, Newark Public Library Clippings File, Subject: Domestics. Domestics' unions also existed in Washington, D.C., and San Diego. See "Domestic Workers Organize," n.d., box 3, folder 33, National Council on Household Employment Records; and Elisabeth Christman to Lula Jane Cotter,

June 1, 1936, National Women's Trade Union League Papers, reel 2, frames 539–40, in James, *Papers of the Women's Trade Union League*.

60. Marvell Cooke, "Some Ways to Kill the Slave Market," *Daily Compass*, January 12, 1950, Schomburg Center for Research in Black Culture, Clipping File, 1925–74, Subject: Domestic Workers.

61. Domestic Workers Union Local 149, All-Day Symposium on Household Employment, n.d., box 3, folder 33, National Council on Household Employment Records; Domestic Service Help Union Agreement, 1936, reel 97, Young Women's Christian Association of the USA, National Board, Records, 1876–1970; Vivian Morris, "Domestic Workers' Union," February 2, 1939, Records of the Works Progress Administration, Federal Writers' Project Collection, Folklore Project.

62. Esther Cooper Jackson, "Negro Domestic Worker in Relation to Trade Unionism," 41.

63. Vivian Morris, "Domestic Workers' Union," February 2, 1939, 2, Records of the Works Progress Administration, Federal Writers' Project Collection, Folklore Project.

64. Esther Cooper Jackson, "Negro Domestic Worker in Relation to Trade Unionism," 46.

65. Ibid., 54.

66. Vivian Morris, "Domestic Workers' Union," February 2, 1939, Records of the Works Progress Administration, Federal Writers' Project Collection, Folklore Project.

67. Historian Cheryl Lynn Greenberg argued that Harlem's "black men and women from all walks of life had been politicized and sometimes even radicalized by Depression-era political organizing." Greenberg, *Or Does It Explode*, 5.

68. Vivian Morris, "Domestic Workers' Union," February 2, 1939, 2, Records of the Works Progress Administration, Federal Writers' Project Collection, Folklore Project.

69. Esther Cooper Jackson, "Negro Domestic Worker in Relation to Trade Unionism," 54.

70. Ibid.; Eugene Gordon, "300 Shout Demand for 60-Hr. Week," ca. March 5, 1939, Schomburg Center for Research in Black Culture, Clipping File, 1925–74, Subject: Domestic Workers. Reporters and investigators have estimated that between 75 and 89 percent of DWU membership was African American. See Esther Cooper Jackson, "Negro Domestic Worker in Relation to Trade Unionism," 41; Ellis, *A Socio-economic Study of the Female Domestic Worker in Private Homes*, 67; and Cooke, "Modern Slaves."

71. Vivian Morris, "Domestic Workers Union," February 7, 1939, 1–2, Records of the Works Progress Administration, Federal Writers' Project Collection, Folklore Project.

72. Ibid.

73. Meeting of the Organization Committee, January 17, 1938, Records of the New York Women's Trade Union League, reel 4, frame 214, in James, *Papers of the Women's Trade Union League*; Wesley Courtwright, "Brief History of the Domestic Workers' Association Brooklyn Local," reel 3, no. 27, Writer's Program Collection.

74. Vivian Morris, "Domestic Workers' Union," February 7, 1939, 3, Records of the Works Progress Administration, Federal Writers' Project Collection, Folklore Project.

75. Ibid.

76. Confidential Report of the Committee on Street Corner Markets to Frieda S. Miller, Industrial Commissioner State of New York, May 15, 1940, reel 228, frame 2310, Papers of Mayor Fiorello LaGuardia.

77. Ibid., frame 2385.

78. Ibid.

79. Bessie O'Banyon Interview, New York City Immigrant Labor Project.

80. Vivian Morris, "Price War in the Bronx Slave Market," 2, Records of the Works Progress Administration, Federal Writers' Project Collection, Folklore Project.

81. Resolution introduced to New York State Federation of Labor Convention (passed by the AFL), by Local 130 of the DWU BSEIU, of Westchester County, box 3, folder 33, National Council on Household Employment Records; Minutes of the Negro Labor Assembly, April 12, 1940, reel 4, box 8, folder b83, Negro Labor Committee Records; Mary Ford to Dear Friend, April 15, 1937, part 10, reel 12, frame 532, in Bracey and Harley, *Papers of the NAACP*.

82. Ellis, *A Socio-economic Study of the Female Domestic Worker in Private Homes*, 70.

83. "Domestic Workers Demand 6-Day-Week."

84. Eugene Gordon, "300 Shout Demand for 60-Hr. Week," ca. March 5, 1939, Schomburg Center for Research in Black Culture, Clipping File, 1925–74, Subject: Domestic Workers.

85. Ibid.

86. Ibid.

87. Cooke, "Help Wanted for the Help."

88. "Maid Loses Assault Case against Couple."

89. Ibid.

90. Ibid.

91. Mary Ford to Julia Brown, June 18, 1936, reel 98, Young Women's Christian Association of the USA, National Board, Records, 1876–1970; Esther Cooper Jackson, "Negro Domestic Worker in Relation to Trade Unionism," 49.

92. Josephine Hall to Dorothy Wells, September 20, 1937, box 3, folder 33, National Council on Household Employment Records.

93. New York Household-Placement Association Flyer, box 3, folder 68, ibid.

94. Cara Cook, "Help Wanted," 1939, reel 2, frame 715, National Women's Trade Union League Papers, in James, *Papers of the Women's Trade Union League*.

95. New York Household-Placement Association Flyer, box 3, folder 68, National Council on Household Employment Records.

96. Ellis, *A Socio-economic Study of the Female Domestic Worker in Private Homes*, 16.

97. Offord, "Slave Markets in the Bronx," June 29, 1940, 781.

98. Esther Cooper Jackson, "Negro Domestic Worker in Relation to Trade Unionism," 48.

99. "Code for Domestic Servants Prepared."

100. Mary Ford to Julia Brown, Young Women's Christian Association of the USA, National Board, Records, 1876–1970.

101. Ellis, *A Socio-economic Study of the Female Domestic Worker in Private Homes*, 16.

102. Helene Frankel, "Report on Some of the Work Done in the Domestic Workers' Field," December 27, 1938, 2, reel 97, Young Women's Christian Association of the USA, National Board, Records, 1876–1970.

103. Esther Cooper Jackson, "Negro Domestic Worker in Relation to Trade Unionism," 52.

104. "Report of Activities of the Negro Labor Committee," January 1—December 31, 1938, box 3, folder b1, reel 1, Negro Labor Committee Records.

105. Cooke, "Modern Slaves."

106. Minutes of the Meeting of the Sub-committee on Household Employment, February 24, 1939, reel 97, Young Women's Christian Association of the USA, National Board,

Records, 1876–1970; Minutes of the Negro Labor Assembly, September 10, 1937, box 8, folder b82, reel 4, Negro Labor Committee Records.

107. Minutes of Executive Board Meeting, Tuesday, December 21, 1937, reel 4, frame 200, New York Women's Trade Union League Papers, in James, *Papers of the Women's Trade Union League.*

108. Work Report for March, April, May, June 1938, reel 4, frame 363, New York Women's Trade Union League Papers, ibid.

109. Minutes of the Executive Board Meeting, January 3, 1939, reel 4, frame 414, New York Women's Trade Union League Papers, ibid.

110. Orleck, *Common Sense and a Little Fire*, 161–62.

111. See Dye, *As Equals and as Sisters*; and Orleck, *Common Sense and a Little Fire.*

112. Ellis, *A Socio-economic Study of the Female Domestic Worker in Private Homes*, 69–70.

113. Report of Work Ending December 1937, reel 4, frame 203, Records of the New York Women's Trade Union League, in James, *Papers of the Women's Trade Union League.*

114. Minutes of the Legislative Committee, December 13, 1939, reel 4, frame 529, Records of the New York Women's Trade Union League, ibid.

115. Although some scholars have addressed public health measures aimed at domestics during this period, there has been no discussion of domestics' widespread resistance. See Brandt, *No Magic Bullet*, esp. 155–57; and Holloway, *Sexuality, Politics, and Social Control in Virginia*, esp. 93–107.

116. *New Rochelle City Council Minutes for 1937*, May 17, 1937, 386.

117. Public Hearing on the Medical Examination of Domestics, *New Rochelle City Council Minutes for 1937*, June 21, 1937, 471.

118. "Domestic Law Foes Surpass Advocates."

119. "Many to Attend Open Hearing on Domestics' Test."

120. "Wallace's Letter."

121. See "The Forum," June 10, 1937; "The Forum," June 11, 1937; "The Forum," June 12, 1937; "The Forum," June 15, 1937; "The Forum," June 17, 1937; and "The Forum," June 21, 1937.

122. "Domestic Exam Hearing Date Spread Anew by Various Agencies."

123. "Many to Attend Open Hearing on Domestics' Test."

124. "Opponents Rally against Law for Domestic Tests."

125. Ibid.

126. Communists were often more willing than even the most liberal labor activists to organize black workers. Although it is not surprising to find them working on behalf of domestics, I have no specific evidence that they played a large role in organizing New York domestic workers. See also McDuffie, "Long Journeys"; Kelley, *Hammer and Hoe*; William J. Maxwell, *New Negro, Old Left*; and Mullen, *Popular Fronts.*

127. "Opponents Rally against Law for Domestic Tests."

128. "Mrs. Gurenson Answers Points Raised in Wallace's Letter."

129. Ibid.

130. "Opponents Rally against Law for Domestic Tests."

131. "The Forum," June 21, 1937.

132. "The Forum," June 11, 1937.

133. "Opponents Rally against Law for Domestic Tests."

134. "The Forum," June 15, 1937.

135. "Wallace's Letter."

136. Ibid.

137. "The Forum," June 17, 1937.

138. "The Forum," June 11, 1937.

139. "Wallace's Letter."

140. "Opponents Rally against Law for Domestic Tests."

141. Ibid.

142. "Mrs. Gurenson Answers Points Raised in Wallace's Letter"; "Opponents Rally against Law for Domestic Tests."

143. "Opponents Rally against Law for Domestic Tests."

144. *New Rochelle City Council Minutes for 1937*, May 17, 1937, 473.

145. Ibid.

146. "Opponents Rally against Law for Domestic Tests."

147. Katherine Gardner to Emma Gunther, June 28, 1934, box 1, folder 24, National Council on Household Employment Records.

148. Ibid.

149. "Domestics Organize to Fight Ordinance."

150. Katherine Gardner to Emma Gunther, June 28, 1934, box 1, folder 24, National Council on Household Employment Records.

151. Department of Health, *Health Report for the City of Newark, Covering the "Depression Years," 1930–1935*, 1935, 8–9.

152. Department of Health, *Health Report for the City of Newark*, 1936, 26.

153. Ellis, *A Socio-economic Study of the Female Domestic Worker in Private Homes*, 12.

154. Transcript of Conference on Employer-Employee Relationships in the Home, October 17, 1928, 44, box 2, folder 27, National Council on Household Employment Records.

155. Ibid.

156. Note written by Benjamin Andrews to writer of National Council on Household Employment Bulletin, box 1, folder 5, ibid.

157. Suggestions for Revision of the Voluntary Agreement, November 4, 1938, 3, reel 97, Young Women's Christian Association of the USA, National Board Records.

158. Ibid.

Epilogue

1. Bernstein, "Invisible to Most."

2. Ibid.

3. Census data puts the number of domestics at work in New York City today at about 200,000. The union argues that the actual number is closer to 600,000. See Domestic Workers United and Datacenter, "Home Is Where the Work Is."

4. Klieman, "Maid Services Clean Up"; Ehrenreich, "Maid to Order," 90.

5. Scelfo, "Trickledown Downsizing."

6. Ruiz, "Giving Rights to Caregivers."

7. Lieber, "Doing the Right Thing by Paying the Nanny Tax."

8. Phyllis Palmer argues that the women's movement was the catalyst for changes not only in domestic labor law but also in the cultural definition of housework as constituting actual labor. The women's movement and the civil rights movement, Palmer argues, made the 1974 amendments to the FLSA possible. See Palmer, "Outside the Law."

9. U.S. House of Representatives, *Hearings before the General Subcommittee on Labor of the Committee on Education and Labor*, 242.

10. Ibid., 232.

11. Ibid., 207.

12. Ibid., 242.

13. Ibid., 205.

14. Ibid., 206.

15. On political movements of domestics in the wake of the civil rights movement and the women's movement, see Cobble, "Spontaneous Loss of Enthusiasm," 34; and Cobble, *The Other Women's Movement*, 198–200.

16. U.S. House of Representatives, *Hearings before the General Subcommittee on Labor of the Committee on Education and Labor*, 206.

17. See Jacqueline Jones, *Labor of Love, Labor of Sorrow*, esp. 275–330.

18. See Ehrenreich and Hochschild, "Introduction," 6.

19. See Zarembka, "America's Dirty Work," 151.

20. Chang, *Disposable Domestics*, 93–121.

21. Ehrenreich and Hochschild, "Introduction," 8; Sassen, "Global Cities and Survival Circuits," 266–67. See also Chang, *Disposable Domestics*, 123–54; and DeParle, "A Good Provider Is One Who Leaves."

22. DeParle, "A Good Provider Is One who Leaves."

23. Ehrenreich and Hochschild, "Introduction," 5.

24. Ehrenreich, "Maid to Order," 101.

25. Anderson, "Just Another Job?," 105.

26. Ibid., 113.

27. Cheever, "Nanny Dilemma," 37.

28. Domestic Workers United and Datacenter, "Home Is Where the Work Is."

29. See ibid., 3, 8. The Union credits Rachel S. Coen and Hena Mansori from the Immigrant Rights Clinic at New York University School of Law with this research.

30. Ibid., 8. A similar law was later enacted in Nassau County in 2006. See Lambert, "New Nassau County Law."

31. Domestic Workers United and Datacenter, "Home Is Where the Work Is," 35. Domestic Workers United considers a "living wage" in New York City to be $13.47 per hour.

32. Ibid., 36.

Bibliography

Archival Collections

Albany, New York
   Legislative Reference Section, New York State Library
      New York Bill Jacket Collection
Cambridge, Massachusetts
   Schlesinger Library, Radcliffe Institute, Harvard University
      Annie Ware Winsor Allen Papers
      Clara Mortenson Beyer Papers
Ithaca, New York
   Kheel Center for Labor-Management Documentation and Archives,
        M. P. Catherwood Library, Cornell University
      Consumers' League of New York City Records, #5307
      National Council on Household Employment Records, #5226
Newark, New Jersey
   Newark Public Library
      Clippings File, Subjects: Newark—Health, 1927–30; Domestics
New Rochelle, New York
   New Rochelle Public Library

New Rochelle City Council Minutes for 1937 (New York, 1937)
New York, New York
    Butler Library, Rare Book and Manuscript Library, Columbia University
        Records of the Citizens Union
        Records of the Goddard-Riverside Community Center
        Records of the League of Women Voters of the City of New York
    Ellis Island Immigration Museum
        Ellis Island Oral History Collection
    Lindquist Group
        A. E. Johnson Employment Registry Book, A. E. Johnson Agency
    Lloyd Sealy College, John Jay College of Criminal Justice
        John Jay Trial Transcript Collection
    New York City Municipal Archives
        Files of Office of the Mayor, Gaynor Administration
        Files of Office of the Mayor, McClellan Administration
        Files of Office of the Mayor, Mitchel Administration
        Papers of Mayor Fiorello LaGuardia
        The People v. Annie Kane
        The People v. Bertha Schade
    New-York Historical Society
        General Collections
            F. E. V. Odell & Co., *Servant's Exchange Pamphlet* (1890)
        Manuscript Collections
            Henrietta MacLauren Richards Diary
    New York Public Library, Manuscripts and Archives Division, Stephen A.
        Schwarzman Building, Astor, Lenox, and Tilden Foundations
        Grace Eulalie Matthews Ashmore Papers
    92nd Street Y
        Records of the Clara de Hirsch Home for Working Girls
    Our Lady of the Rosary Roman Catholic Parish
        Our Lady of the Rosary Home for Immigrant Girls Registry Book, 1906–7
    Schomburg Center for Research in Black Culture, New York Public Library
        General Collections
            Clipping File, 1925–74, Subject: Domestic Workers
            National Negro Congress Records, 1933–47, microfilm edition
            Negro Labor Committee Records, 1925–69, microfilm edition
            Universal Negro Improvement Association, Central Division,
                New York Records, 1918–59, microfilm edition
            Writer's Program Collection, microfilm edition
        Manuscripts, Archives, and Rare Books Division
            Records of the White Rose Mission and Industrial Society
    New York University
        Robert F. Wagner Labor Archives, Tamiment Library
            New York City Immigrant Labor Project
            New Yorkers at Work Oral History Collection

Northampton, Massachusetts
   Sophia Smith Collection, Smith College
      Young Women's Christian Association of the USA, National Board,
         Records, 1876–1970
Poughkeepsie, New York
   Archives and Special Collections, Vassar College Library
      Lucy Maynard Salmon Papers
Princeton, New Jersey
   Seely G. Mudd Manuscript Library, Princeton University
      Arthur von Briesen Papers, 1895–1920
Washington, D.C.
   Library of Congress
      Records of the National Council of Jewish Women
      Records of the National Urban League
      Records of the Works Progress Administration
         Federal Writers' Project Collection, Folklore Project
   National Archives
      Records of the Women's Bureau, Record Group 86
   National Park Service
      Mary McLeod Bethune Council House National Historic Site
         Records of the National Council of Negro Women, DcWaMMB,
            catalog no. 001

Newspapers and Periodicals

The Aframerican Woman's Journal	Hygeia
American Journal of Sociology	Independent
American Magazine	Ladies' Home Journal
Arena	Legal Aid Review
Atlantic Monthly	Leslie's Weekly
Brooklyn Daily Eagle	Liberator
Chautauquan	Literary Digest
Chicago Daily Tribune	McClure's Magazine
Collier's	The Nation
Cosmopolitan	New Rochelle Standard-Star
Current Literature	New York Amsterdam News
Daily Worker	New York Daily News
Delineator	New York Journal American
Everybody's Magazine	New York Times
Forum	New York Tribune
Gaelic American	Opportunity
Good Housekeeping	Our Day
Hampton's Magazine	Outlook
Harper's Bazaar	Parents Magazine
Harper's Weekly	Saturday Evening Post

Published Sources, Dissertations, and Theses

Abel, Mary Hinman. "A Training School for Servants." *Outlook*, October 28, 1899, 501–3.

"About Servants in Liveries—and in General." *Harper's Weekly*, May 3, 1902, 567.

Addams, Jane. "A Belated Industry." *American Journal of Sociology* (March 1896): 536–50.

Aldrich, Mark. "The Gender Gap in Earnings during World War II: New Evidence." *Industrial and Labor Relations Review* 42, no. 3 (1989): 415–29.

Aldrich, Mark, and Robert Buchele. *The Economics of Comparable Worth*. Cambridge: Ballinger, 1986.

Allen, Annie Ware Winsor. *Both Sides of the Servant Question*. Boston: American Unitarian Association, 1910.

Anderson, Bridget. "Just Another Job? The Commodification of Domestic Labor." In *Global Woman: Nannies, Maids, and Sex Workers in the New Economy*, edited by Barbara Ehrenreich and Arlie Russell Hochschild, 104–14. New York: Henry Holt, 2002.

Annual Report of the Alliance Employment Bureau of the New York Association of Working Girls' Societies. New York: 1897.

Annual Report of the Mission of Our Lady of the Rosary. New York, 1885.

Annual Report of the Mission of Our Lady of the Rosary. New York, 1887.

Annual Report of Our Lady of the Rosary of the City of New York. New York, 1891.

Annual Report of the Mission of Our Lady of the Rosary. New York, 1899.

Annual Report of Our Lady of the Rosary of the City of New York. New York, 1905.

"Another View of the Matter." *New York Tribune*, January 20, 1887, 3.

Bacon, Josephine Daskam. "We and Our Servants." *American Magazine*, February 1907, 349–60.

Baer, Judith A. *The Chains of Protection: The Judicial Response to Women's Labor Legislation*. New York: Greenwood Press, 1978.

Bailey, Alice Ward. "Livin'-Out Girls." *Outlook* 73 (February 7, 1903): 307–12.

Baker, Ella, and Marvel Cooke. "The Bronx Slave Market." *Crisis*, November 1935, 330–31, 340.

Baker, S. Josephine. *Fighting for Life*. New York: Macmillan, 1939.

Barker, C. Hélène. *Wanted, a Young Woman to Do Housework: Business Principles Applied to Housework*. New York: Moffat, Yard, 1915.

Batchelder, Grace E. "Healthy Help." *Parents Magazine*, March 1935, 26, 58–59.

Bensley, Martha S. "Experiences of a Nursery Governess." *Everybody's Magazine*, January 1905, 25–31.

———. "Experiences of a Nursery Governess—VIII." *Everybody's Magazine*, August 1905, 180–84.

Bernstein, Nina. "Invisible to Most, Immigrant Women Line Up for Day Labor." *New York Times*, August 17, 2005, A1, B6.

"Bills Passed in Albany." *New York Times*, April 15, 1904, 3.

Boehm, Randolph, and Lillian Serece Williams, eds. *Records of the National Association of Colored Women's Clubs, 1895–1992*. Microfilm edition. Bethesda, Md.: University Publications of America, 1994.

"Bold Man Defends the Servant Girl." *New York Times*, December 19, 1907, 16.

Boris, Eileen. *Home to Work: Motherhood and the Politics of Industrial Homework in the United States*. Cambridge: Cambridge University Press, 1994.

Boris, Eileen, and Rhacel Salazar Parreñas, eds. *Intimate Labors: Cultures, Technologies, and the Politics of Care*. Stanford, Calif.: Stanford University Press, 2010.

Boydston, Jeanne. *Home and Work: Housework, Wages, and the Ideology of Labor in the Early Republic*. New York: Oxford University Press, 1990.

Brace, Charles Loring. *The Dangerous Classes of New York, and Twenty Years' Work among Them*. New York: Wynkoop & Hallenbeck, 1872.

Bracey, John H., Jr., and Sharon Harley, eds. *Papers of the NAACP*. Microfilm edition. Bethesda, Md.: University Publications of America, 2002.

Brandt, Allan M. *No Magic Bullet: A Social History of Venereal Disease in the United States since 1880*. New York: Oxford University Press, 1987.

————. "Racism and Research: The Case of the Tuskegee Syphilis Experiment." In *Tuskegee's Truths: Rethinking the Tuskegee Syphilis Study*, edited by Susan M. Reverby, 15–33. Chapel Hill: University of North Carolina Press, 2000.

Browder, Dorothea. "A 'Christian Solution of the Labor Situation': How Workingwomen Reshaped the YWCA's Religious Mission and Politics." *Journal of Women's History* 19 (Summer 2007): 85–110.

————. "From Uplift to Agitation: Working Women, Race, and Coalition in the Young Women's Christian Association, 1908–1950." Ph.D. diss., University of Wisconsin-Madison, 2008.

Brown, Jean Collier. *Concerns of Household Workers: Program with Household Workers in the YWCA*. New York: Woman's Press, 1941.

Bulletin of the Inter-Municipal Committee on Household Research 1, no. 1 (November 1904).

Bulletin of the Inter-Municipal Committee on Household Research 1, no. 2 (December 1904).

Bulletin of the Inter-Municipal Committee on Household Research 1, no. 4 (February 1905).

Bulletin of the Inter-Municipal Committee on Household Research 1, no. 5 (March 1905).

Bulletin of the Inter-Municipal Committee on Household Research 1, no. 7 (May 1905).

Butler, Amy E. *Two Paths to Equality: Alice Paul and Ethel M. Smith in the ERA Debate, 1921–1929*. Albany: State University of New York Press, 2002.

"By Women, for Women." *New York Tribune*, March 21, 1896, 14.

Campbell, Helen. *Prisoners of Poverty: Women Wage-Workers, Their Trades and Their Lives*. Boston: Roberts Brothers, 1890.

Carby, Hazel V. "Policing the Black Woman's Body in an Urban Context." *Critical Inquiry* 18, no. 4 (Summer 1992): 738–55.

"Card from Servant Girls." *Brooklyn Daily Eagle*, January 24, 1899.

Cash, Floris Barnett. *African American Women and Social Action: The Clubwomen and Volunteerism from Jim Crow to the New Deal, 1896–1936*. Westport, Conn.: Greenwood Press, 2001.

Chang, Grace. *Disposable Domestics: Immigrant Workers in the Global Economy*. Cambridge: South End Press, 2000.

Cheever, Susan. "The Nanny Dilemma." In *Global Woman: Nannies, Maids, and Sex Workers in the New Economy*, edited by Barbara Ehrenreich and Arlie Russell Hochschild, 31–38. New York: Henry Holt, 2002.

Christian Aid Association. *Annual Report*. New York: 1890.

Christian Aid to Employment Society. *Annual Report*. New York: 1892.

Christiansen, Lars. "The Making of a Civil Rights Union: The National Domestic Workers Union of America." Ph.D. diss., Florida State University, 1999.

"City Missionary Work." *New York Tribune*, November 9, 1896, 5.

Claghorn, Kate Holladay. *The Immigrant's Day in Court*. New York: Arno Press, 1969.

Clark-Lewis, Elizabeth. *Living-In, Living-Out: African American Domestics in Washington, DC, 1910–1940*. Washington, D.C.: Smithsonian Institution Press, 1994.

"The Club and the Domestic Problem." *New York Tribune*, January 27, 1901, 5.

Cobble, Dorothy Sue. *The Other Women's Movement: Workplace Justice and Social Rights in Modern America*. Princeton: Princeton University Press, 2004.

———. "'A Spontaneous Loss of Enthusiasm': Workplace Feminism and the Transformation of Women's Service Jobs in the 1970s." *International Labor and Working-Class History* 56 (Fall 1999): 23–44.

Coble, Alana Erickson. *Cleaning Up: The Transformation of Domestic Service in Twentieth Century New York City*. New York: Routledge, 2006.

"Code for Domestic Servants Prepared." *New York Amsterdam News*, November 29, 1933, 3.

Coffey, Michael, ed. *The Irish in America*. New York: Hyperion, 1997.

Coman, Katharine. "The Problem of Domestic Service in Its Industrial Aspects." *Chautauquan*, March 1898, 651–53.

"Commissioner Keating Names His Inspectors." *New York Times*, June 5, 1904, 10.

Comstock, Sarah. "The Mistress Problem." *Collier's*, February 1, 1913, 15–16, 30, 33.

Cooke, Marvel. "Bronx Slave Market as Active as Ever." *Amsterdam News*, May 27, 1939, 17.

———. "Bronx Slave Market Flourishes." *Amsterdam News*, July 9, 1938, 7.

———. "Help Wanted for the Help." *New York Amsterdam News*, October 7, 1939, Section 2, 11.

———. "Modern Slaves." *Amsterdam News*, September 27, 1937, 19.

———. "Slavery . . . 1939 Style." *Amsterdam News*, May 27, 1939, 17.

Cott, Nancy. *The Grounding of Modern Feminism*. New Haven: Yale University Press, 1987.

Cowan, Ruth Schwartz. *More Work for Mother: The Ironies of Household Technology from the Open Hearth to the Microwave*. New York: Basic Books, 1983.

Cumming, Robert Cushing, Owen L. Potter, and Frank B. Gilbert, eds. *The Constitution of the State of New York with Notes, References and Annotations, Together with the Articles of Confederation, Constitution of the United States, New York State Constitutions of 1777, 1821, 1846, Unamended and as Amended and in Force in 1894, with an Index of the Revised Constitution and the Constitution of the United States*. Albany: James B. Lyon, 1894.

Cusack, Mary Frances. *Advice to Irish Girls in America, by the Nun of Kenmare*. New York: McGee, 1872.

Daniels, Roger. *Coming to America: A History of Immigration and Ethnicity in American Life*. New York: Harper Perennial, 2002.

———. *Guarding the Golden Door: American Immigration Policy and Immigrants since 1882*. New York: Hill and Wang, 2004.

Davidson, Cathy N., and Jessamyn Hatcher, eds. *No More Separate Spheres! A Next Wave American Studies Reader*. Durham: Duke University Press, 2002.

Davis, Rebecca Harding. "The Recovery of Family Life." *Independent*, September 21, 1905, 673–75.

Dawley, Alan. *Struggles for Justice: Social Responsibility and the Liberal State*. Cambridge: Belknap Press, 1991.

"Days Out." *Atlantic Monthly*, September 1911, 426–29.

"A Defense of Servant Girls." *New York Tribune*, February 17, 1877, 4.

DeParle, Jason. "A Good Provider Is One Who Leaves." *New York Times Magazine*, April 22, 2007.

Department of Health. *Health Report for the City of Newark, Covering the "Depression Years," 1930–1935*. Newark, N.J., 1935.

———. *Health Report for the City of Newark*. Newark, N.J., 1936.

———. *Health Report for the City of Newark*. Newark, N.J., 1937.

———. *Health Report for the City of Newark*. Newark, N.J., 1939.

———. *Health Report for the City of Newark*. Newark, N.J., 1944.

Department of Public Affairs. *The Health Report*. March 1944.

Deshon, Rev. George. *Guide for Catholic Young Women, Especially for Those Who Earn Their Own Living*. New York: Catholic Book Exchange, 1893.

Deutsch, Sarah. *Women and the City: Gender, Space, and Power in Boston, 1870–1940*. New York: Oxford University Press, 2000.

Diner, Hasia. *Erin's Daughters in America: Irish Immigrant Women in the Nineteenth Century*. Baltimore: Johns Hopkins University Press, 1983.

"Discovered: A Modern Slave Block." *Liberator*, June 15, 1938, 5.

"A Dishonest Servant Arrested." *New York Times*, February 16, 1880, 8.

"The Domestic Chaos." *New York Tribune*, November 25, 1904, 5.

"Domestic Exam Hearing Date Spread Anew by Various Agencies." *New Rochelle Standard-Star*, June 9, 1937, 1.

"Domestic Law Foes Surpass Advocates." *New York Amsterdam News*, June 26, 1937, 19.

"Domestic Servants Needed." *New York Tribune*, December 27, 1897, 5.

"Domestic Service." *The Nation*, January 3, 1884, 7–8.

"Domestics' Medical Test Hearing Sought June 14." *New Rochelle Standard-Star*, May 15, 1937, 1.

"Domestics Organize to Fight Ordinance." *New York Times*, April 30, 1934, 17.

"Domestics Plan to Form Union." *New York Amsterdam News*, October 17, 1936, 12.

"Domestic Workers Demand 6-Day-Week." *New York Amsterdam News*, October 10, 1936, 3.

Domestic Workers United and Datacenter. "Home Is Where the Work Is: Inside New York's Domestic Work Industry." July 14, 2006, ⟨http:// www.domesticworkersunited.org/homeiswheretheworkis.pdf/⟩, accessed October 21, 2010.

Dorr, Rheta Childe. "The Prodigal Daughter: Second Article—What Organized Women Can Do to Take Domestic Service Out of the List of Dangerous Trades." *Hampton's Magazine*, May 1910, 679–88.

"Do Servants Need a Code?" *Forum*, July 1934, 34–41.

Doughty, Frances Albert. "Evolution in the Kitchen." *Chautauquan*, January 1899, 386–89.

"A 'Downtrodden' Mistress." *New York Tribune*, July 16, 1903, 5.

Du Bois, W. E. B. *The Philadelphia Negro: A Social Study*. Philadelphia: University of Pennsylvania Press, 1899.

Dudden, Faye E. "Experts and Servants: The National Council on Household Employment and the Decline of Domestic Service in the Twentieth Century." *Journal of Social History* 20, no. 2 (Winter 1986): 269–89.

———. *Serving Women: Household Service in Nineteenth-Century America*. Middletown, Conn.: Wesleyan University Press, 1983.

Dye, Nancy Schrom. *As Equals and as Sisters: Feminism, the Labor Movement, and the Women's Trade Union League of New York*. Columbia: University of Missouri Press, 1980.

Ehrenreich, Barbara. "Maid to Order." In *Global Woman: Nannies, Maids, and Sex Workers in the New Economy*, edited by Barbara Ehrenreich and Arlie Russell Hochschild, 85–103. New York: Henry Holt, 2002.

———, and Arlie Russell Hochschild. "Introduction." In *Global Woman: Nannies, Maids, and Sex Workers in the New Economy*, edited by Barbara Ehrenreich and Arlie Russell Hochschild, 1–14. New York: Henry Holt, 2002.

Ekman, Katri, Corinne Olli, Dr. John B. Olli, eds. and translators. *A History of Finnish American Organizations in Greater New York, 1891–1976*. New York: Greater New York Finnish Bicentennial Planning Committee, 1976.

Ellis, Benson. *A Socio-economic Study of the Female Domestic Worker in Private Homes, with Special Reference to New York City*. New York, 1939.

"Employment Office Evils." *New York Tribune*, March 16, 1904, 7.

Enstad, Nan. *Ladies of Labor, Girls of Adventure: Working Women, Popular Culture, and Labor Politics at the Turn of the Twentieth Century*. New York: Columbia University Press, 1999.

"The Experiences of a 'Hired Girl.'" *Outlook*, April 6, 1912, 778–80.

Fifth Annual Report of the Young Women's Christian Association of the City of New York. New York: 1876.

"Finns of New York." *New York Times*, November 3, 1901, SM4.

Fitzgerald, Maureen. *Habits of Compassion: Irish Catholic Nuns and the Origins of New York's Welfare System, 1830–1920*. Urbana: University of Illinois Press, 2006.

Fitzpatrick, Ellen. *Endless Crusade: Women Social Scientists and Progressive Reform*. New York: Oxford University Press, 1990.

Flagg, James Montgomery. "I Should Say So! Come Live with Me and Be My Cook!" *American Magazine*, February 1913, 111–14.

Flanagan, Maureen. *Seeing with Their Hearts: Middle-Class Women and the Vision of the Good City, 1871–1933*. Princeton: Princeton University Press, 2002.

Foner, Phillip. *Women and the American Labor Movement: From Colonial Times to the Eve of World War I*. New York: Free Press, 1979.

Forbath, William. *Law and the Shaping of the American Labor Movement*. Cambridge: Harvard University Press, 1991.

Forrester, Izola. "The 'Girl' Problem." *Good Housekeeping*, September 1912, 375–82.

Forsyth, Anne. "Seven Times a Servant." *Delineator*, September 1910, 157–58.

"The Forum." *New Rochelle Standard-Star*, June 10, 1937, 15.

"The Forum." *New Rochelle Standard-Star*, June 11, 1937, 21.

"The Forum." *New Rochelle Standard-Star*, June 12, 1937, 4.

"The Forum." *New Rochelle Standard-Star*, June 15, 1937, 11.

"The Forum." *New Rochelle Standard-Star*, June 17, 1937, 15.

"The Forum." *New Rochelle Standard-Star*, June 21, 1937, 9.

Fraser, Elizabeth. "The Servant Problem." *Saturday Evening Post*, February 25, 1928, 10–11, 36–40.

Frederick, Christine. "Suppose Our Servants Didn't Live with Us." *Ladies' Home Journal*, October 1914, 102.

Garfield, Belle. "An Afternoon on the Auction Block." *Daily Worker*, July 24, 1935, 5.

Giddings, Paula J. *In Search of Sisterhood: Delta Sigma Theta and the Challenge of the Black Sorority Movement*. New York: Morrow, 1988.

Gilman, Charlotte Perkins. *Concerning Children*. [1900.] New York: Rowman & Littlefield, 2003.

———. "The Irresponsible Nursemaid." *Harper's Bazaar*. March 1909, 282–83.

———. *Women and Economics: A Study of the Economic Relation between Women and Men*. Amherst, N.Y.: Prometheus Books, 1994.

Gilmore, Glenda Elizabeth. *Gender and Jim Crow: Women and the Politics of White Supremacy, 1896–1920*. Chapel Hill: University of North Carolina Press, 1996.

Godman, Inez. "A Nine-Hour Day for Domestic Servants." *Independent*, February 13, 1902, 397–400.

———. "Ten Weeks in a Kitchen." *Independent*, October 17, 1901, 2459–64.

"Golden Rule Club." *New York Tribune*, March 6, 1905, 5.

Goodwin, Christina. "An Appeal to Housekeepers." *Forum*, August 1895, 753–60.

Gordon, Linda. *The Great Arizona Orphan Abduction*. Cambridge: Harvard University Press, 2001.

———. *Pitied but Not Entitled: Single Mothers and the History of Welfare, 1890–1935*. Cambridge: Harvard University Press, 1994.

Gray, Brenda Clegg. *Black Female Domestics during the Depression in New York City*. New York: Garland, 1993.

Greater New York Federation of Churches. *The Negro Churches of Manhattan: A Study Made in 1930*. New York: The Federation, 1930.

Greenberg, Cheryl Lynn. *"Or Does It Explode?" Black Harlem in the Great Depression*. New York: Oxford University Press, 1991.

Guy-Sheftall, Beverly. *Daughters of Sorrow: Attitudes toward Black Women, 1880–1920*. Brooklyn, N.Y.: Carlson, 1990.

Habermas, Jürgen. *The Structural Transformation of the Public Sphere: An Inquiry into a Category of Bourgeois Society*, translated by Thomas Burger and Frederick Lawrence. London: Polity Press, 1989.

Harley, Sharon. "When Your Work Is Not Who You Are: The Development of a Working-Class Consciousness among Afro-American Women." In *Gender, Class, Race, and Reform in the Progressive Era*, edited by Noralee Frankel and Nancy S. Dye, 42–55. Lexington: University Press of Kentucky, 1991.

Harris, Ruth-Ann M. "'Come You All Courageously': Irish Women in America Write Home." *Eire-Ireland* 36 (Spring/Summer 2001): 166–84.

Hart, Vivien. *Bound by Our Constitution: Women, Workers, and the Minimum Wage*. Princeton: Princeton University Press, 1994.

Haynes, George Edmund. *The Negro at Work in New York City*. New York: Arno Press, 1968.

Heath, Sarah. "Negotiating White Womanhood: The Cincinnati YWCA and White Wage Earning Women, 1918–1929." In *Men and Women Adrift: The YMCA and the YWCA and the City*, edited by Nina Mjagkij and Margaret Spratt, 86–110. New York: New York University Press, 1997.

Hedgeman, Anna Arnold. *The Trumpet Sounds: A Memoir of Negro Leadership*. New York: Holt, Rinehart and Winston, 1964.

"Helping Irish Girls." *Gaelic American*, October 1904, 2.

Hewitt, Nancy A. *Women's Activism and Social Change: Rochester, New York, 1822–1872*. Lanham, Md.: Lexington Press, 2001.

Higginbotham, Evelyn Brooks. *Righteous Discontent: The Woman's Movement in the Black Baptist Church, 1880–1920*. Cambridge: Harvard University Press, 1993.

Holloway, Pippa. *Sexuality, Politics, and Social Control in Virginia, 1920–1945*. Chapel Hill: University of North Carolina Press, 2006.

"A Home for Working Girls." *New York Tribune*, May 8, 1886, 2.

Hood, Clifton. "Subways, Transit Politics, and Metropolitan Spatial Expansion." In *The Landscape of Modernity: Essays on New York City, 1900–1940*, edited by David Ward and Olivier Zunz, 191–212. New York: Russell Sage Foundation, 1992.

Hotchkiss, T. W. "Advice to Employers." *Good Housekeeping*, September 1909, 244.

Hotten-Somers, Diane M. "Relinquishing and Reclaiming Independence: Irish Domestic Servants, American Middle-Class Mistresses, and Assimilation, 1850–1920." In *New Directions in Irish-American History*, edited by Kevin Kenny, 227–42. Madison: University of Wisconsin Press, 2003.

"Household Work." *New York Tribune*, March 6, 1887, 4.

"Housewives Want No Servants' Union." *New York Times*, January 27, 1938, 23.

Hoxie, Charles De Forest. *Civics for New York State*. New York: American Book Company, 1901.

Hunter, Tera. "The 'Brotherly Love' for Which This City Is Proverbial Should Extend to All: The Everyday Lives of Working-Class Women in Philadelphia and Atlanta in the 1890s." In *African American Urban Experience: Perspectives from the Colonial Period to the Present*, edited by Joe W. Trotter, Earl Lewis, and Tera Hunter, 76–98. New York: Palgrave Macmillan, 2004.

———. *To 'Joy My Freedom: Southern Black Women's Lives and Labors after the Civil War*. Cambridge: Harvard University Press, 1997.

Huntington, Emily. *Little Lessons for Little Housekeepers*. New York: A. D. F. Randolph, 1875.

Ignatiev, Noel. *How the Irish Became White*. New York: Routledge, 1995.

Ingalls, Robert P. "New York and the Minimum-Wage Movement, 1933–1937." *Labor History* 15, no. 2 (Spring 1974): 179–98.

"An Insane Woman as a Servant." *New York Times*, February 23, 1881, 8.

"Invitations to Theft." *New York Tribune*, September 27, 1896, Section III, 5.

"Irish Servants Are Scarce." *New York Tribune*, October 13, 1902, 4.

"Is the Home Disappearing?" *New York Tribune*, December 4, 1900, 7.

"Its Care of Servants." *New York Tribune*, May 2, 1904, 5.

Jackson, Esther Cooper. "The Negro Domestic Worker in Relation to Trade Unionism." Master's thesis, Fisk University, 1940.

Jackson, Kenneth T. *Crabgrass Frontier: The Suburbanization of the United States*. New York: Oxford University Press, 1985.

Jacobson, Matthew Frye. *Whiteness of a Different Color: European Immigrants and the Alchemy of Race*. Cambridge: Harvard University Press, 1998.

James, Edward T., ed. *Papers of the Women's Trade Union League and Its Principal Leaders, 1855–1964*. Woodbridge, Conn.: Research Publications, 1979.

Jeffries, Leroi. "New York Slave Markets." *Opportunity*, March 17, 1939, 85.

Jones, Beverly W. "Race, Sex, and Class: Black Female Tobacco Workers in Durham, North Carolina, 1920–1940, and the Development of Female Consciousness." *Feminist Studies* 10 (Autumn 1984): 445.

Jones, Dora. "A Self-Help Program of Household Employees." *The Aframerican Woman's Journal* 2 (Summer/Fall 1941): 26–31.

Jones, Jacqueline. *Labor of Love, Labor of Sorrow: Black Women, Work, and the Family from Slavery to the Present*. New York: Vintage Books, 1985.

Jones, James. *Bad Blood: The Tuskegee Syphilis Experiment: A Tragedy of Race and Medicine*. New York: Free Press, 1981.

Kamphoefner, Walter D., Wolfgang Helbich, and Ulrike Sommer, eds. *News from the Land of Freedom: German Immigrants Write Home*, translated by Susan Carter Vogel. Ithaca: Cornell University Press, 1988.

Katzman, David. *Seven Days a Week: Women and Domestic Service in Industrializing America*. Urbana: University of Illinois Press, 1978.

"Keating, Solomon, of New York Employment Agencies." *New York Times*, November 20, 1904, SM6.

Kelleher, Patricia. "Young Irish Workers: Class Implications of Men's and Women's Experiences in Gilded Age Chicago." In *New Directions in Irish-American History*, edited by Kevin Kenny, 185–208. Madison: University of Wisconsin Press, 2003.

Kelley, Robin D. G. *Hammer and Hoe: Alabama Communists during the Great Depression*. Chapel Hill: University of North Carolina Press, 1990.

Kellor, Frances A. "The Criminal Negro: I. A Sociological Study." *Arena*, June 1901, 59–68.

———. "Criminal Sociology: II. Criminality among Women." *Arena*, May 1900, 516–24.

———. "The Immigrant Woman." *Atlantic Monthly*, September 1907, 401–7.

———. "The Intelligence Office." *Atlantic Monthly*, October 1904, 458–64.

———. *Out of Work: A Study of Employment Agencies, Their Treatment of the Unemployed, and Their Influence upon Homes and Business*. New York: Knickerbocker Press, 1904.

———. "The Problem of the Young Negro Girl from the South." *New York Times*, March 19, 1905, X8.

Kerber, Linda K. "Separate Spheres, Female Worlds, Woman's Place: The Rhetoric of Women's History." *Journal of American History* 75, no. 1 (June 1988): 9–39.

Kessler-Harris, Alice. *Out to Work: A History of Wage-Earning Women in the United States.* New York: Oxford University Press, 2003.

———. *In Pursuit of Equity: Women, Men, and the Quest for Economic Citizenship in 20th Century America.* New York: Oxford University Press, 2001.

Kingsley, Florence Morse. "The Maid and the Mistress." *Outlook,* October 1, 1904, 295–97.

"Kitchen Autocrats Stirred Up." *New York Tribune,* November 30, 1900, 8.

"The Kitchen Drama." *New York Tribune,* April 26, 1900, 6.

"The 'Kitchen-Garden.'" *New York Times,* March 24, 1878, 6.

"Kitchen versus Slop Shop." *New York Times,* March 5, 1893, 12.

Klapper, Melissa. "Jewish Women and Vocational Education in New York City, 1885–1925." *American Jewish Archives Journal* 53, no. 1 and 2 (2001): 113–46.

Kleinberg, S. J. "Gendered Space: Housing, Privacy, and Domesticity in the Nineteenth-Century United States." In *Domestic Space: Reading the Nineteenth-Century Interior,* edited by Inga Bryden and Janet Floyd, 142–61. Manchester: Manchester University Press, 1999.

Klieman, Carol. "Maid Services Clean Up as Demand Escalates." *Chicago Tribune,* August 17, 1986, 1.

Klink, Jane Seymour. "The Housekeeper's Responsibility." *Atlantic Monthly,* March 1905, 372–80.

———. "Put Yourself in Her Place." *Atlantic Monthly,* February 2, 1905, 169–77.

Kneeland, George J. *Commercialized Prostitution in New York City.* New York: Century, 1913.

Kruglick, J. Sanford. "The Real Servant Problem." *Hygeia,* May 1938, 400–401.

The Ladies' Protective Union and Directory, Its Object and Its Work. New York: 1877.

Lambert, Bruce. "New Nassau County Law to Protect Domestic Workers." *New York Times,* May 16, 2006.

Lane, Janet. "Listen Mrs. Legree." *Collier's,* December 9, 1939, 27, 43.

"Laundry Reforms Needed." *New York Tribune,* January 30, 1881, 5.

Lawrence, Carl Dunbar. "Uncover Job Racket in Case of Virginia Girl." *Amsterdam News,* May 7, 1939, 4.

Leavitt, Judith Walzer. *Typhoid Mary: Captive to the Public's Health.* Boston: Beacon Press, 1996.

Lebsock, Suzanne. *The Free Women of Petersburg: Status and Culture in a Southern Town, 1784–1860.* New York: Norton, 1984.

Lehrer, Susan. *Origins of Protective Labor Legislation for Women, 1905–1925.* Albany: State University of New York Press, 1987.

Lemann, Nicholas. *The Promised Land: The Great Black Migration.* New York: Vintage Books, 1991.

Lieber, Ron. "Doing the Right Thing by Paying the Nanny Tax." *New York Times,* January 23, 2009, B1.

Lintelman, Joy K. "'America Is the Woman's Promised Land': Swedish Immigrant Women and American Domestic Service." In *The Work Experience: Labor, Class, and Immigrant Enterprise,* edited by George E. Pozzetta, 385–99. New York: Garland, 1991.

————. "'More Freedom, Better Pay': Single Swedish Immigrant Women in the United States, 1880–1920. Ph.D. diss., University of Minnesota, 1991.

Lipschultz, Sybil. "Hours and Wages: The Gendering of Labor Standards in America." *Journal of Women's History* 8, no. 1 (1996): 114–36.

Lynch-Brennan, Margaret. *The Irish Bridget: Irish Immigrant Women in Domestic Service in America, 1840–1930.* Syracuse: Syracuse University Press, 2009.

M., Agnes. "The True Life Story of a Nurse Girl." *Independent*, September 24, 1903, 2261–66.

Mackenzie, Catherine. "Domestic Help: National Issue." *New York Times*, June 5, 1938, 57.

MacLean, Annie Marion. "The Diary of a Domestic Drudge." *The World To-Day*, June 1905, 601–5.

Mageean, Deirdre. "Making Sense and Providing Structure: Irish-American Women in the Parish Neighborhood." In *Peasant Maids—City Women: From the European Countryside to Chicago*, edited by Christiane Harzig, 223–60. Ithaca: Cornell University Press, 1997.

"Maid Loses Assault Case against Couple." *New York Amsterdam News*, December 2, 1939, 24.

"The Maidservant." *New York Tribune*, February 10, 1894, 23.

"Maids' Union Is Dying." *Chicago Daily Tribune*, October 25, 1901, 3.

"Many to Attend Open Hearing on Domestics' Test." *New Rochelle Standard-Star*, June 21, 1937, 1.

Marsh, Margaret. *Suburban Lives.* New Brunswick, N.J.: Rutgers University Press, 1990.

"Martyrdom of the Housewife." *The Nation*, October 22, 1903, 317.

Matovic, Margareta. "Embracing a Middle-Class Life: Swedish-American Women in Lake View." In *Peasant Maids—City Women: From the European Countryside to Chicago*, edited by Christiane Harzig, 261–98. Ithaca: Cornell University Press, 1997.

Matthews, Glenna. *Just a Housewife: The Rise and Fall of Domesticity in America.* New York: Oxford University Press, 1987.

Maxwell, Mary Mortimer. "The Family Washing: Another Domestic Problem." *New York Times*, September 2, 1906, SM5.

Maxwell, William J. *New Negro, Old Left: African American Writing and Communism between the Wars.* New York: Columbia University Press, 1999.

May, Elaine Tyler. *Homeward Bound: American Families in the Cold War Era.* New York: Basic Books, 2008.

McArdell, Roy L. "Help! Help! Help!" *Everybody's Magazine*, October 1906, 477–84.

McCook, Philip J. "The Judicial Aspect of the Work of the Legal Aid Society." *Legal Aid Review* 5, no. 3 (July 1907): 17–19.

McCulloch-Williams, Martha. "The Logic of the Servant Problem." *Harper's Bazaar*, November 1908, 1146–47.

McDannell, Colleen. "Going to the Ladies' Fair: Irish Catholics in New York City, 1870–1900." In *The New York Irish*, edited by Ronald H. Bayor and Timothy Meagher, 234–51. Baltimore: Johns Hopkins University Press, 1996.

McDuffie, Erik S. "Long Journeys: Four Black Women and the Communist Party, USA, 1930–1956." Ph.D. diss., New York University, 2003.

McGuire, John Thomas. "A Catalyst for Reform: The Women's Joint Legislative Conference (WJLC) and Its Fight for Labor Legislation in New York State, 1918–1933." Ph.D. diss., State University of New York at Binghamton, 2001.

McMahan, Anna B. "Something More about Domestic Service." *Forum*, June 1886, 399–403.

Mettler, Suzanne. *Dividing Citizens: Gender and Federalism in New Deal Public Policy*. Ithaca: Cornell University Press, 1998.

Meyerowitz, Joanne J. *Women Adrift: Independent Wage Earners in Chicago, 1880–1930*. Chicago: University of Chicago Press, 1988.

Mintz, Stephen, and Susan Kellogg. *Domestic Revolutions: A Social History of American Family Life*. New York: Free Press, 1988.

Mitchell, Louise. "Slave Markets Typify Exploitation of Domestics." *Daily Worker*, May 5, 1940, 5.

Moloney, Deirdre M. "A Transatlantic Reform: Boston's Port Protection Program and Irish Women Immigrants." *Journal of American Ethnic History* 19, no. 1 (Fall 1999): 50–66.

"Mr. Coster's Servant Girl." *New York Times*, December 4, 1880, 2.

"Mrs. Gurenson Answers Points Raised in Wallace's Letter." *New Rochelle Standard-Star*, June 4, 1937, 19.

Mullen, Bill V. *Popular Fronts: Chicago and African American Cultural Politics, 1935–1946*. Urbana: University of Illinois Press, 1999.

Muncy, Robyn. *Creating a Female Dominion in American Reform, 1890–1935*. New York: Oxford University Press, 1991.

Murolo, Priscilla. *The Common Ground of Womanhood: Class, Gender, and Working Girls' Clubs, 1884–1928*. Urbana: University of Illinois Press, 1997.

Nadel, Stanley. *Little Germany: Ethnicity, Religion, and Class in New York City, 1845–1880*. Urbana: University of Illinois Press, 1990.

National Council of Catholic Women. *Directory of Boarding Homes for Young Women under Catholic Auspices in the United States*. Washington, D.C., 1929.

New York Women's Trade Union League. *Annual Report, 1938–1939*. New York: 1939.
———. *Annual Report, 1939–1940*. New York: 1940.
———. *Annual Report, 1941–1942*. New York: 1942.
———. *Annual Report, 1945*. New York: 1945.
———. *Annual Report, 1946*. New York: 1946.

"Not Enough 'Green Girls.'" *New York Tribune*, August 1, 1902, 7.

"No Union for Servant Girls." *New York Times*, May 31, 1901, 16.

Odem, Mary P. *Delinquent Daughters: Protecting and Policing Adolescent Female Sexuality in the United States, 1885–1920*. Chapel Hill: University of North Carolina Press, 1995.

Offord, Carl. "Slave Markets in the Bronx." *The Nation*, June 29, 1940, 780–81.
———. "Slave Markets in the Bronx." *The Nation*, August 3, 1940, 100.

"One Who Tried Domestic Service." *New York Tribune*, January 20, 1887, 3.

"Opponents Rally against Law for Domestic Tests." *New Rochelle Standard-Star*, June 22, 1937, 15.

Orleck, Annelise. *Common Sense and a Little Fire: Women and Working-Class Politics in the United States, 1900–1965*. Chapel Hill: University of North Carolina Press, 1995.

Ovington, Mary White. *Half a Man: The Status of the Negro in New York*. New York: Longmans, Green, 1911.

Palmer, Phyllis. *Domesticity and Dirt: Housewives and Domestic Servants in the United States, 1920–1945*. Philadelphia: Temple University Press, 1989.

———. "Outside the Law: Agricultural and Domestic Workers under the Fair Labor Standards Act." *Journal of Policy History* 7, no. 5 (1995): 416–40.

Pascoe, Peggy. *Relations of Rescue: The Search for Female Moral Authority in the American West, 1874–1939*. New York: Oxford University Press, 1990.

Patterson, James T. *The New Deal and the States: Federalism in Transition*. Princeton: Princeton University Press, 1969.

"The People to Whom We Confide Our Children." *Delineator*, February 1911, 95.

Perry, Elisabeth Israels. "Women's Political Choices after Suffrage: The Women's City Club of New York, 1915–1990." *New York History* 71 (October 1990): 417–34.

Pettengill, Lillian. *Toilers of the Home: The Record of a College Woman's Experience as a Domestic Servant*. New York: Doubleday, Page, 1903.

"Phases of Domestic Service." *New York Tribune*, December 25, 1886, 4.

Piess, Kathy. *Cheap Amusements: Working Women and Leisure in Turn-of-the-Century New York*. Philadelphia: Temple University Press, 1986.

"The Plague of the Household." *New York Times*, March 13, 1881, 6.

"Plans a Union of Housemaids." *Chicago Daily Tribune*, June 17, 1901, 3.

"The Privileges of Servants." *Outlook*, March 17, 1900, 614–15.

"Problem Hard to Solve." *New York Tribune*, April 7, 1904, 7.

Quadagno, Jill. *The Transformation of Old Age Security: Class and Politics in the American Welfare State*. Chicago: University of Chicago Press, 1988.

Ramsey, Annie R. "How a Bride Can Train a Cook." *Ladies' Home Journal*, April 1909, 48.

"The Reason Why." *New York Tribune*, July 22, 1903, 9.

Records of the National Consumers' League. Microfilm edition. Washington, D.C.: Library of Congress Photoduplication Service, 1982.

Regan, Francis, Alan Paterson, Tmara Goriely, and Don Fleming, eds. *The Transformation of Legal Aid: Comparative and Historical Studies*. Oxford: Oxford University Press, 1999.

Rembiénska, Aleksandra. "A Polish Peasant Girl in America." In *America's Immigrants: Adventures in Eyewitness History*, edited by Rhoda Hoff, 118–20. New York: Henry Z. Walck, 1967.

Report of the Commissioner of Licenses John N. Bogart submitted to the Hon. George B. McClellan, New York: 1906.

Report of the Commissioner of Licenses John N. Bogart, Submitted to the Hon. George B. McClellan. New York: 1907.

Report of the Commissioner of Licenses John N. Bogart, Submitted to the Hon. George B. McClellan. New York: 1908.

Report of the Commissioner of Licenses John N. Bogart, Submitted to the Hon. George B. McClellan. New York: 1909.

Report of the Commissioner of Licenses Herman Robinson, Submitted to the Hon. William Gaynor. New York: 1910.

Report of the Commissioner of Licenses Herman Robinson, Submitted to the Hon. William Gaynor. New York: 1912.

Report of the Commissioner of Licenses Submitted to the Hon. William J. Gaynor by Herman Robinson, Commissioner of Licenses, New York: 1913.

Report of the Department of Licenses, Submitted to the Hon. Mayor John F. Gilchrist, by John F. Hylan Commissioner. New York: 1922.

Report of the Tenement House Committee of the Working Women's Society. New York: Freytag Printing Co., 1892.

Rhode, Deborah L. *Justice and Gender: Sex Discrimination and the Law.* Cambridge: Harvard University Press, 1991.

Richardson, Dorothy. *The Long Day: The Story of a New York Working Girl.* Charlottesville: University of Virginia Press, 1990.

Richter, Amy G. *Home on the Rails: Women, the Railroad, and the Rise of Public Domesticity.* Chapel Hill: University of North Carolina Press, 2005.

Riis, Jacob A. *How the Other Half Lives: Studies among the Tenements of New York.* New York: Sagamore, 1957.

Ritter, Gretchen. *The Constitution as Social Design: Gender and Civic Membership in the American Constitutional Order.* Stanford: Stanford University Press, 2006.

Robb, Juliet Everts. "Our House in Order." *Outlook,* June 18, 1910, 353–60.

Rodgers, Daniel. *Atlantic Crossings: Social Politics in a Progressive Age.* Cambridge: Belknap Press, 1998.

Roediger, David R. *The Wages of Whiteness: Race and the Making of the American Working Class.* London: Verso Press, 1991.

Romero, Mary. *Maid in the U.S.A.* New York: Routledge, 1992.

Rorer, S. T. "How to Train a Green Cook." *Ladies' Home Journal,* January 1900, 24.

———. "How to Treat and Keep a Servant." *Ladies' Home Journal,* May 1900, 26.

Rose, Heloise Durant. "The White Woman's Burden." *New York Times,* December 31, 1900, 7.

Rosenberg, Carroll Smith. "The Female World of Love and Ritual: Relations between Women in Nineteenth Century America." *Signs* 1 (Autumn 1975): 1–29.

Ross, Carl. *The Finn Factor in American Labor, Culture and Society.* New York Mills, Minn.: Parta Printers, 1977.

Ross, Carl, and K. Marianne Wargelin Brown, eds. *Women Who Dared: The History of Finnish American Women.* St. Paul, Minn.: Immigration History Research Center, University of Minnesota, 1986.

Rubinow, I. M., and Daniel Durant. "The Depth and Breadth of the Servant Problem." *McClure's Magazine,* March 1910, 576–85.

Ruiz, Albor. "Giving Rights to Caregivers without a Voice." *New York Daily News,* April 6, 2009, ⟨http://www.nydailynews.com/ny_local/brooklyn/2009/04/05/2009-04-05_giving_rights_to_caregivers_without_a_vo.html⟩, accessed October 21, 2010.

Ryan, Mary P. *Cradle of the Middle Class: The Family in Oneida County, New York, 1790–1865.* Cambridge: Cambridge University Press, 1981.

Sacks, Marcy S. *Before Harlem: The Black Experience in New York City before World War I.* Philadelphia: University of Pennsylvania Press, 2006.

Salem, Dorothy. *To Better Our World: Black Women in Organized Reform, 1890–1920.* Brooklyn, N.Y.: Carlson, 1990.

Salmon, Lucy Maynard. *Domestic Service.* New York: Macmillan, 1911.

Sassen, Saskia. "Global Cities and Survival Circuits." In *Global Woman: Nannies, Maids, and Sex Workers in the New Economy*, edited by Barbara Ehrenreich and Arlie Russell Hochschild, 254–74. New York: Henry Holt, 2002.

Scacchi, Anna. "American Interiors: Redesigning the Home in Turn-of-the-Century New York." In *Public Space, Private Lives: Race, Gender, Class, and Citizenship in New York, 1890–1929*, edited by William Boelhower and Anna Scacchi, 15–38. Amsterdam: VU University Press, 2004.

Scelfo, Julie. "Trickledown Downsizing." *New York Times*, December 11, 2008, D1.

Schmitt, J. P. *History of the Legal Aid Society of New York, 1876–1912.* New York, 1912.

Schrier, Arnold. *Ireland and the American Emigration, 1850–1900.* Minneapolis: University of Minnesota Press, 1958.

Schudson, Michael. "Was There Ever a Public Sphere? If So, When? Reflections on the American Case." In *Habermas and the Public Sphere*, edited by Craig Calhoun, 143–63. Cambridge: MIT Press, 1992.

Schuyler, Lorraine Gates. *The Weight of Their Votes: Southern Women and Political Leverage in the 1920s.* Chapel Hill: University of North Carolina Press, 2006.

Scobey, David. *Empire City: The Making and Meaning of the New York City Landscape.* Philadelphia: Temple University Press, 2002.

Scott, Anne Firor. *Natural Allies: Women's Associations in American History.* Urbana: University of Illinois Press, 1991.

Scott, Anne Firor, and Elisabeth Israels Perry, eds. *Grassroots Women's Organizations: Records of the Women's City Club of New York, 1916–1980.* Microfilm edition. Frederick, Md.: University Publications of America, 1989.

Seely, Evelyn. "Our Feudal Housewives." *The Nation*, May 28, 1938, 613–15.

Seely, L. *Mrs. Seely's Cook Book.* New York: Macmillan, 1914.

Seller, Maxine Schwartz, ed. *Immigrant Women.* New York: State University of New York Press, 1994.

Sergel, Ruth, ed. *The Women in the House: Stories of Household Employment.* New York: Woman's Press, 1938.

"A Servant Girl for Her Class." *New York Tribune*, March 24, 1877, 3.

"The Servant Girl Question: Miss M. C. Jones in the Pittsburgh Dispatch." *New York Times*, July 17, 1892, 12.

"Servant Girls." *New York Times*, September 2, 1877, 5.

"Servant Girls Extravagant." *New York Tribune*, February 24, 1877, 5.

"A Servant Girl's Fiendish Revenge." *New York Times*, September 8, 1882, 8.

"A Servant Girl's Letter." *Independent*, January 2, 1902, 36–37.

"Servant Girls Make Rules." *New York Times*, July 29, 1901, 1.

"The Servant Girl's Union." *New York Times*, August 1, 1901, 6.

"A Servant on the Servant Problem." *American Magazine*, September 1909, 502–4.

"The Servant Question." *New York Times*, December 10, 1882, 4.

"Servant Quest Now." *New York Tribune*, July 9, 1903, 7.

"The Servants' Side." *New York Tribune*, March 12, 1903, 7.

"A Servant's View of the Situation." *Leslie's Weekly*, April 5, 1906, 328.

Sharer, Wendy B. *Vote and Voice: Women's Organizations and Political Literacy, 1915–1930.* Carbondale: Southern Illinois University Press, 2004.

Sheldon, Rev. Charles M. "Servant and Mistress." *Independent*, December 20, 1900, 3018–21.

Sinke, Suzanne M. *Dutch Immigrant Women in the United States, 1880–1920.* Urbana: University of Illinois Press, 2002.

Sinkoff, Nancy B. "Educating for 'Proper' Jewish Womanhood: A Case Study in Domesticity and Vocational Training, 1897–1926." *American Jewish History* 77, no. 4 (June 1988): 572–99.

Sklar, Kathryn Kish. "Hull House in the 1890s: A Community of Women Reformers." *Signs* 10, no. 4 (1985): 658–77.

———. *Florence Kelley and the Nation's Work.* New Haven: Yale University Press, 1995.

Skocpol, Theda. *Protecting Soldiers and Mothers: The Political Origins of Social Policy in the United States.* Cambridge: Harvard University Press, 1992.

"Slave Markets." *New York Journal American*, June 26, 1938, 38.

Smith, Goldwin. "The Passing of the Household." *Independent*, August 24, 1905, 422–24.

Smith, Mary Bancroft. *Practical Helps for Housewives, Written by a Housekeeper.* Rutherford, N.J.: Bergen County Herald Publishing Co., 1896.

Smith, Mary Roberts. "Domestic Service: The Responsibility of Employers." *Forum*, August 1899, 679–89.

"The Spectator." *Outlook*, May 30, 1908, 240–42.

Spofford, Harriet Elizabeth. *The Servant Girl Question.* Boston: Houghton Mifflin, 1881.

Stanley, Amy Dru. *From Bondage to Contract: Wage Labor, Marriage, and the Market in the Age of Slave Emancipation.* Cambridge: Cambridge University Press, 1998.

Stansell, Christine. *City of Women: Sex and Class in New York, 1789–1860.* Urbana: University of Illinois Press, 1982.

State of New York. *Public Papers of Thomas E. Dewey, Fifty-first Governor of the State of New York, 1945.* Albany: Williams Press, 1946.

Stiehm, Judith Hicks. "Government and the Family: Justice and Acceptance." In *Changing Images of the Family*, edited by Virginia Tufte and Barbara Myerhoff, 361–75. New Haven: Yale University Press, 1979.

Stone, C. H. *The Problem of Domestic Service.* St. Louis: Nelson Printing Co., 1892.

Storrs, Landon R. Y. *Civilizing Capitalism: The National Consumers' League, Women's Activism, and Labor Standards in the New Deal Era.* Chapel Hill: University of North Carolina Press, 2000.

Strasser, Susan M. "Mistress and Maid, Employer and Employee: Domestic Service Reform in the United States, 1897–1920." *Marxist Perspectives* 1, no. 4 (Winter 1978): 52–67.

———. *Never Done: A History of American Housework.* New York: Henry Holt, 2000.

"A Sunday Night Stroll." *New York Times*, April 9, 1883, 5.

Sutherland, Daniel. *Americans and Their Servants: Domestic Service in the United States from 1800 to 1920.* Baton Rouge: Louisiana State University Press, 1981.

"Swedes in Brooklyn." *Brooklyn Daily Eagle*, February 8, 1891.

Taft, M. A. "How Is the Refined New York Family of Moderate Income to Solve a Question Which Daily Becomes More Difficult?" *New York Times*, October 16, 1904, SM2.

Tarbell, Ida M. "The Woman and Democracy." *American Magazine*, June 1912, 217–20.

Taylor, Clarence. *The Black Churches of Brooklyn*. New York: Columbia University Press, 1994.

Taylor, Elvira P. "Housework as a Business." *Outlook*, August 29, 1908, 1005–6.

Thompson, Flora McDonald. "The Servant Question." *Cosmopolitan*, May 1900, 521–28.

"Tiring of Factory Life." *New York Tribune*, February 23, 1902, Section II, 8.

"To Found a Training School." *New York Tribune*, September 11, 1901, 5.

"To Save the Great American Home." *Literary Digest*, January 2, 1926, 1, 11.

"Training Girls for Servants." *New York Times*, November 21, 1881, 8.

"Trials of a Governess." *New York Tribune*, December 26, 1886, 5.

Turbin, Carole. "Refashioning the Concept of Public/Private: Lessons from Dress Studies." *Journal of Women's History* 15, no. 1 (Spring 2003): 43–51.

————. *Working Women of Collar City: Gender, Class, and Community in Troy, New York, 1864–1886*. Urbana: University of Illinois Press, 1992.

"Union Maid the Kitchen Queen." *Chicago Daily Tribune*, July 28, 1901, 1.

"The Union Servant Girl." *Chicago Daily Tribune*, July 29, 1901, 3.

U.S. Bureau of the Census. *Twelfth Census of the United States*. Washington, D.C.: Government Printing Office, 1900.

————. *Thirteenth Census of the United States*. Washington, D.C.: Government Printing Office, 1910.

————. *Fifteenth Census of the United States*. Washington, D.C.: Government Printing Office, 1930.

U.S. House of Representatives. *Hearings before the General Subcommittee on Labor of the Committee on Education and Labor, House of Representatives, 93rd Congress, First Session on H.R. 4757 and H.R. 2831*. Washington, D.C.: Government Printing Office, 1973.

"An Unsettled Question." *Outlook*, July 14, 1894, 59–60.

Van Raaphorst, Donna L. *Union Maids Not Wanted: Organizing Domestic Workers, 1870–1940*. New York: Praeger, 1988.

Vapnek, Lara. *Breadwinners: Working Women and Economic Independence, 1865–1920*. Urbana: University of Illinois Press, 2009.

von Briesen, Arthur. "Servant Problem Involves a Recognition of Rights." *New York Times*, December 22, 1912, X10.

Vrooman, G. "Manual Training for Women and the Problem of Domestic Service." *Arena*, September 1895, 308–16.

Wagner, Lola D. "Into Such Hands Do We Commit Our Children." *Ladies' Home Journal*, May 1907, 63.

"Wallace's Letter." *New York Amsterdam News*, June 5, 1937, 19.

Walter, Bronwen. *Outsiders Inside: Whiteness, Place, and Irish Women*. London: Routledge, 2001.

"War Prices for Servant Girls." *New York Tribune*, February 10, 1877, 2.

Warren, Carl. "Venereal Tests for Servants Proposed." *New York Daily News*, January 7, 1939, 6.

Weatherford, Doris. *Foreign and Female*. New York: Facts on File, 1995.

Wehner, Silke. "German Domestic Servants in America, 1850–1914: A New Look at German Immigrant Women's Experiences." In *People in Transit: German Migrations in Comparative Perspective, 1820–1930*, edited by Dirk Hoerder and Jörg Nagler, 267–93. Cambridge: Cambridge University Press, 1995.

Weisenfeld, Judith. *African American Women and Christian Activism: New York's Black YWCA, 1905–1945*. Cambridge: Harvard University Press, 1997.

Weiss, Nancy J. *The National Urban League, 1910–1940*. New York: Oxford University Press, 1974.

Welter, Barbara. "The Cult of True Womanhood: 1820–1860." *American Quarterly* 18, no. 2 (Summer 1966): 151–74.

West, Mary Allen. "Domestic Service." *Our Day*, November 1889, 401–15.

"What the Servant Sells." *Current Literature*, June 1903, 685.

Whipple, Edwin P. "Domestic Service." *Forum*, March 1886, 25–36.

White, Deborah Gray. *Too Heavy a Load: Black Women in Defense of Themselves*. New York: W. W. Norton, 1999.

"Why Domestic Service Is a Problem: Being the Humble Opinion of Barbara—the Commuter's Wife." *Outlook*, October 1, 1904, 299–301.

"Why Is It That So Many Servant Girls Go Insane?" *New York Times*, January 17, 1909, SM5.

"Why 100,000 Domestics Are Needed Here." *New York Times*, May 19, 1912, SM1.

"Why There Is a Servant Question." *New York Tribune*, July 13, 1903, 5.

Wikander, Ulla, Alice Kessler-Harris, and Jane Lewis, eds. *Protecting Women: Labor Legislation in Europe, the United States, and Australia, 1880–1920*. Urbana: University of Illinois Press, 1995.

Willoughby, K. R. "Mothering Labor: Difference as a Device towards Protective Labor Legislation for Men, 1830–1938." *Journal of Law and Politics* 10, no. 3 (1994): 445–89.

Wilson, Thane. "How We Treat Servants and How They Treat Us." *American Magazine*, October 1923, 64–65, 114–18.

Woloch, Nancy, ed. *Muller v. Oregon: A Brief History with Documents*. New York: Bedford Books, 1996.

"Women and Business." *New York Tribune*, June 12, 1881, 6.

"Working Women Organize." *New York Times*, July 21, 1901, 1.

Working Women's Protective Union. *A Report of Its Condition and the Results Secured*. New York: 1879.

Young, Louise B. *In the Public Interest: The League of Women Voters, 1920–1970*. New York: Greenwood Press, 1989.

Young Women's Christian Associations, U.S. National Board. *Commission on Household Employment, First Report of the Commission on Household Employment to the Fifth National Convention of the Young Women's Christian Associations of the United States*. Los Angeles, 1915.

Zarembka, Joy M. "America's Dirty Work: Migrant Maids and Modern-Day Slavery." In *Global Woman: Nannies, Maids, and Sex Workers in the New Economy*, edited by Barbara Ehrenreich and Arlie Russell Hochschild, 142–53. New York: Henry Holt, 2002.

Zelizer, Viviana. *The Purchase of Intimacy*. Princeton: Princeton University Press, 2005.

Index

Abyssinian Baptist Church, 160. *See also* Black churches

Addams, Jane, 13, 75

Adkins v. Children's Hospital, 108–9

A. E. Johnson Agency, 46

African American domestic workers, 8, 9, 15, 90–93, 94, 100–101, 114–15; and health examinations, 166–72; live-out vs. live-in, 9, 115; and racism, 91–92; and unions, 146–49, 155–65. *See also* Domestic service; Domestic Workers Union; Race; Unions

Allen, Annie Ware Winsor, 30

American Federation of Labor, 15, 50, 106, 120, 147. *See also* Unions

Amundsen, Lillian, 47, 52, 54

Anderson, Mary, 109, 122, 124

Andrews, Benjamin, 118, 120, 171

Archer, Theodore, 167

Ashcroft, Henry, 152

Ashmore, Grace Eulalie, 36, 66

Bacon, Josephine Daskam, 34

Baker, Ella, 123

Beckermann, Anna, 53, 54

Black churches, 150, 154–55, 160

Briesen, Arthur von, 67, 69, 81

Brietbart, Charles H., 128, 133. *See also* Health examinations; Middle-class reformers: and fears of contagion

Bronx "slave markets." *See* Street corner markets

Brown, Bessie, 161, 164

Brown, Jean Collier, 157

Building Services Employees International Union, 147. *See also* American Federation of Labor; Domestic Workers Union; Unions

Garvey, Marcus, 9

Gilman, Charlotte Perkins, 22, 33, 34

Gilroy, Ellen, 60

Gilroy, Thomas F., 68

Godman, Inez, 72, 79

Golden Rule Club, 96

Goodwin, Christina, 27, 30

Great Depression, 119–20, 124, 131, 133, 136–37, 138, 148, 149, 155, 170, 172–73; effect on domestic work, 121–23, 150–53, 158, 163

Great Migration, 4, 8, 14, 99, 113–15, 149

Gurenson, Rose, 166, 167, 169

Haener, Dorothy, 177

Harty, Norabell, 151

Haynes, Elizabeth Ross, 150

Haynes, George Edmund, 113

Health examinations, 9, 15, 107, 127–33, 135–36, 137, 153–54, 165–72. *See also* Craster, Thomas V.; Middle-class reformers: and fears of contagion; Newark Health Department

Heany, Mary, 52, 53

Hedgeman, Anna Arnold, 119, 152

Henning, Astrid, 49, 52, 55, 60, 62, 67

Hill, T. Arnold, 153

Hired girls, 5–6

Holmes, Josephine Pinyon, 152

Hordi, Kate, 62

Household Economics Association, 83

Household Employees of New York, 167

Household Technicians of America, 178

Housekeeper's Alliance and Civic Club, 99

Howard, Aili, 47, 66–67

Immigrant domestic workers, 15, 18, 19, 20–21, 28, 30, 43–47, 72, 85, 100; and Catholicism, 7, 26, 29–30, 56, 58, 59, 82, 87; and collective resistance, 50–51, 60–65, 191 (n. 12); and ethnic community institutions, 57–60; and Legal Aid, 67–70; and quitting, 65– 67, 69, 70, 196 (n. 153); and sexual harassment,

38–39, 49, 93, 190 (n. 120); and sexuality, 30–32, 37–38; and working-class amusements, 15, 34–35, 52–57, 60, 71, 96, 104, 189 (n. 91), 193 (n. 57). *See also* Domestic service; Finnish immigrants; Immigrant homes; Immigration; Irish immigrants

Immigrant Girls' Home and Home Co-operative Society, 86

Immigrant homes, 15, 85–94, 97, 100, 102, 103, 105, 199 (n. 59), 201 (n. 110)

Immigration, 4, 6, 44–46, 58, 93, 99, 111, 175, 179–80

Innovation Club, 95

Intelligence agencies. *See* Employment agencies

Inter-Municipal Council on Household Research, 86, 89, 99, 103

International Labor Defense, 161

Irish immigrants, 24, 34, 51, 52, 53, 54, 55, 59, 63, 64, 69, 115; and ethnic institutions, 58; and immigration demographics, 6, 44–45, 58; relationship with employers, 7–8, 29–30. *See also* Catholic Church; Immigrant domestic workers; Immigrant homes; Immigration; Our Lady of the Rosary Home for Immigrant Girls

Jones, Dora, 106, 126, 147, 148, 155–65, 172–73. *See also* Domestic Workers Union

Kane, Annie, 59

Kelley, Florence, 75, 110

Kellor, Frances, 10, 19, 27, 31, 37, 74, 86, 89, 96–98, 117, 202 (n. 134); and employment agencies, 24, 26, 32, 35, 61–63; and employment agency law, 4, 98–105. *See also* Middle-class reformers

Klink, Jane Seymour, 20, 37, 39, 72, 96, 103

Kneeland, George, 31

Komula, Betty, 43